W9-ALJ-540

THE LAST ICON

The Last Icon
Tom Seaver and His Times

Steven Travers

TAYLOR TRADE PUBLISHING
Lanham • New York • Boulder • Toronto • Plymouth, UK

Published by Taylor Trade Publishing
An imprint of The Rowman & Littlefield Publishing Group, Inc.
4501 Forbes Boulevard, Suite 200, Lanham, Maryland 20706
http://www.rlpgtrade.com

Estover Road, Plymouth PL6 7PY, United Kingdom

Distributed by National Book Network

British Library Cataloguing in Publication Information Available

Library of Congress Cataloging-in-Publication Data

Travers, Steven.
The last icon : Tom Seaver and his times / Steven Travers.
p. cm.
Includes bibliographical references and index.
ISBN 978-1-58979-660-7 (hardback) – ISBN 978-1-58979-661-4 (electronic)
1. Seaver, Tom, 1944- 2. Baseball players–United States–Biography. I. Title.
GV865.S4T73 2011
796.357092—dc22

2011016699

∞™ The paper used in this publication meets the minimum requirements of American National Standard for Information Sciences—Permanence of Paper for Printed Library Materials, ANSI/NISO Z39.48-1992.

Printed in the United States of America

To the memories of Bud Furillo and Rod Dedeaux

CONTENTS

ACKNOWLEDGMENTS

THANK YOU TO MY FRIEND RICK RINEHART AT ROWMAN & LITTLEfield; to Flannery Scott, Alden Perkins, and Patricia MacDonald at Taylor Trade Publishing; to my agent, Ian Kleinert of Objective Entertainment in New York City; to John Horne and the Baseball Hall of Fame; to Matt Merola; to Bud Harrelson and Tom Seaver.

STEVEN R. TRAVERS
USCSTEVE1@aol.com
redroom.com/member/STWRITES
(415) 455-5971

1

THE BASEBALL CAPITAL OF THE WORLD: 1944–1964

HE WAS THE "24-YEAR-OLD REINCARNATION OF CHRISTY MATHEWSON, Hobey Baker and Jack Armstrong" according to sportswriter Ray Robinson. He was "so good blind people [came] out to hear him pitch," said Reggie Jackson. He was, wrote legendary *Los Angeles Times* sports columnist Jim Murray, "too good to be true," except that he was.

At the height of his fame he elicited media verbiage surpassing any previous sports star. He was the primary, dominant figure in a story generally accepted to be the greatest in athletic history, so impossible it is still viewed as much an act of God as an earthly event. He was like a U.S. Senator who also happened to be the best pitcher in the world, a statue come to life.

He came to the toughest, most hard-core city in the world, where the greatest of the great set standards impossible to attain. He matched them, entering the pantheon reserved for a precious few that include Babe Ruth and Lou Gehrig; Joe DiMaggio and Mickey Mantle; Jackie Robinson and Willie Mays; Frank Gifford and Joe Namath. In a year in which American heroes bestrode Manhattan's concrete canyons in ticker-tape splendor, he engendered the greatest adoration.

He represented greatness and excellence during the waning days of innocence, before Watergate, free agency, and steroids. In his prime he was the best pitcher in baseball, and arguably the best either of all time or in the post–World War II time span, depending upon how one analyzes the records and eras. He enjoyed several of the most spectacular single seasons in history and sustained a career built on consistent success over a long period. He transcends sports and New York City.

In a rough 'n' tumble town, a town of Irish Catholics, of rough-hewn neighborhood Italians, of Brooklyn Jews and Harlem blacks, he was a Park Avenue, or to be precise, a Connecticut WASP, yet somehow he was also this fresh-faced Californian who remains the only Mets player to be selected among that rarest of the New York pantheon—in many ways really, the last icon.

He was born George Thomas Seaver on November 17, 1944, in Fresno, California. He went by the name Tom, except from his wife, Nancy, who called him George. Charles Seaver, Tom's father, played football and basketball at Stanford University. He was also one of the finest golfers in the world at one time. In 1932 he competed for the United States in the prestigious Walker Cup, an amateur trophy named for the family of two presidents: George W. Bush and his father, George Herbert *Walker* Bush. Famed radio broadcaster Ted Husing announced Seaver defeating his British opponent, Eric Fiddian, thus securing for the U.S. their seventh Walker Cup title. Seaver also competed in the 1934 Los Angeles Open.

After winning the Walker Cup, Charles returned to Stanford and defeated a golf teammate named Lawson Little. When courting his wife, Betty Lee (a former high school basketball player), their dates more often than not were putting contests for nickels and dimes. Two good athletes and good genetics.

"I've got my mother's hands and fingers and my father's legs and butt," Tom explained.

After graduation came marriage; membership in the aptly named Sunnyside Country Club in Fresno, California; and a rising executive career with the Bonner Packing Company.

This was the central California of John Steinbeck's novels, but Charles Seaver was a successful businessman who protected his young family from the Great Depression. Fresno and environs were "America's fruit basket" or "salad bowl," providing grapes, figs, peaches, oranges, and vegetables to fruit stands and grocery stores.

Charles raised a family in idyllic California suburbia. Fresno is a town that gets very hot in the summer and is subject to strange "tule fogs" in the winter. Despite being in California, it is a place with a passion for sports that more resembles Texas or Oklahoma. Of those sports, baseball is king. When Tom was growing up, it could be argued that Fresno was the "baseball capital of the world." It may still be.

The family backyard included cherry, orange, and fig trees. The streets were safe for the kids to ride bikes and get into mischief. The Little League fields were well kept, supported by an enthusiastic community. Charles kept up his golf game, winning the Fresno city tournament six times. Weekends were spent at the country club. Charles and his wife watched their four children splash in the pool, play golf, and whack tennis balls.

The kids included Charles Jr., who took to golf like his old man. Next was Katie, a swimmer in the manner of her aunt, who had surfed Hawaii's wild rides. Carol was also a swimmer.

"There was good clean competition in our home, and you earned what you got," said Charles. "The only thing provided for you was emotional security."

George Thomas was the youngest. The Battle of the Bulge was about to get under way when he was born in the late fall of 1944. Victory in Europe came less than six months later; the conquering of Japan a few months after that. He would grow up in a postwar Baby Boomer environment that has been mythologized by such books as David Halberstam's *The Fifties*: California barbecuing, drinks on the patio, socializing with neighbors, the kids' fast friends. Capitalism had not just survived, it had thrived. The Great Depression, the New Deal; done, dead. These were the Dwight Eisenhower years, and this was the middle class, the American dream. But in this West Coast version of the Kennedys, being youngest meant fighting for everything you got.

"When you are the fourth child in a family, you probably have to be a little tougher to survive," his mother told friends.

"His dad was Tom's idol," Charles Jr. said. "Our father was a perfectionist and he taught his boys to be the same way."

For reasons that have never really been explained, Tom went by his middle name from an early age. Tom played in the backyard with imaginary friends, one of whom was his alter ego, "George." He took to baseball over and above all other activities. The game was coming into its own as a televised sport. Tom imitated the players, sliding into "home," declaring himself "safe," arguing with the "umpire."

Eventually he was allowed to leave the house on his own, to venture into a street past sprinklers watering lawns. The music of the era was Pat Boone, not Nirvana. It was the age of innocence, the last vestiges of a bygone era before drugs, the antiwar protests of the 1960s, pornography, and the bone-chilling fear of child molestation.

Tom's mother read him a children's book called *The Little Engine That Could.*

"The lesson got through to me," he said. "I grew to share my mother's optimism, her feeling that everything would work out, that any goal could be achieved."

Tom made fast friends with a neighbor boy named Russ Scheidt. They played baseball together. Seaver learned control early on. Not allowed yet to cross the street, they played catch by throwing the ball across it. It required discipline and concentration lest the ball end up in "no man's land." Charles began playing "pepper" with him, which honed his all-around skills more. Tom had baseball tools. His father encouraged him. In 1953, with the Korean War coming to an end, eight-year-old Tom Seaver showed up for Little League tryouts. The coach, a high school teacher named Hal Bicknell, noticed that he was the smallest boy and told him he needed to be at least nine. He ran home bawling into the arms of his mother but resolved to come back the next year. When the time finally came, he made the North Rotary team of the Fresno Spartan League.

Tom was given uniform number 13 and immediately installed as a pitcher, the most important position on the field. One day an adult rooting for the opposing team shouted a stream of insults at young Tom, who cried but kept on pitching.

"He had this tremendous desire to succeed, to win," recalled Bicknell. He "didn't complain, didn't quit, just poured it right in there."

Charles Sr. went to the games but was never a "Little League parent," pushing his kids to be something they did not want to be. He sometimes sat not behind home plate but watched with the rest of the family from beyond the outfield fence with their dog, Little Bit. He encouraged his son as he did all his children, but he always stressed education above everything else. Charles was a perfectionist and instilled that in young Tom, but the desire extended beyond baseball to all things he endeavored in.

"I started playing ball when I was nine, but I was always a big fan," Seaver recalled. "Everything seemed so magical then. I remember the first time I ever saw Candlestick Park in San Francisco—I thought it was the greatest place in the world!" Later it was "my least favorite park in the National League. But as a child the Major Leagues were just very, very special.

"Although my friends liked the Yankees, I was more a fan of the underdog. My favorite teams were the Milwaukee Braves, the Pittsburgh Pirates, and the Philadelphia Phillies. It was some thrill for me when the Braves beat the Yankees in the 1957 World Series and when the Pirates did it in 1960. My two favorite players were Henry Aaron and Sandy Koufax, but I always seemed to follow hitters more than pitchers. How I loved those old Braves with those beautiful uniforms—Aaron, Eddie Mathews, Wes Covington, Jim Pendleton—that's right, even little-known guys like Covington and Pendleton were heroes to me.

"I was an avid reader of box scores. I could spend hours over them. They contain so much. I especially loved the Monday newspapers, with all those doubleheaders from the day before, when you could add the two games together to see how the players had done. That's one habit that hasn't left me—to this day, I love going over box scores.

"I saved baseball cards—wish I knew whatever became of all of them—and read *Sports Illustrated,* and I remember reading a biography of Ty Cobb called *The Georgia Peach.* Sometimes my dad would drive me 180 miles north from Fresno to San Francisco, and I could see the Giants play. My father often had business up there, or we would visit my sister at Stanford or my brother at Berkeley. Any excuse to visit San Francisco was okay with me. I think I saw the Giants play in Seals Stadium four times before Candlestick was opened. What powerhouse teams the Giants had in those days, with Willie Mays, Willie McCovey, Orlando Cepeda, Willie Kirkland, Leon Wagner, Felipe Alou—I guess I always liked guys who could hit it out of the park. Later on, though, when I became a pitcher, I grew to prefer guys who hit into double plays.

"I'd also follow the Major Leagues through the *Game of the Week,* and I'd listen to the local Fresno Cardinals on the radio. Larry Jackson, a right-hander who later starred in the Majors and killed the Mets, was 28–4 with 351 strikeouts for Fresno in 1952 . . .

"I was a nine-year-old Little League ballplayer," Seaver continued. "I loved baseball. Professional ballplayers were my idols. I collected baseball cards because I wanted to know everything about the game of baseball and the players.

"I was a student of the game of baseball. I read sports magazines and newspapers to learn everything I could about baseball. But I can honestly say that the best way I had of learning about the game was by studying my baseball cards.

"Lots of players do not go into baseball as 'fans.' They have spent, perhaps, too many hours on the field to study the backs of baseball cards or thumb through the record books. While most players can tell you who Babe Ruth and Ty Cobb were, you draw some blank stares when you get to Rogers Hornsby, Pie Traynor, or Jimmie Foxx. Forget about if you're talking about Hal Newhouser, Bucky Harris, or Gene Bearden."

Young Tom engrossed himself in dusty old baseball books.

"I must confess, I tended to enjoy the older stories more than the modern ones, the ones I'd lived through. The thought of Christy Mathewson and Walter Johnson standing on the mound, facing the same circumstances I encountered, having the infield play at double-play depth or in close, walking a man to get to a weaker hitter, fascinated me." Seaver recalled a time when Teddy Roosevelt was the president.

"It's still a tough 60 feet six inches between pitcher and batter, after all these years," he philosophized.

Young Seaver loved corny old baseball movies, too.

"To see the Lou Gehrig movie, or to read about his life, it's hard not to have tears in your eyes," he recollected. "It's happened to me—every time I see Gary Cooper making that famous speech, 'Today I consider myself the luckiest man on the face of the Earth.'"

Tom achieved the pinnacle of his Little League world, batting .543 and throwing a perfect game. Getting back to that level of perfection would drive his pitching career well into the big leagues.

For some reason, he could not master golf as he did baseball, which angered and frustrated him. His mother told him she would not play with him as long as he threw his clubs after bad shots, but he did follow Charles Sr. on the course, learning the art of quiet concentration.

"I've got the ability of self-control and discipline on the mound, and I certainly got that from my dad," he said.

Fresno in the 1950s and 1960s may well have been not just the baseball capital but also the sports capital of America. It was a competitive environment, producing young kids who went on to great success on the diamond. Jim Maloney came out of Fresno to become one of the hardest-throwing strikeout pitchers in baseball, the ace of the Cincinnati Reds. Dick Ellsworth was another hard-throwing chucker who went to the Mets. Wade Blasingame was a top infielder with the Reds. The 1959 Fresno State Bulldogs made it to the College World Series.

The town also produced Tom Flores, a quarterback hero who would star for the Oakland Raiders, later leading them to two Super Bowl titles as their coach. Daryle Lamonica followed Flores. After Notre Dame he became a two-time American Football League Most Valuable Player, quarterbacking the Raiders into the 1968 Super Bowl.

Little League ends at age 12. When the boys turn 13, they move on to Babe Ruth League play, which means making the enormous leap from small-field dimensions to a regular diamond: pitcher's mound 60 feet, six inches from home plate; the bases 90 feet apart. It is the end of many a "career." It almost was the end for Tom Seaver.

He had a friend named Dick Selma. He and Selma were rivals throughout Little League, competing for star status, their teams for supremacy. It was an even rivalry until junior high school. Selma continued to grow. As he entered Fresno High School he was reaching six feet in height with a muscular build. Tom was still five foot six and 140 pounds as a high school sophomore. On top of all else, Tom was by virtue of being born in November younger than most of his classmates, some of whom were born in January and therefore were almost a year older at a time when that year meant everything in a kid's development.

"He was the runt of our crowd," Selma recalled.

Selma made the Fresno High varsity as a sophomore, a singular honor that separates a young man from the pack. Tom barely made the junior varsity. While Selma impressed the local prep media and professional scouts, Seaver remained a JV. To still be a JV in one's junior year, as he was, invariably means that one lacks the skills to go beyond high school if indeed he makes the varsity in his last try as a senior. Tom did not throw hard, but he was smart. He learned how to set up hitters, to change speeds, developing a curve and even a knuckler.

"Tom was a hell of a pitcher, as contrasted to a thrower, even when he was on the JVs," Selma recalled after they both reached the big leagues. "He knew how to set up hitters, and him just in high school; I'm still learning now."

"As a teenager I had the widest assortment of pitches imaginable," Tom reminisced. "And I needed all the off-speed pitches I could find, because I just wasn't big enough to throw hard. When I was 13 I started throwing a slider, a pitch that dipped sharply down and away from right-handed hitters. At 14 I started throwing an exaggerated changeup, and by the time I was 15 I was throwing every kind of curve, sidearm, overhand, and three-quarters overhand. I was very lucky that all those freaky pitches I threw before I really was physically mature didn't strain or hurt my arm. I guess I was lucky."

High school sports success often dictates one's place in the social hierarchy. Being a career JV was a comedown after Little League stardom, but Tom had much more going for him. Despite his lack of size, he was a good-looking kid with an outgoing personality. Tom had easygoing charm and the gift of repartee. He was popular with teachers, with teammates, but most importantly with pretty girls. Above all other things, this is the prized attribute that determines a high school boy's place in the pecking order. He was a good student who decided he wanted to become a dentist.

"He was a real happy-go-lucky guy," Selma said. "He had a lot of friends and he always dated all the good-looking girls."

In his senior year, Tom wanted to play football, but his mother would not allow him. He went out for basketball, mainly to stay in shape for baseball. He was determined that he would make the most of what looked to be his last year of athletic competition. He was a 5-foot-10, 165-pound guard whose natural athleticism shone through. Surprisingly, he made the all-city team.

The scouts were out in force, but not to see him. Selma was on everybody's radar and would eventually sign with the expansion New York Mets for $20,000. Tom did manage to make it into the starting rotation under Fresno High coach Fred Bartels. Still lacking any heat, he was effective enough throwing off-speed pitches with control to win six games against five losses and a place on the all-city baseball team, "mostly because there wasn't anyone else to choose," he recalled. "When the professional scouts came around, looking over the local talent, some of the other kids got good offers. I didn't even get a conversation; not one scout approached me."

He was a natural leader. His teammates gravitated to him. During a road trip to Ontario for the playoffs, Seaver kept his team loose. Bartels gave him leeway, realizing that while he was small and not a star, he had star power via his charisma.

It was the beginning of the magical "summer of '62," the year depicted by filmmaker George Lucas, who grew up in nearby Modesto and would attend the University of Southern California with Seaver. The world Lucas showed in *American Graffiti* was the only one Tom Seaver knew. It was a unique central California culture of cars and girls. Tom Seaver's Fresno was not quite The Beach Boys'

Southland surf magic, nor the brewing, dangerous mix of angry protest, harmful drugs, and unprotected sex that would have such ultimately devastating consequences in the San Francisco Bay Area.

Songwriter Stephen Stills wrote a famous line: "There's something happening here; what it is ain't exactly clear." Indeed, in California something *was* happening there. It had been going on there for decades. Tom Seaver would come to symbolize what it was.

He hung out with a guy named Mike Podsakoff, who owned a 1958 Chevy, which they often drove to the local hangout, a barber shop, or they would tear about on the open roads dotting the agricultural lots surrounding Fresno.

California's political ethos can be traced back to the Civil War. Abraham Lincoln promoted the building of the Transcontinental Railroad. He received his greatest financial backing from the railroad companies. A look at the map leaves one pondering why the line was built over the difficult terrain of the Rocky and Sierra Mountain ranges, to San Francisco, instead of the relatively flat lands of Texas, Arizona, Nevada, the Southern California desert, and on into Los Angeles. The reason is that had it been built over the "Southern route," slaves would have built it. Lincoln could not condone that.

When the Civil War ended, a large migration to California occurred. Northerners from Boston and New York who supported the Union tended to favor San Francisco. Former Confederates favored Los Angeles. Later, when the Rose Bowl became popular, Midwesterners flocked to the warm lands of Southern California. As a result, the north took on a more liberal, secular nature. The south became more conservative and Christian.

However, intermixing within California created a general mind-set popular statewide. It became a progressive place, a trendsetter, a place of new ideas. In the north, a strong civil rights movement developed. Orange County and environs remained right wing, but on matters of race its white, Christian citizenry developed a sense of moderation unlike their Southern brethren, who thought like them on most other matters such as anti-Communism and small government.

Two Southern California political figures embodied this way of thinking. Both Richard Nixon and Ronald Reagan ascended to the White House in large measure on the strength of Southern support. Together, they husbanded the South "into the Union," so to speak, by making palatable to the South the conservative yet racially moderate views of Orange County and California in general.

So it was that in the 1950s and 1960s, a young white boy growing up in an affluent California suburb would feel free to choose as his sports hero a black man without thinking twice about it, with no repercussions from disapproving friends and family. When Tom Seaver was a young boy in Fresno, California, the Dodgers and Giants were still in New York. There were no Pacific Coast League teams near him. As a fan, he was a "free agent." He was not predisposed to root for white stars such as Mickey Mantle of the Yankees or Ted Williams of the Red Sox. After the clubs moved west, he lived in the fan bases of Willie Mays of the Giants and Sandy Koufax of the Dodgers, yet he chose as his favorite Henry Aaron, the smooth-swinging outfielder of the Milwaukee Braves. At that time he was an emerging superstar.

In later years, Seaver said he was "prejudiced" growing up in Fresno, that to look down upon black people was accepted. Perhaps Seaver was correct, but what he considered prejudice in the 1950s and early 1960s was moderate by American standards. It did not stop him from admiring Hank Aaron, at least as an athlete. Interracial dating and full-scale integration may not have been subjects on his radar screen, but whatever predisposed social constructs he was raised with did not affect his view of black baseball stars.

"It must have been his form that made me pick him," he said. "I sat through entire ball games, just looking at Henry Aaron, nothing else, fascinated by him, studying him at the plate and on the bases and in the field."

He was also impressed by the hustle and professionalism of Stan Musial.

"I have a very vivid recollection of Stan Musial when I was about 14," he once wrote. "The Cardinals were playing the Giants in the old Seals Stadium in San Francisco around 1958 or 1959. I went to the game especially to see Musial play. Well, he didn't have a particularly good day—he hit four routine grounders to second. Never got the ball out of the infield. But on every one he hustled as hard as he could to first base. I mean, he was a superstar, a legend, and he was almost 40, but that didn't stop him from playing the game the way it was supposed to be played. I'll never forget it."

He was a National League fan but did not relegate his rooting interests to the senior circuit.

"If there was one team in the American League I followed more than any other while growing up, I guess it would have been the Chicago White Sox . . . somehow the way the White Sox played ball got to me," he declared. "They weren't a big team, but they were good." Nellie Fox "stood out" and Billy Pierce was a "stylish pitcher."

Seaver once expressed some question as to why he, a pitcher, chose as his idol an outfielder. Later, when he went to the University of Southern California, he attended many Dodgers games on season tickets owned by his uncle.

"Sandy Koufax became my hero," he said. "But he never really replaced Aaron."

The choice of the Jewish Koufax is also emblematic. Tom Seaver, raised a Protestant, became a race-neutral white man. As he matured and broadened his horizons, he chose his heroes, idols, associates, roommates, and friends strictly on merit and personal commonalities. At USC his roommate would be Mike Garrett, a black running back on the football team (also a baseball outfielder who later played professionally for the Dodgers organization) from the inner-city Los Angeles neighborhood of Boyle Heights. Seaver would bring his California attitude with him to New York. He would be part of the "new breed" of modern athletes in the late 1960s.

But that was all a long ways away in 1962. The dream of big-league glory was gone. Tom had no reason to believe he had a chance, but his love of the game would never go away. There was also the matter of college. Coming from a solidly middle-class family, his father undoubtedly could have paid his tuition, but he had already put Tom's three older siblings through school, interestingly enough attending three of the four great California universities.

Katie was a swimmer and volleyball player at Stanford who once punched a fresh guy in an off-campus bar. Charles Jr. swam at the University of California. Carol majored in physical education at UCLA before joining the Peace Corp in Nigeria.

Charles Seaver's plans for his youngest son were quite pedestrian: study business at Fresno City College while working for the Bonner Packing Company, then begin as an executive, rising up the ranks. Tom, however, saw a world beyond Fresno. He had his heart set on studying dentistry at the fourth of the great California colleges, USC, a private school with steep tuition costs and one of the best dental schools in the nation. He wanted to spare his father from fronting the money. A plan was hatched: Instead of college after high school, he would serve in the U.S. Marines. He would save and earn some money, getting some help from the G.I. Bill. That would only assuage a little bit of the cost. A tiny voice in the back of Tom Seaver's mind would not go away.

What about a baseball scholarship?

This seemed to be a ludicrous proposition. USC had the best baseball program in the nation, led by legendary coach Rod Dedeaux. They had their choice of the best players. If a hot prospect did not wish to go directly into professional baseball, his college choices were basically USC, SC, Southern California, or Southern Cal; at least it seemed that way. Dedeaux had no more interest in a junk-baller from Fresno than the pro scouts who ignored him did.

First things first. While waiting to report for Marine Corps basic training, Tom worked for the Bonner Packing Company. It was not an internship in his father's plush office suites. Rather, he got up each day before dawn and spent the day wrestling enormous boxes of raisins along a loading platform. Two or three men were needed to lift the "sweat boxes." The temperature in the un-air-conditioned warehouse was 100 degrees in the summertime. Sometimes snakes, rats, and spiders slithered out of the boxes.

"After six months it was almost a relief to go into the Marines," he stated. At night, Tom pitched for an American Legion team. Something was already happening to Tom Seaver. As he approached his 18th birthday, he was getting taller, was putting on weight, and was stronger after lifting "sweat boxes." Tom could feel his clothes tightening on his body, his pants becoming too short. He could not help but think that he was throwing harder in July than he had in April. His baseball dreams would not die.

He joined the Marines with his boyhood friend, Russ Scheidt. First came three months at Camp Pendleton, the famed home of the so-called Hollywood Marines (as opposed to those who train in Parris Island, South Carolina) near San Diego.

"I hated the Marine Corps boot camp," Seaver wrote in *The Perfect Game*, an autobiographical review of his 1969 World Series victory over Baltimore, written in collaboration with Dick Schaap. Caught with a dirty rifle, for three-and-a-half hours he had to do an exercise called "up-and-on shoulders, first holding out my rifle, which weighed 11 pounds, then lifting it over my head, then holding it out again."

"No, no, no, you don't stop 'til *I get tired*!" the drill instructor yelled in typical Southern Marine voice cadence, when Seaver seemed too exhausted to go on.

The DI in fact *did* get tired, and several had to take turns "supervising" Seaver, who "thought I was going to die." After getting caught whispering to Scheidt, verboten during chow time, one DI jumped on the table, running toward him, food and plates flying everywhere. He took Seaver outside, kicking him over and over again. By this time Seaver had been in boot camp for 10 weeks. He was a "trained-to-kill Marine, and nothing could hurt me short of an M-14 rifle in the chest." He had tears in his eyes . . . to keep from laughing!

Seaver graduated from boot camp a new man.

"It was all part of the psychology of being a Marine," Seaver stated. "They were going to keep only those who stand it, and they tried hard to make guys quit. At the same time they kept pushing at each individual, appealing to him, that he was different—he was a Marine. Marines are different."

He joined a Marine Reserve unit and by the fall of 1963 enrolled at Fresno City College. For more than a year since high school, he had eaten three squares a day and done countless push-ups, pull-ups, and "up-and-on shoulders." As he got older he had grown. In this period of time he had gone from 5 foot 10, 165 pounds to 6 foot 1, 195 pounds. He was a grown man, physically and mentally. He had pitched a little for a Marine team and had a sneaking suspicion that he was able to throw harder than ever, and if so . . .

Strolling down the street in Fresno, Tom passed a man he had known all his life. The man did not recognize him.

"Hey, remember me?" he called out to him.

"My God," he said. "Is that little Tom Seaver?"

There still seemed no hope of that scholarship from USC, and none of Major League glory, but Seaver had the indomitable optimism of his mother.

The Little Engine That Could.

The Fresno City College Rams have one of the greatest J.C. baseball traditions in the country. Jim Maloney, Dick Ellsworth, and Dick Selma all pitched there before going to the big leagues. Scouts and college coaches paid attention to them. In September of 1963, a couple months shy of his 19th birthday, Seaver came out for what the coaches and players call "fall ball." He was known for having made all-city pitcher at Fresno High, even if it had been "because there wasn't anyone else to choose."

But his new height, the 30 pounds of muscle, the newfound strength, gave Tom confidence that he could not help but be noticed by coaches and players alike. After the initial period of conditioning came the moment of truth: tryouts on the mound. After warming up, Seaver got set, went into his motion, and delivered *a 90-mile-per-hour fastball.*

The ball sailed up and in, smacking into the catcher's mitt with a loud thud. Suddenly, USC did not look like such a pipe dream. In the spring of 1964, freshman right-hander Tom Seaver was the ace of coach Les Bourdet's conference champion Fresno City College Rams, winning his last eight decisions to compile an 11–2 record against stiff competition, earning team MVP honors. This created an entirely new dynamic. Fred Bartels was stunned that Seaver, whom he coached when he was a "runt" at Fresno High, was now a hard-throwing star. Charles and Betty Seaver had to change their minds, too.

They wanted him to stay in Fresno and go to work for the Bonner Packing Company. If he went on to a four-year school, Charles intended to pay for it, but his son had an independent streak. He wanted a baseball scholarship and wanted to go to college beyond Fresno's borders, just like the Ron Howard character in *American Graffiti.*

2

THE NEW YORK YANKEES OF COLLEGE BASEBALL: 1964–1966

WHAT WAS HAPPENING TO SEAVER WAS LESS A PHENOMENON AND more common than many realize. The high school "blue chipper" is accorded great attention, but many times he has physically matured sooner than his peers have. Sometimes he peaks at the age of 17 or 18. Others, like Seaver, grow, gain strength, and mature in more ways than one. Few make the kind of transition that Tom Seaver would ultimately make, but many high school "suspects" in various sports go on to become prospects in college, in the minor leagues, and in their 20s. Some attain stardom. Scouting is a very tricky, unpredictable business.

Still, Seaver's case was more unusual than the normal "late bloomers." The impossible seemed to have occurred. His 11–2 record at Fresno City College earned the recruiting attention of Rod Dedeaux. Seaver was a legitimate fastball artist. Dedeaux called him the "phee-nom from San Joaquin."

But Dedeaux needed to know for sure that Seaver could compete for the Trojans. "I only have five scholarships to give out," the coach told him. Before the ride would be offered, Seaver would have to prove himself with the Fairbanks, Alaska, Goldpanners.

Today, collegiate summer baseball is a well-known commodity. Many scouts place more credence on a player's performance in one of these leagues than they do on college seasons. The Cape Cod League uses only wooden bats, which proves to be a great equalizer for pitchers and a shock for aluminum-bat sluggers who find themselves batting .250 on the Cape. Summer ball has a long tradition in Canada, where American collegians test themselves in such exotic locales as Calgary, Edmonton, and Red Deer, Alberta. The Kamloops International Tournament in British Columbia has attracted some of the fastest baseball for decades. The Jayhawk League, consisting of teams from Boulder, Pueblo, and Colorado Springs plus Kansas and Iowa, was once a leading destination for college players. The California Collegiate Summer League, consisting of teams from the Humboldt Crabs in the north to the San Diego Aztecs in the south, has produced many stars in its various forms over the years.

But the Alaskan Summer Collegiate League is the most legendary. For a time, the league became the Alaska-Hawaii League, with teams flying in for extended road trips on the islands and the "land of the midnight sun."

"The team was put together by a man named Red Boucher," said former Mets pitcher Danny Frisella, who was a teammate of Seaver's in Fairbanks. Boucher was the mayor of Fairbanks. "He got all the best young ballplayers up there." Andy Messersmith of the University of California became a 20-game winner with the California Angels. Mike Paul pitched for Cleveland. Graig Nettles played for Minnesota. USC quarterback Steve Sogge, a baseball catcher, played on that team. Rick Monday was an All-American at Arizona State, where he was a teammate of Reggie Jackson and Sal Bando in a program that captured the 1965 national championship (also producing Mets pitcher Gary Gentry). In the very first amateur draft ever held in 1965, Monday became the first player chosen, by the Kansas City A's.

"Monday was there the year I was and he couldn't even make our team," said Frisella. "I think 13 guys were signed off that team. It was semi-pro ball, and we played eight games a week. We didn't get paid. Not for playing ball. But I earned $650 a month for pulling a lever on a dump truck. And I didn't have to pull the lever too often."

The man most responsible for the growth of summer collegiate baseball was Dedeaux. In 1963, when his Trojans won their fourth national championship, the press dubbed his team the "New York Yankees of college baseball." He eventually retired with 11 College World Series titles, having produced such stalwarts as Ron Fairly, Don Buford, Bill "Spaceman" Lee, Jim Barr, Dave Kingman, Rich Dauer, Steve Kemp, Fred Lynn, Steve Busby, Roy Smalley, Mark McGwire, and Randy Johnson. His successor, Mike Gillespie, won the school's 12th College World Series in 1998 (Louisiana State is second with six) while producing such talented stars as Bret Boone, Aaron Boone, Jeff Cirillo, Geoff Jenkins, Jacque Jones, Morgan Ensberg, Barry Zito, and Mark Prior.

If a young player wanted to test himself among the best of the best, he could find no more competitive environment than the USC baseball program. For Tom Seaver, having tasted real success for the first time in his life at Fresno City College, it represented the ultimate challenge. He needed that scholarship—not just to save his father from paying the steep tuition but also to give himself imprimatur as opposed to "walk-on" status.

Dedeaux had come out of Hollywood High School to become the captain of the Trojan baseball team. He had the briefest of Major League "careers" with the Brooklyn Dodgers but befriended his manager, Casey Stengel. Later, Stengel brought his Yankees to Los Angeles for exhibition games against USC, giving college players the chance to play against Mickey Mantle and Whitey Ford. After retirement from managing the Mets, he became a banking executive in Glendale, the L.A. suburb where Dedeaux lived. For years Casey was a regular at Trojan baseball games.

Dedeaux was a key figure in organizing and growing the popularity of the College World Series. The first CWS was held in Kalamazoo, Michigan, and featured the University of California Golden Bears beating Yale for the national title. Yale's first baseman was a war veteran named George H. W. Bush. Bush and Yale came back the next year, only to be beaten this time by Dedeaux's Trojans. Eventually, the CWS found a permanent home in Omaha, Nebraska.

"He never looked like a ballplayer, but he had eyes in the back of his head," said Bill Lee, who played four years under him from 1965 to 1968, winning the national title in his senior year. "He knew in the first inning what would happen in the fifth; in the fifth what to expect in the eighth." The greatest teams Lee ever saw were "the 1975 Cincinnati Reds, any Taiwanese little league team, and the 1968 USC Trojans!"

"Dedeaux was the sharpest tack in the box," recalled Mike Gillespie, who played on his 1961 College World Series champions.

An extraordinary amount of athletic talent flowed to the professional sports leagues from USC and California in general. Huge crowds watching Trojan football games at the L.A. Memorial Coliseum played a large role in luring the Dodgers and Lakers out west. Dedeaux modernized the collegiate game from a "club sport" to a pipeline for the pros. Utilizing the perfect California weather, he turned his into a year-round program. There was "fall ball" from September to Thanksgiving, followed by a full slate of 50 to 60 games in the spring instead of a paltry 20 or 25. But it was summer ball that Dedeaux turned into breeding grounds for diamond success.

A college player generally returned to his hometown after school let out and played on a pickup team or a ragamuffin semipro outfit. The competition was not good and players benefited little, returning to school without having progressed. Dedeaux wanted his players to experience something akin to minor league life—playing nightly games, traveling, and handling a fast brand of ball that prepared them for the college season, then a pro career.

In the 1950s he sent his players to Canada, where in addition to good baseball experience they enjoyed the educational aspects of life in a locale far from home. When Alaska became a state, Red Boucher raised money to build a first-class facility and began recruiting the best collegians to Fairbanks. Dedeaux and USC were his number one source. A league was developed with teams in Fairbanks, Anchorage (the Glacier Pilots and later the nearby North Pole Knicks), Palmer Valley (the Green Giants), and the Kenai Peninsula (the Oilers). Teams from Canada and the contiguous lower 48 states traveled to Alaska. The sun almost never set in the summer. Lights were not needed. On June 21 a "midnight sun" game starting at 11:00 p.m. was played without any lighting. The Alaskan teams also traveled, playing in an end-of-summer tournament called the National Baseball Congress in Wichita, Kansas. The NBC featured all the best teams from across America. The Canadian teams generally played in the Kamloops International Tournament.

Years later, when Tom Seaver became a broadcaster even before his playing career ended, he told partner Joe Garagiola of his Alaskan experience during a World Series telecast.

"They play baseball in Alaska?" asked Garagiola.

"Really good baseball, Joe," replied Seaver.

"Tell me about it," inquired Garagiola, and Seaver did just that.

In June 1964, Seaver boarded a plane for Fairbanks to join a team consisting of future big leaguers Monday, Nettles, Curt Motton, Ken Holtzman, and Gary Sutherland of USC. They were All-Americans with national reputations. Seaver was immediately intimidated, wondering whether he, a junior college pitcher still battling the insecurities of a nothing prep career, could compete at this level. He had little time for contemplation once he arrived, however. Boucher's wife met him at the airport.

"We're playing a game right now," she told him. "I brought a uniform with me. You can put it on at the field. We may need you."

The beautiful stadium and the large crowd struck Seaver. In a town of 20,000, some 50,000 people attended Goldpanners games each summer.

"I dressed in a shack near the field," Seaver recalled.

There was no time for introductions when he arrived in the dugout, beyond Boucher's handshake and orders to get to the bullpen and warm up *right now.* The score was tied 2–2 with the Bellingham, Washington, Bells in the fifth inning as Seaver hurriedly got loose, was waved into the game, and "met my catcher on the way to the mound."

He proceeded to retire the side, then met his teammates in the dugout. That night, Seaver pitched effectively in relief, earning a hard-fought victory and the respect of his all-star mates. He was used mainly in relief, later rating himself the "third- or fourth-line pitcher" on the 'Panners. He lived with the Bouchers. Aside from being a community leader, Red was a sharp baseball man who taught young Seaver important lessons on the psychology of pitching. He was very much like Tom's optimist mother. Seaver came to understand that half the battle was believing in himself. Through psychology and the experience of successfully testing himself against the best, he was gaining invaluable confidence. Boucher told him that each morning he needed to wake up and say to himself, "I *am* a Major Leaguer."

One of Tom's good friends in Fairbanks was Rick Monday, who also did a tour in the Marine Reserves. They often went fishing together. Dedeaux coached a summer team of USC players in Los Angeles that traveled to Fairbanks. Seaver pitched and mowed them down with high heat. When Boucher yelled at Dedeaux from across the field to ask how it was going, the USC coach cracked, "How the hell would I know? I haven't seen the ball since the second inning." Seaver made the Alaska all-star team, a huge honor that often meant a player was considered an All-American prospect when the college season began. Seaver's scholarship offer was seemingly secured that night, but there were still bumps in the road.

"Alaska was something else," Seaver remembered. "You simply can't realize what a magnificent place it is unless you've been there. And it's a lot different than most people picture it. . . .

"The weather in July and August is ideal. It's in the high 60s and 70s every day and no humidity. It's the time of year when they have 24 hours of sunlight and it's pretty weird."

In August the Goldpanners made their way to Wichita for the NBC, stopping in Grand Junction, Colorado, for a tune-up against a fast semi-pro outfit. Seaver started but was hammered off the mound. NBC rules required the roster be reduced to 18 players. Boucher had to decide between Seaver and Holtzman, an All-American at the University of Illinois. He visited Seaver in his hotel room to inquire of his confidence, but the young Californian just told him to "try me." Boucher kept Seaver.

Against the Wichita Glassmen, Seaver was called on in relief with the Goldpanners winning 2–0. The bases were loaded in the fifth inning with one out. Boucher tried to steady his reliever, but

Seaver just growled that he had "listened to you all summer long. Now it's up to me. Give me the ball and get out of here."

Confident or not, it took some doing for Seaver to steady himself. Two walks and an infield hit pushed across three runs and now the Goldpanners trailed, 3–2. A double play kept the damage down. Over the next innings Seaver gained command. It was before the days of the designated hitter. In the eighth inning with the bases loaded, Seaver came to the plate. Boucher saw something in the young man who had once batted .543 with 10 home runs in Little League. He decided to let him hit. Seaver responded with a grand slam to win the game. He pitched and won a second game in the tournament, earning summer All-American honors from the National Baseball Congress. For the first time, professional scouts were evaluating him.

"We had a lot of players who could throw the ball harder than Tom," Boucher recalled. "His fastball moved well, but he was no Sandy Koufax. His curve and slider were not much better than average by college standards. His greatest asset was his tremendous will to win. And he had this super concentration. He believed he could put the ball right *through* the bat if he wanted to."

Dedeaux called Boucher and inquired of several USC players on the Fairbanks roster. Boucher interrupted him to say that Seaver would be "your best pitcher." Boucher assured him that he would "bet on it," to which Dedeaux replied that the Alaska manager was so high on the kid, "I really don't have any choice."

Seaver had finally assured himself of the scholarship. His matriculation at USC completed a full educational cycle within his family: Charles Jr. (University of California), sister Katie (Stanford like their father), and sister Carol (UCLA Bruins). Now Tom was a Trojan. Despite his quick rise, he still did not allow himself to dream of big-league glory. His immediate goal was to attain a degree in dental studies, leading to a career in dentistry.

He arrived at USC during a golden age on campus and in Los Angeles. That fall of 1964, quarterback Craig Fertig led the Trojans to a breathtaking comeback victory over Notre Dame, 20–17. USC running back Mike Garrett would go on to become the first of the school's seven Heisman Trophy winners.

The actor Tom Selleck, a basketball, baseball, and volleyball star out of Van Nuys High School, was on campus. A few years separated them, but Seaver and Bill Lee were in the program at the same time. It was a dominant age, under athletic director Jess Hill the greatest sustained sports run in college history. Aside from Dedeaux's perennial champions, John McKay's football team won two national titles and two Heismans in the decade. The track, swimming, and tennis teams won NCAA titles with regularity.

Crosstown, John Wooden's UCLA basketball dynasty was just heating up that year. Big-league baseball was in full swing on the West Coast. The Los Angeles Angels were an expansion team. The Giants and Dodgers had continued their rivalry in California. Sandy Koufax and the Dodgers sold out the beautiful new Dodger Stadium and won the World Series twice in three years.

The famed USC film school also became world class at that time. Two of their most famous students were in school when Seaver was there. George Lucas would create the blockbuster *Star Wars* series. John Milius wrote the screenplays *Dirty Harry* and *Magnum Force* and then directed *The Wind and the Lion* and *Red Dawn*, among many others. He would become known as the most conservative filmmaker in notoriously liberal Hollywood. Another aspiring film student was turned down by USC. Steven Spielberg had to settle for Cal State, Long Beach, but as friends with Lucas and Milius, Spielberg was hanging around the campus so much he seemed to have matriculated there.

Those three became friends with Francis Ford Coppola, who was attending film school at UCLA along with future Doors' rock legends Jim Morrison, Ray Manzarek, and John Densmore. Together, Lucas, Milius, Spielberg, and Coppola hatched a harebrained scheme to go to Vietnam with actors to film a "docudrama" in the style of *Medium Cool*, which was half movie, half footage from the 1968 Democratic National Convention in Chicago. The Vietnam idea was nixed (for some odd reason) by the Pentagon but eventually became *Apocalypse Now*, featuring the haunting music of Morrison singing "The End." All of it was detailed in a fabulous 1998 Hollywood book by Peter Biskind called *Easy Riders, Raging Bulls* and in the documentary *Hearts of Darkness.*

The USC campus had always been conservative, fraternity oriented, and traditional, but even more so when Seaver arrived. That fall, Republican presidential candidate Barry Goldwater energized a conservative movement based in nearby Orange County, embodied by Republican student politics at USC. Numerous USC (and UCLA) graduates made up the campaign and later administration staffs of Richard Nixon. Among them were Watergate figures H. R. Haldeman, John Ehrlichman, Dwight Chapin, and Donald Segretti. In the 1976 film *All the President's Men,* the Segretti character tells Dustin Hoffman, playing Carl Bernstein, about the so-called USC Mafia of that era.

Bill Lee got a taste of the stuck-up nature of social life on campus, which he described in his riotous 1984 autobiography, *The Wrong Stuff.* Lee was dating a beautiful sorority sister until movie star "Alan Ladd's kid snaked her away from me," presumably with a show of wealth.

Dedeaux was a gregarious character who knew everybody who was anybody, including Casey Stengel.

"My baseball coach at USC, Rod Dedeaux, was a very close personal friend to Casey, and he'd often tell us stories about him, probably all true," recalled Tom.

Seaver enrolled as a predental student, joined the Sigma Chi fraternity, and quickly made friends with Dedeaux's son, Justin. His Marine experience immediately separated him from the silly frat boys. Seaver and the younger Dedeaux roomed together and hunted pheasant on occasion. They learned how to cook them, and they became the specialty of the house. The Trojans made an annual trip to Hawaii, where Seaver had an unusual meeting with Stan Musial.

"The first time I met Musial I was in Hawaii with my college baseball team, and we were ordered off the beach because there was a tidal wave warning," Seaver remembered. "So we ran into the nearest hotel and up to the third floor. As we were running down the hall, I saw Musial in his room, watching the ocean with his wife and a friend. I couldn't resist the opportunity to just walk into his room and say hello. I didn't usually have that much nerve, but I couldn't let that moment pass. I reminded him about it once, and he said he remembered, but maybe he was just being polite."

He also befriended Mike Garrett. This arrangement came to symbolize all that is righteous about college sports. Here was Seaver, the white middle-class son of an affluent business executive, "prejudiced" while in high school, paired with Garrett, the black inner-city son of a single mother. Had they not been teammates at USC, these two never would have found each other. Instead they became the best of friends.

Garrett was an introspective young man bound and determined to make the most of his opportunity. He had been an All-American at Roosevelt High School in Los Angeles and of course made his name on the football field, winning the Heisman Trophy in 1965 and helping the Kansas City Chiefs win the 1970 Super Bowl. Eventually, he graduated from law school and became USC's athletic director, where he hired the great Pete Carroll in 2000. Garrett was just as serious about baseball, too.

"Mike was serious about things," said assistant USC football coach Dave Levy. "One time he and I got into a big discussion, and he expressed frustration that he could not rent an apartment in Pasadena because he was black. I just told him he needed to understand there were white folks of good conscience and that you had to let people change. I had discussions with black kids at USC, and I said they needed to take advantage of the educational opportunities that sports provided them. Mike came to agree with me."

"If you'd told me that a black kid from Boyle Heights would win the Heisman Trophy," Garrett said on the *History of USC Football* DVD (2005), "I'd have just said, 'You're crazy.'"

Seaver and Garrett were both intensely dedicated. They worked out together. Justin Dedeaux was amazed that Seaver could keep up with Garrett stride-for-stride running wind sprints. The Garrett-Seaver relationship also directly marks the beginning of a revolution in sports training, with profound consequences. Baseball players were told not to lift weights, that to do so would "tie up" their muscles, making them unable to throw and swing the bat. But Seaver had seen how much better he had gotten when he got stronger lifting boxes and later doing push-ups, pull-ups, and rifle exercises in the Marines.

Jerry Merz, a friend of Seaver's who studied physical education, recommended that Seaver lift weights to increase his strength. Garrett lifted weights for football, and Seaver asked him to help start a regimen, which he did. Seaver's stocky body responded to weight training, with immediate good results on the field. He would take his weight training routine with him into professional baseball, influencing a change in the perception of weights in the 1970s. Over time, all baseball players would bulk up on weights, and eventually this led to the rampant use of steroids.

Seaver's casual, open relationship with Garrett was an eye-opener for him. Despite idolizing Henry Aaron from a young age, he had met few blacks. He had adopted the country club racism accepted by whites of that era, probably without fully realizing it. Charles "Tree" Young was a black track, basketball, and football star at Edison High School in Fresno a few years after Seaver came out of Fresno High. He became an All-American tight end on the 1972 USC football team generally considered the greatest in history and later a star with the 1981 world champion San Francisco 49ers before entering the Christian ministry.

"I most certainly knew all about Tom Seaver," Young said. "He was from Fresno, had starred at USC, and made good with the New York Mets. But the Fresno of the 1960s was a place where you needed to know your place."

Young lived in the "black section" of Fresno. It was not a segregated society, certainly not like the South. Edison High was integrated and Young a popular student-athlete.

"If you are good in athletics, you can go places and do things unavailable to others," Young said. "When I arrived at USC, my first question was, *Where's the blacks?* I quickly discerned that there was double meaning in the term *Southern* California. But through sports, black brethren and white brethren became one. It took some doing, and on our football team it did not happen overnight."

Young was a member of the 1970 USC football team that traveled to Birmingham and, behind running back Sam "Bam" Cunningham, defeated Alabama, thus effectuating great racial change in the South. The Trojan team he played on, ironically, was racially divided as a result of the playing of black quarterback Jimmy Jones over white hotshot Mike Rae.

The nature of USC—its conservatism and traditions—has been credited by those who were there at the time with allowing social change to freely occur. By contrast, angst and war protests dominated life at rival campuses Cal-Berkeley and Stanford. According to John McKay, the supposedly "enlightened" Stanford student body directed "the most vile, foul racial epithets I ever heard" at his team, one in which McKay had provided more and greater opportunities for black athletes than any in the nation, when they made their way onto the Stanford Stadium field.

A few years prior to that, Tom Seaver brought a certain amount of white conservatism with him. After all, his father ran a large company, and he had never been exposed to radical politics. But USC was a place where ideas could flow more easily than at a segregated Southern campus, yet be tempered by the kind of respect for tradition that seemed to have been lost at Berkeley. The Cal campus was allowing itself to become the de facto staging grounds of American Communism in the 1960s.

In the hierarchy of Trojan sports, Mike Garrett towered above a junior college baseball transfer like Seaver. But as teammates they gravitated to each other, finding their similarities more compelling than their differences. Garrett was considered undersized, and Seaver—at least until his recent growth spurt—had always identified himself as "the runt of our crowd," as Dick Selma put it. He felt only admiration for Mike, who forged success for himself without the kinds of physical gifts of a later Trojan superstar, O. J. Simpson.

In 1965, Seaver worked hard to make it onto USC's starting rotation, although his NBC All-American status gave him great imprimatur. Oddly, it was a down year for the Trojans, who finished 9–11 in conference play, in fourth place behind cochampions Stanford and California, and one game back of crosstown rival UCLA. But Seaver was excellent, winning 10 games overall against only two defeats with a 2.47 earned run average, establishing himself as the undisputed staff ace. He was named to the all-conference team along with Garrett and Justin Dedeaux. A major boost in his confidence came in an alumni game when Seaver got Dodgers first baseman

Ron Fairly, a former Trojan, to pop up on a slider. As Fairly ran past Seaver on the mound he said, "Pretty good pitch, kid." Seaver had retired a big-league hitter and allowed himself to dream big-league dreams (three years later in the Major Leagues, Fairly connected on a Seaver slider for a home run).

"Even at USC, I was a six-pack-and-a-pickup-truck guy, but Tom was a champagne-and-cigar-in-the-back-of-a-limousine guy," recalled ex-Trojan and Boston Red Sox favorite Bill "Spaceman" Lee.

"I knew Tom from the fraternity," recalled football All-American Tim Rossovich. "He was a tough guy. He was like a football mentality in a baseball player, but also really smart and a great athlete."

In June of 1965, the very first Major League draft was held. Rick Monday, an All-American outfielder for national champion Arizona State, was the number one pick. Because he had not gone into the Marines his first year after high school, the sophomore Seaver's college class was in its third year, making him eligible for the draft. Already, the strategy behind obtaining maximum signing bonuses meant that college juniors would get more, since they had the bargaining leverage of returning for their senior year. A graduated senior had to take whatever was offered him or go home, his eligibility gone.

His favorite team, the Los Angeles Dodgers, drafted Seaver. He and his USC pals regularly went to nearby Dodger Stadium on his uncle's tickets to watch the great Sandy Koufax pitch.

"He had an artistic style," recalled Seaver. "He used every part of his body in pitching. His mechanics were what I watched. He was so smooth." One night Seaver saw Koufax knocked out of the box, a rarity. Koufax walked off the mound with his head held high. Four days later Tom was back at Dodger Stadium. Koufax blew his opponent away, back in form.

Scout Tom Lasorda came around to negotiate. If Seaver had lacked any confidence before, making All-American at the National Baseball Congress, retiring Fairly, and compiling a 10–2 mark for Troy took care of that. Lasorda offered $2,000. Seaver came back with $50,000, arguing that Selma had received $20,000 from the Mets out of junior college, and he was a seasoned Trojan star. Lasorda came up to $3,000, but that was that. The tantalizing possibility of Tom Seaver's forging a career on the great Dodgers teams of the 1970s would be only that, tantalizing.

"Good luck in your dental career," Lasorda told him.

It was a real-world business lesson Seaver was not going to learn in any economics class. It also meant a return to Fairbanks in the summer of 1965. This time Seaver did not arrive in Alaska as an unknown, dressing in a shack and introducing himself to his catcher on the mound. There was a sense of hierarchy on the Goldpanners, and the ace pitcher at the University of Southern California was tops on that hierarchy. It was as talented a team as any in the country, the "all-star" concept of picking the best collegians from around the nation making the Goldpanners better than most college teams and probably better than a lot of minor league clubs.

The "pitching staff was so deep and talented—Andy Messersmith, Al Schmelz, Danny Frisella, and I were the starters," recalled Seaver. As can happen when a young athlete achieves success, a sense of overconfidence—some call it "senioritis"—can affect his performance and often requires some "negative feedback" in order to right the tilting ship. Seaver again made the Alaska all-star team. He thought pretty highly of himself as the Goldpanners again made it to the NBC in Wichita, but the plethora of talented pitchers, all vying for mound time to gain experience, strengthen their college resumes, and of course get visibility for the scouts, meant that Seaver's toughest competition came on his own team. In Wichita, "I had a chance to win only one game before we reached the semi-finals" against the Wichita Dreamliners.

A big crowd and lots of scouts came out for a ballyhooed matchup between the hotshot Trojan hurler and a semi-pro outfit consisting of four recent big-league performers: Bobby Boyd, Jim Pendleton, Charlie Neal, and Rod Kanehl. Neal and Kanehl had played for the New York Mets. Neal led off the game with a triple, Boyd added three hits, and Kanehl stole home as the Dreamliners defeated Seaver, 6–3. Seaver probably could have pitched around some of the former big leaguers but challenged them instead, paying the price. He hated walking hitters even if it meant giving them a pitch they could hit. After getting knocked from the mound, Boyd approached him.

"Kid, you got a great future ahead of you," he told him. "You're going to be a big-league pitcher."

"I just stared at him," said Seaver. "I didn't believe a word he said." Seaver felt the veteran was mocking him. That night, Tom and some teammates went out for beers. Kanehl joined them, repeating what Boyd had said. Fairly had expressed admiration for his ability, too. *Maybe they're right.*

"The thought had me walking on air for a couple of weeks," Seaver recalled.

Schmelz and Frisella both signed with the Mets instead of returning to school. Seaver came back to Southern Cal and immediately noticed a bevy of scouts at the "fall ball" games. He attended a number of Dodgers games that September, focusing on Koufax as he pitched his team to the world championship. The consensus among the scouts was that Seaver was one of the top young prospects in amateur baseball and that the Dodgers had blown it by not signing him in the summer.

While Seaver's baseball future was developing, so too was his personal future. In 1964 he sat in a class at Fresno City College a few seats away from a pretty blonde named Nancy Lynn McIntyre. His smooth repartee and way with the girls deserted him, and he never said "two words to her the entire semester."

At the end of the spring semester before heading north to Alaska, Seaver and some pals blew off steam drinking beers and playing softball when he spotted her. Impulsively he ran toward her and, in what had to be one of the most awkward "first dates" in history, was unable to stop himself; he ran into her, knocking her flat. He then picked her up and asked if she wanted to go to a softball game.

"No," she replied.

"It definitely was not love at first sight," she said, laughing. "He had his hair plastered, was skinny, and had big teeth and hands—a late developer."

Seaver then, for all practical purposes, kidnapped her. She endured the softball game and agreed to a second "date" if it would be less violent. Nancy was born in Kansas but grew up in Fresno with three brothers. Her father owned a liquor store. She attended a rival high school.

Over the next year and a half, the relationship faced challenges with Nancy in Fresno and Tom in Alaska for two summers and in Los Angeles going to school. She occasionally came to visit. He saw her on vacations back to Fresno. Their casual agreement was that they would see other people. In Los Angeles, Tom knew that a pretty girl like Nancy would have no trouble finding a guy. He had always been popular with girls. Dick Selma expressed amazement at how, despite being a JV pitcher, he dated all the best-looking girls in high school.

Now he was a "big man on campus," best friend of the Heisman Trophy winner, star of the baseball team, rumored to be a bonus baby when the draft came around. Girls at USC were plentiful and he dated his share of them. Perhaps his Marine experience, or the up-and-down nature of baseball, had matured him beyond his years, but for whatever reason he did not want to "play the field" anymore. He and Nancy agreed to be exclusive, and after some initial difficulties both realized that they wanted marriage, a family, and stability. He told Nancy USC girls seemed only interested in "clothes and parties."

"Nancy and I," he wrote in *The Perfect Game,* "seemed . . . to realize at the same time that life wasn't about all parties, that we could be serious about ourselves and about other things without being pretentious or somber." They both wanted to "live in a real world."

They decided to marry, and more importantly, never to hurt each other—easier said than done. Tom's prospects were certainly excellent. If baseball did not pan out, he would have a USC degree, followed by dental school and a nice practice back in Fresno. The only friendly glitch in the relationship was the fact that Nancy's father argued the merits of Notre Dame football while Tom supported his Trojans. The Tom-Nancy partnership would prove to be a remarkable love story.

3

THE CHOSEN ONE: 1966–1967

TOM SEAVER WAS EXPECTED TO BE A JUNIOR AT USC IN THE SPRING of 1966, but he was one year older than most juniors since he had not attended college in 1962–1963, when he served in the Marines (although being born in November made him closer to their age). In January of 1966 a winter draft was held. Because of what eventually happened to Tom Seaver, the rules of the winter draft were later changed, but despite being in school he was selected number one by the Milwaukee Braves, who were that year in the process of moving to Atlanta. Braves' scout Johnny Moore, who had seen 'em all in Fresno, arrived at the Seaver household in a Cadillac. When he left, Tom was $51,500 richer. He was a hot young prospect ticketed for the big leagues, where his teammate would be the great Henry Aaron!

Charles and Betty Seaver were slightly disappointed that their son was dropping out of school but understood that his future in professional baseball was bright. Tom also assured them he intended to go to school each off-season until graduating. He arranged with the Braves for his continuing education to be paid for by the club.

"I had two years of college before I signed a contract," Seaver assessed. "With two years completed, it's not so difficult to finish the last two years of college. It's awfully hard to do four years of college, one semester at a time in the off-season. I admire anyone who can do it. Your education will stay with you forever, long after your last fastball has faded."

No sooner did he sign with the Braves than he discovered the contract was invalid. USC had played a few early-season games. A player could sign only prior to the playing of games on the spring schedule, and the Trojans always got off to an early start. Coach Dedeaux was none too happy about losing his ace pitcher and alerted baseball officials that Seaver was not eligible for the draft. Seaver would have to wait until the June draft, but he was not disappointed. He would pitch for Southern Cal. Then the NCAA declared he was ineligible since he had signed a pro contract. He was like Ko-Ko in *The Mikado,* caught in the middle of a "pretty state of things," wrote sportswriter John Devaney.

Tom and Charles researched baseball's rules in order to find some solution to the dilemma. Finally, after receiving an impassioned letter from Charles Seaver, the commissioner's office got involved. It was decided that a "lottery" would be held. Any team willing to match the Braves' offer could enter it. Three teams—Philadelphia, Cleveland, and the New York Mets—did just that. The Dodgers wanted in, too, but general manager Buzzie Bavasi was so consumed in contract talks with Sandy Koufax and Don Drysdale, both holdouts that spring, that he forgot to get the team's name in. For the second time, the Dodgers passed up a chance to get Tom Seaver.

"Tom Seaver changed baseball history," said longtime Los Angeles talk show host Fred Wallin. "If he had signed with the Dodgers when he was first drafted, L.A. would not have gone from 1965 to 1988 without winning the World Series. If the commissioner had allowed the Braves to control his rights, who knows what would have happened to that franchise? But assuredly if Tom Terrific had not signed with the Mets, the miracle of 1969 could not have happened."

The Mets almost failed to enter the draft, as well. General manager George Weis needed to be talked into it.

"We felt he could be a great addition," said club president Bing Devine. "I don't know if we felt he'd become as great as he did. I don't know if anyone knows for sure when they make what looks like a great pickup. . . . Who knows if he's going to mature?"

The Mets were afraid Seaver would sue, "and George Weis was against it. Yes, he was against taking Seaver. Let's be honest about it: He didn't know anything about him. And so he just said, 'We can't do it,' and Joe McDonald and I had a private meeting, and we agreed I had to make a case for that. I made a big case, and I recall it was only hours before we had to make a decision and agree to that, and George Weis finally shook his head, I'm sure not wanting to do it, and said, 'If you people make such a big case of it, go ahead.'"

The Mets were selected, and Seaver was the chosen one. Seaver was pleased.

"What I remember about Seaver was he was a student of the game and a student of pitching," Devine recalled years later. "He was a very smart guy. He could have done anything else. I recognized that about him, that he had a lot of things going for him that a lot of young ballplayers didn't and probably never would—this was aside from his ability to pitch and the stuff he had."

The Mets were an expansion team without established pitchers. His path to the big leagues would be swifter. Scout Nelson Burbrink arrived at the Seaver home on El Rancho Drive in a Chevy, not as fancy as Moore's Caddy. He signed him to the same deal the Braves agreed to, though. Seaver reported to Homestead, Florida, where their minor leaguers were well under way for Spring Training. The experience was extraordinary for him. Four years earlier, he had been less than a "suspect"—a warehouse "sweat box" lifter and a lowly Marine recruit with drill instructors screaming in his face. Year by year things had gotten better for him: junior college ace; proving himself with the Alaska Goldpanners; "big man on campus" at USC; now a bonus baby; and a few months later, married to the beautiful Nancy Lynn McIntyre.

He was also one of the first baseball players to lift weights, which raised eyebrows.

"I remember walking into my first Mets' Spring Training clubhouse carrying the 10-pound dumbbell I used at the University of Southern California," Seaver recalled.

"Whaddya got there, Atlas?" somebody wisecracked.

The guy who could not make the Fresno High varsity until his senior year found himself trailed by curious glances and murmurs at Homestead. "That's the guy from USC." "That's Seaver; they paid him over 50 grand." Bud Harrelson, Jerry Koosman, and Nolan Ryan were all in camp, but Seaver was singled out for the special treatment accorded to the most important prospects. It was dizzying, but Seaver had "class" according to Harrelson, who said that despite his place at the top of the totem pole, the bonus baby did not put on airs or try to show anybody up.

Harrelson recalled that in batting practice Seaver "lay the ball right in there" instead of trying to show off. "Right away I thought, I like that guy. He's not trying to impress anybody. He's getting loose; he doesn't care; his ego doesn't need to strike out the team. This kid's got some class!"

Harrelson, a scrawny shortstop from Northern California, quickly became Seaver's friend and roommate. Most players start out at class A ball and have to fight for years to move up the ladder. The combination of Seaver's college record, his bonus money, and the team's lack of success meant that he started at triple-A Jacksonville, Florida. Manager Solly Hemus, who had seen a few in his long baseball career, declared him "the best pitching prospect the Mets have ever signed" and then paid him the ultimate compliment: "Seaver has a 35-year-old head on top of a 21-year-old body. Usually, we get a 35-year-old arm attached to a 21-year-old head."

Seaver was teammates with Dick Selma at Jacksonville. Immediately he had success and was ticketed as a "can't miss" prospect who would be in the Major Leagues soon, maybe even in September. His first professional game was played on April 25, 1966. Seaver struck out nine and allowed six hits in 8⅓ innings, defeating the Rochester Red Wings. He followed that up with a masterful 6–0 shutout of Buffalo, striking out 11. One Bisons player remarked that his fastball "just exploded when it reached the plate."

"We may be watching the development of one of the great ones of our time," said Buffalo manager Red Davis. "This kid didn't pitch and beat a bunch of rookies. He beat a veteran team. From what I saw, Seaver could be one of the great ones."

After beating Buffalo again, 2–1, there were predictions that he would be pitching at Shea Stadium "before the end of June." Sportswriters called him the "Jacksonville wonder boy."

Seaver was perfecting his "drop and drive" pitching motion, which has been described as the most "perfect" of any pitcher ever. It was a compact, beautifully constructed use of the big muscles in his powerful legs, relieving stress on his arm, with a minimum amount of gyration. He was not as liquid or artistic as Koufax, but for a man built like Seaver, it was just right. It reminded many of Robin Roberts, a Philadelphia Phillies Hall of Famer who retired the year Tom broke into organized ball. The comparisons were meant to be flattering, and they were.

He was given the nickname Super Rookie, or Supe for short. His future was secured, oddly, after losing four straight games after starting 3–0. Hemus said he reminded him of Bob Gibson, adding when most minor league pitching prospects get hit, they are removed so as to protect their gentle psyches. Hemus realized Seaver had the mental toughness of a 35-year-old. When his rough patches came, as they always do, he kept him in to gain from the experience. He led the team in victories (12) and strikeouts.

The roughest patch came off the field. Seaver planned to marry Nancy in September when he returned to Los Angeles, continuing his studies at USC. While many minor leaguers play the field with "groupies," Tom determined to remain true to Nancy, holding to the promise both made to each other when he was at USC, to be faithful.

He wrote that he was "going crazy" at the Roosevelt Hotel. Reports differ on how Seaver proposed and carried out the wedding. In one story, he enclosed a one-way ticket to Jacksonville and proposed they be married. A traditional couple, neither wanted to live in sin. Nancy agreed, flew to Florida, and they were quietly married on June 9. However, according to a *People* magazine feature in 1977, Tom made a fast cross-country flight to California, formally asked Nancy's father for his daughter's hand in marriage, then impulsively rushed her to Florida for a wedding between games.

"I thought I was marrying a dentist," Nancy insisted. "But it didn't make the society page, it made the sports page." On their wedding night, she said, "We went to dinner, to our room, and then out again for hot fudge sundaes. Finally, back in our room, we called our parents, just stalling."

"Does she mean that before they were married they actually hadn't . . . ?" wrote Martha Smilgis in *People*. "Oh, Tom would kill me if I told," Nancy blushed.

The wedding, not coincidentally, spurred Seaver back on a winning streak.

When the "wizened" wives and girlfriends of the Jacksonville players set the naive California girl Nancy "straight" on the notorious sexual habits of ballplayers, Tom assured her of his commitment to her, but her mind was filled with dreadful thoughts while Tom was on the road. They remained true to each other. It was a trait Tom Seaver would become known for: the faithful husband. He would not be the only faithful husband in professional sports, but he was in a distinct minority.

After a heavy workload at Jacksonville, the Mets decided not to call him up in September. It was expected that he would make the Mets' Major League roster in 1967. Seaver and his new bride drove across the country to Los Angeles. The young Nancy began crying, still not convinced that life as a ballplayer's wife was for her. She was experiencing doubts about her marriage.

"As much as we're going to be separated you're going to have to trust me," he told her. "When you married me, I think you knew that I could be trusted." Instinctively, she did. Tom had been raised right by his parents. Interestingly, while throughout his career he avoided temptation on the road, he was never a Goody Two-shoes. He enjoyed drinking beer, chewing tobacco, telling jokes, using bawdy language, and playing cards. He was always one of the boys. Seaver had a talent for nonjudgment. His teammates did what they did, and he did what he did. Seaver never admonished or chastised and was never ostracized for being "too good" for his teammates.

When he said good-bye to Hemus at season's end, the manager told him, "I'll see you in the 'biggies' next season."

After a year in the minors, "I was rolling in dough, making $500 a month," Tom joked.

"Yeah," Nancy interrupted, "you splurged and bought me a hair dryer."

In the fall of 1966, Seaver reenrolled at the University of Southern California, where he was now just another student. Suddenly Seaver saw a new future in baseball and began to think about broadcasting on the side. He transferred his major from predentistry to public relations. Instead of living near campus, notorious for being near a high crime zone and at that time only a year removed from the nearby Watts riots, they lived in upscale Manhattan Beach.

"Being a successful pitcher is not just being able to throw the ball, but being able to weigh and make quick decisions," he said. "College refines that and has helped me to make the right decisions on the mound. More than ever before, now I know pitching is using your mind." Seaver stayed in shape pitching, running, and lifting weights with Rod Dedeaux's team and numerous off-season pros working out with the Trojans.

"When I was going to college at USC, I'd go to Dodger Stadium a lot to catch him pitch," Seaver recalled of Sandy Koufax. "Once my uncle got me tickets right behind the Dodger dugout, and just watching Sandy warm up was a phenomenal experience. I remember after I pitched at Jacksonville in 1966, and our season ended before the Major Leagues, Nancy and I went back to California, and I made her come with me two nights in a row to watch Koufax and then Don Drysdale pitch. She was bored, but I was in Heaven just watching Sandy work."

Prior to the 1967 season, Nancy took a call from the Mets asking Tom to report to St. Petersburg, Florida, for Spring Training. She did not think much of it until she passed the message along to her husband. When Seaver heard it he explained what it meant: St. Pete meant the bigs. The *minor leaguers* were assigned to Homestead, as he had been the previous spring. He was joyous, exclaiming that this meant they would live in New York, and they would make a lot of money. Nancy was unable to grasp what it all meant, not understanding the difference between St. Petersburg and Homestead, or even the ramifications of their future life in the Big Apple.

Seaver entered Spring Training amid speculation that he would be a starting pitcher. Had Seaver not been with the lowly Mets, he probably would not have made it to "the Show," as the majors are referred to, as quickly. He would have started out at single A or double A, then worked his way up. Instead, he did start as a rookie in 1967. In truth, he was as ready as can be. Manager Wes Westrum not only put him in the starting rotation at the beginning of the season, he was talked out of starting him on Opening Day only out of caution.

The Mets were as bad as ever in 1967, only now they were just terrible, not funny. The old Casey Stengel stories, the wacky Marvelous Marv Throneberry antics, were gone. Now they just lost. Seaver was appalled. The "advantage" of being selected by the Mets was not an advantage anymore. Seaver's performance at Jacksonville, in Spring Training, and early in the 1967 campaign made it plainly obvious that he not only was worthy of being in the big leagues, he was star material. But the Mets were still a joke. Herein lies the key to Tom Seaver's legend.

In the entire history of athletics, the New York Mets of the 1960s were the worst outfit of all time. There was no close second. If some other bad team, like the old St. Louis Browns or the Pittsburgh Steelers before their glory days, might compare statistically, nobody matched them for sheer comedic looniness. Books were written about their antics and errors.

Born out of expansion after the Dodgers and Giants abandoned New York in 1957–1958, the Mets began playing at the Polo Grounds in 1962. Under former Yankees manager Casey Stengel, they were 40–120, the worst record—then and still—in baseball history. Stengel was old and engendered laughter with his famed "Stengelese," but what passed for genius with the champion Yankees looked like buffoonery with the Mets.

Every possible joke seemed to be played on his team. Players were late for the team's first game because they were stuck in an elevator. They ran into each other, passed each other on the bases, and made errors that defied reality. This act continued unabated between 1962 and 1966.

During this time, a funny thing happened. The New York press did not cover them simply in the sports pages. They made them a feature story, liberally pointing out their comically endearing ways. In a city that demanded winners, in which the Yankees seemed a symbol of Roman power, having "conquered Gaul" by driving out the competition of the Dodgers and Giants, the Mets filled a gap among National League aficionados who disdained the methodical champion Bronx Bombers in favor of the all-too-human "Metsies."

The team moved to Shea Stadium in 1964 and drew enormous attendance despite their record in the decade. When the Yankees began to slide in 1965, the Mets were unquestionably the more popular team. But by 1967, their comedy routine was wearing thin. Gone were Stengel, Marvelous Marv, Choo Choo Coleman, Rod Kanehl, and other floundering favorites.

During Spring Training Tom's teammates laughed about an error. Seaver had yet to throw his first big-league inning, but he stored the event away mentally, determined that if he rose to a leadership role by dint of success on the field, he would assert his will.

Pitching an exhibition game against Minnesota in 90-degree heat at Orlando, Florida, Seaver challenged the great slugger Harmon Killebrew, striking him out with fastballs.

He recalled "striking Killebrew out during Spring Training of 1967, the year I first made the Majors," he reminisced. "Every time you retire a Major Leaguer in that situation, it really builds your confidence."

But another Twins slugger, Tony Oliva, opened his eyes.

"In the same inning I faced Oliva, and he ripped a double off me. As much confidence as the Killebrew at-bat gave me, Oliva's had the opposite effect until I realized that not too many Major League pitchers ever got him out easily."

After a few more impressive outings, he was given a five-inning start against Kansas City, allowing one run in a strong outing. He followed that up with five scoreless innings against the defending world champion Orioles.

Seaver impressed the coaches and his teammates with his work ethic, running endless wind sprints, doing sit-ups, pick-ups, and training on his own even on off days. When asked what drove him he replied, "Pitching has always been hard work for me. I never had anything handed to me. At 14, I already knew my physical limitations. It appeared to be a burden then, but it obviously helped."

The New York press was too used to the comical Mets legend to realize what was happening. When Maury Allen of the *New York Post* found out manager Wes Westrum was planning to start the rookie on Opening Day, he was flabbergasted. Seaver was very boyish looking. His nickname was Spanky. Westrum backed off and decided to start Seaver in the second game of the year.

"I'll admit he doesn't have much experience, but he gets people out," Westrum observed.

4

THE NEW YORKER: 1967–1968

On the morning of April 12, Seaver awoke in his Queens apartment, his belly filled with butterflies. He was scheduled to start against Roberto Clemente and the Pittsburgh Pirates that day. Nancy fixed some bacon (modern dietary rites were not yet established), but her husband just nibbled on a small piece. Finally he left, got a haircut, and drove to Shea Stadium.

About 20,000 fans were on hand. It was still cool in Manhattan. Seaver felt strong warming up. He threw hard with pinpoint control. For five innings in his debut, he was effective, but he had not pitched a complete game since 1966. After giving up a hit in the sixth he admitted to Westrum that his legs were tiring. The manager was impressed with his honesty, which worked out when Chuck Estrada was brought on in relief, held, and the Mets prevailed, 3–2.

In his next start against Ernie Banks, Ron Santo, and Billy Williams of the Chicago Cubs, Seaver was magnificent for seven innings. In the eighth he tired, but outfielder Tommy Davis made a running catch of a long drive by Glenn Beckert. Seaver again admitted he was weary. Don Shaw held Chicago, the Mets added a couple more runs, and Tom Seaver had his first Major League victory, having held the

Cubs—an upcoming powerhouse under manager Leo Durocher—to eight hits with five strikeouts and just one run.

The writers crowded around his cubicle. Seaver admitted he was tired, a rather rare thing, but an aspect of his personality his managers over the years appreciated. Rather than stay in and blow leads, he preferred to see fresh-armed relievers preserve his victories. This was the beginning of a trend that over time changed baseball.

After the game Tom and Nancy celebrated at a favorite Chinese restaurant, Lums. Tom enjoyed a whiskey sour and a big dinner, which went down well as he was often too nervous to eat much prior to his starts. It was all coming together—fame and baseball success, marriage to a beautiful young bride. At times it seemed still a dream to the young man who was relegated to the Fresno High JVs his junior year and entered the Marines because no scouts or colleges noticed him after graduation. Seaver was that rarest of athletes, the wide-eyed fan suddenly elevated to greatness, or at least what looked like it could be greatness.

But Seaver was too smart and disciplined, too much Charles Seaver's son, to let it go to his head. He developed a sleeping pattern that helped maximize his strength on the day of his starts. He developed a detailed notebook of National League hitters and worked out slavishly, devoted to a routine, in between appearances.

At age 10, Seaver had been introduced by his father to the great Pittsburgh Pirates slugger Ralph Kiner at a Crosby Pro-Am golf tournament. Charles requested an autograph for "my boy who one day will be in the big leagues." Kiner was now one of the Mets' radio announcers, hosting the *Kiner's Korner* interview program. Tom approached him to get his insight, to try to understand what went on in the hitters' heads. He looked for every edge, every advantage. He also wanted tips on broadcasting, a future vocation he was already interested in someday pursuing.

Tom was such a huge fan of the game he took advantage of every opportunity to hear stories from the old days. He asked Kiner about the Hall of Famer Honus Wagner.

"He coached in Pittsburgh so long that a lot of people I've met knew him well, particularly the Mets' broadcaster Ralph Kiner, who played for the Pirates then" and often talked "about what a nice man he was."

Seaver would ask old-timers about the likes of Babe Ruth and Christy Mathewson. Of Ruth he said, "I'd have loved to have seen him play a whole season, or even a whole game, and thus learn to appreciate him fully."

Early in Seaver's career people began to see similarities with Mathewson. "You see, when I came up to the Major Leagues in 1967, a lot of old writers, some of whom even knew Mathewson, thought I looked a little like him," he recalled. "We were both built about the same, both threw right-handed, both had come quickly from college to the Majors, and both pitched for New York. So they had fun comparing us, even suggesting that I was Matty, if you like to believe in reincarnation. I took it all as a compliment, of course, for after all, the guy did win 373 games. . . . Better than reminding people of someone who never got anybody out."

Rogers Hornsby was also a player he asked about: "His last job in baseball was as a coach for the Mets in their first season. It was five years before I got there, but there were still a lot of people in the organization who knew him, and they say he was just as ornery as ever, even in the last year of his life. He wrote a book called *My War with Baseball.* You'd think at 68 he might have mellowed, but he was still the fiery competitor he'd been with the Cardinals. And what a hitter!"

Hall of Famer Frankie Frisch made an acquaintance with Tom.

"I knew Frankie near the end of his life," Seaver recalled. "He lived in the New York area and would show up at Mets games, particularly old-timers' days. He'd always be complaining about how soft the modern players had it, what with wearing batting helmets and using big gloves, but he said it with good humor, and he was a delightful man. He had a lot of confidence, too, and I could see how he would have been a good team leader."

Seaver's rookie card featured him and a player named Bill Denehy. Seaver continued to pitch well. Now a team leader, he felt free to speak up whereas in Spring Training he held his tongue when he observed his teammates laughing at their own ineptitude.

The Mets played well when he pitched but lost the edge on the days Seaver was not on the mound.

Once, when Mets players were fooling around in the dugout during a game Seaver was not pitching, he found some spiders nesting in a corner. He scooped them all up and threw them at the offenders, telling them to wake up and pay attention. His attitude would have been taken exception to except that he was so shockingly good. It earned him immediate respect.

Seaver's work ethic was legendary, his concentration and seriousness unprecedented in Mets history. He was immediately successful. When his brother, Charles Jr., a New York City social worker, visited a client, he saw a poster of his brother hanging in his tenement apartment. It was an era before ESPN, and the lowly Mets were not on national TV very much, so it took him by surprise.

By the end of June Seaver sported an 8–5 record, a singular accomplishment on a last-place club headed for a 61–101 record. Against his hero Henry Aaron, Seaver induced the slugger into a double play but was almost in admiration of his opponent when Aaron adjusted later and hit the same pitch over the fence. Henry told him he was "throwing hard, kid."

"Facing Aaron as a rookie was some kind of thrill for me," recalled Tom. "As I was growing up in Fresno, he was my favorite player, along with Sandy Koufax. For some reason, I had taken a real liking to the Milwaukee Braves, a power-hitting, successful team. I liked their uniforms. I liked their style, and I loved their power. Not only did I like Aaron and Mathews, but guys like Bill Bruton did it for me too.

"Facing him for the first time was like standing on the mound and facing my image of him from TV. I was so in awe of this man that I turned my back as he went through his customary preparations to hit. I knew all his actions—how he would approach the plate, rest his bat against his upper leg, put on his helmet, pick up the bat, and step in.

"He coauthored a book in 1967, and I sheepishly asked him for a copy when the New York Mets played the Braves in Atlanta after my introduction to number 44 on a previous trip there. I also asked Hank if he would autograph it for me and bring it to New

York on his next road trip there—thinking he would certainly forget. On the day the Braves pulled into Shea Stadium for their series with us, I thought not of my opponents and how I might pitch to them, but rather of Henry Aaron and my request. I parked my car in the bullpen lot, walked the dark, musty hall to the clubhouse . . . and there on a stool in front of my locker was a copy of *Aaron R.F.* On that day, Henry Aaron became more than an idol, more than just a symbol of consistent excellence."

Seaver "stalked" Sandy Koufax at the batting cage when the now-retired legend was in town as a broadcaster. When Koufax recognized who he was, Seaver was taken aback but pleased.

"The year after he retired was my rookie season, so I never had the thrill of being on the same field as he as a player," recalled Seaver years later. "But I'm also glad I never had to pitch against him. He was a broadcaster for NBC in 1967 and was going to cover a Mets game at Shea Stadium. I remember driving to work and thinking more about meeting him than the game itself. During batting practice he was standing near our batting cage when a ball rolled under it, and we both went to pick it up. I remember thinking, 'What am I going to say to him?' But he spoke first. 'Hi, Tom, I'm Sandy Koufax.' Wow. But then we just got to yakking about baseball, and over the years we developed a kind of mutual respect for each other that I really value. One spring we just sat and talked pitching for about two hours. It was a very memorable two hours for me."

When Tom Seaver became the Mets' first legitimate star in 1967, it had a discomfiting effect. Seaver's excellence, which he demanded of his teammates, was something new, but fans did not know how to handle it. They did not dare root for their team to actually *win*, but Seaver's bravura performance actually showed them what winning looked like. They began to hope for it, and in so doing began to become disenchanted with the performance of Tom's teammates. The Mets' star rookie in 1967 was not supposed to be Seaver but a center fielder named Don Bosch. Touted as the "next Mickey Mantle," he was instead a 27-year-old neurotic with gray hair. The press dubbed him a "midget," but Tom Seaver was not laughing. This sort of legend was no longer funny.

"I was not raised on the Mets' legend," he said. He had no affinity for any of that stuff. Despite being a rookie, he quickly ascended to a position of leadership on the club. When teammates laughed at their ineptitude, he was aghast. He had played for Rod Dedeaux at USC, the "New York Yankees of college baseball," where he was schooled in fundamentals and expected to win. The Mets did not seem to be any better than the Trojans, a mere college outfit. "I never did find defeat particularly amusing," said Seaver.

Mets play-by-play man Howie Rose grew up a Mets fan.

"I think that people who watched him as a rookie got the sense that they had finally developed a player who was capable of doing special things and therefore capable of helping the Mets achieve some pretty good things on their own along the way," he said.

Cincinnati's Pete Rose openly wondered who "the kid" was at Gallaghers, a New York steak house, when he saw an out-of-place Seaver sitting at a table by himself. Told who he was, Rose then made the connection. This was the guy who beat his Reds, 7–3, on June 13.

"He sure looks young but the kid's got a helluva fastball."

"When I first came into the league in 1967, Rose was in his fifth season and already talking about the goal of being 'the first singles hitter to a make a hundred thousand dollars,'" according to Seaver.

Aside from Aaron, several other stars from his boyhood favorite team, the Braves, were still in the league, including Eddie Mathews.

"Well, as events would have it, I got to face Mathews in my rookie season, which was his last year in the National League," recalled Seaver. "He was playing for Houston then, and this was my first appearance ever in the Astrodome, not exactly known as a home run ballpark.

"Eddie was 35 and clearly slowing down. He'd already hit 496 home runs. I was young and strong and decided to buzz a fastball by him, hero or not. Well, he tore into it and sent it over the Astrodome scoreboard, and the red seats, on a line drive!

"I got back to our dugout and one of our veterans, maybe it was Don Cardwell, came over and said, 'He's a pretty good fastball hitter, you know.'

"Was he ever."

Seaver earned a spot on the National League roster for the All-Star Game, played near his college stomping grounds, at Anaheim Stadium. This meant more embarrassed mistaken identity. Cardinal superstar Lou Brock thought he was the clubhouse boy and asked him to fetch a Coke. Seaver dutifully did that, but Brock had to apologize when he was informed who he was.

Seaver was thrilled to discover his cubicle was next to Aaron's. "I had to pinch myself to prove it was all really happening to me," thinking, "I can't believe that just a year and a half ago, I was sitting back in California just dreaming about playing in the Major Leagues. Now I'm here thinking how I'm going to pitch to guys like Mickey Mantle."

In the game, Seaver came on in extra innings. Trying to alleviate his nerves, Seaver joked with Rose when he arrived on the mound but got his "greatest thrill of the day" when he looked at the outfield only to see Roberto Clemente of Pittsburgh in right, Willie Mays of San Francisco in center, and his idol, Henry Aaron, in left.

Years after first identifying Henry as his hero, "later, in 1967, I had been in the Major Leagues for 12 weeks when I found myself standing on the pitching mound in Anaheim Stadium, wearing my gray Mets road uniform, ready to pitch my first All-Star Game. A year before I had been at Jacksonville, Florida. Two years before, I had been at USC." When he turned and saw Aaron, Mays, and Clemente he thought he "had died and gone to Heaven" because "this wasn't Strat-O-Matic baseball."

Seaver took a deep breath.

"Imagine turning around and seeing all those great players behind you," said Seaver. "That was the greatest thrill I got that day, and one of the great thrills in my life."

To top it off, he knew Sandy Koufax was part of the broadcast team and was *watching him.* The manager was the legendary Walter Alston of the Dodgers. Seaver was asked to save the game for Alston's Hall of Fame ace, Don Drysdale. But Nancy was not confident at all.

"In that first All-Star Game, I prayed and prayed, 'Please, don't put Tom in, don't put him in,'" she admitted years later. "'He's too little. He's just a young guy, don't put him in the game.' And then he walked out on the mound and I couldn't believe it was Tom. I thought: I don't even know him. It was the strongest experience."

The first batter was Boston's great young star, Tony Conigliaro. Seaver induced him to fly out on a low fastball. Conigliaro's Red Sox teammate, the great Carl Yastrzemski stepped in. Yaz was having his greatest year, on his way to the Triple Crown. Seaver walked him, but he easily handled Bill Freehan and Ken Berry to preserve his league's 2–1, 15-inning victory. He was surrounded by congratulations from National League All-Stars, a photo prominently captured in *Sport* magazine. Seaver suddenly felt a hand pound him on the back. It was a smiling Henry Aaron.

"Those two things with Henry are the two biggest thrills I've ever had—the experience of pitching against him for the first time, and then his congratulating me—terrific!" he recalled.

Flying back from Anaheim he told his wife the National Leaguers were "winners" because they took such pride in winning the All-Star Game, which the American League seemed to regard as more of an exhibition. He added, "That's what we need at the Mets." When the second half started, Seaver announced after a dismal performance against Pittsburgh, "Gentlemen, after watching that performance, I would like to take this opportunity to announce my retirement from the game of baseball." His "announcement" was met with nervous laughter, but they got the message.

The New York press—oft-Jewish, cynical, a little scruffy, mostly Democrats—lauded his ability, dubbing him Tom Terrific, one of the great nicknames ever given, but took some time getting used to Seaver's persona. Here was a fresh-scrubbed Westerner and his blonde wife who looked like a college cheerleader. Seaver did not advertise his politics or religion, but it was assumed he was a Christian and a Republican. He certainly was not part of the protest crowd advocating America's leaving Vietnam. Was he too good to be true?

His teammates, however, had a different view. Many were country boys, not politically radical if political at all. Seaver was well spoken, a college man. They respected his intelligence. What they really respected was his no-nonsense, tough-nosed work ethic, the way he played the game hard—brushbacks, handling the bat well—and the fact that despite his All-American image, he was "one of the boys." He was a notorious clubhouse cutup, gaining a reputation as one of the great practical jokers in baseball. His jokes were said to go above and beyond the ordinary. Despite his rookie status, Seaver was the unquestioned leader of the New York Mets. He was also a "stopper," one of the most valuable components any team can ever have. He stopped losing streaks. His nickname from Jacksonville was updated. He lost the Spanky moniker and became Supey, as in Super Rookie, a nickname first given to him at Jacksonville.

Then there was Dick Selma, who introduced Seaver to chewing tobacco. There was something serendipitous about Tom's life and career, something so near perfect that it sometimes seemed it all was crafted by the hand of a higher power. Seaver was in New York City, where he got to know legends like Ralph Kiner, Casey Stengel, and Frank Frisch. He entered baseball during a time when the game's biggest names were still playing, making friends with Aaron, Mays, Clemente, Mantle. But here was his childhood friend sharing all of this with him on the big stage of the Big Apple. How many players get to be big-league teammates with friends from Little League and high school?

By August he was a 12-game winner, but both Seaver and the press openly discussed the fact his team played well when he pitched but floundered on other days. Tom openly said it was not right, urging his mates to come to the park enthused every game, but on a team headed to 100 losses it was easier said than done.

"There was an aura of defeatism about the team, a feeling of let's get it over with," Seaver recalled. "I noticed that the team seemed to play better when I pitched but . . . that wasn't right and I said so. I probably got a few people mad, but I went around and told the guys that if they did that for me and not for somebody else, it was wrong."

"When Seaver's pitching, these guys plain work a little harder," noted catcher Jerry Grote.

"You notice his concentration out there on the mound when he's pitching," said Bud Harrelson. "And playing behind him, you try to match it."

Incredibly, Mets attendance was down somewhat in 1967. The press wrote he was "hurting the Mets' image." Their fan base was used to lovable losers. They cheered Seaver, coming out in good numbers for his starts, but in so doing began to expect more of the team. When they continued to lose, the old ways were not so lovable.

Two years later, when the Mets shocked the baseball world, everybody wanted to know what the turning point had been. Obviously the signing and ascendancy of Tom Seaver was, but in terms of a single game, many pointed to a game late in the 1967 campaign. Seaver held a precarious 1–0 lead against Chicago late in the game when Ron Santo hit an easy ground ball to Bud Harrelson. It scooted under his glove, tying the game. In the 10th inning, Seaver himself singled, advanced to second on a long fly ball by Cleon Jones, and scored the winning run on a base hit.

Joyous, Seaver entered the clubhouse only to see his friend sitting morosely at his cubicle. He went over to Harrelson, put his arm around him, and consoled him. After all, the team won the game, but Bud cost him a shutout. Seaver told him there would be many more shutouts (he was not wrong about that), but winning was a team goal, and they were in it together. It was a bonding moment for Seaver and Bud, a moment of great leadership demonstrated by the young star hurler.

"For the first time, maybe we realized we had guys who cared deeply whether we achieved, that we even had pitchers who could hit occasionally and who wanted to win so desperately," Seaver told a *Sport* magazine reporter years later. "Looking back, I think it was the first time in my experience with the Mets that we believed in each other, the first time I felt that I wasn't there to lose."

Seaver was not superstitious, but he was spiritual. He wore a St. Christopher medal. In Atlanta he left it in his hotel room, but Buddy Harrelson saved the day, bringing it to the park and giving it to him at the last minute.

New York City likes its athletes to be regular guys. With Seaver it was as if they found somebody from the fanciest prep school, a best-selling author, a U.S. Senator or college professor; put a uniform on him; and discovered to their amazement that he could bring high, hard heat with the best of 'em. Over time, Seaver's singular impressiveness as a pitcher and a person wore thin with teammates and the press. He never suffered fools well.

Later, one of his teammates disdainfully thought Seaver read books such as *Bury My Heart at Wounded Knee* on airplanes in order to look smart. Eventually it was demonstrated to be who he was. It was not an act. He was one of the rarest of the breed. He read John Steinbeck, followed politics, and was a genuine intellect.

Other athletes have been smart. Moe Berg was an OSS spy. Bill Bradley was a Rhodes Scholar. Even Wilt Chamberlain was an intellect. But few if any were the complete package as was Seaver—a combination of looks, education, uprightness, and unmatched athletic greatness.

He and Nancy took to the New York scene with feet flying. If ever a "sports couple" was seemingly born for the Big Apple scene, it was the Seavers.

"Nancy and I love this town," Seaver told sportswriter Maury Allen. "We walk around Manhattan, up Fifth Avenue, past Carnegie Hall, down Broadway. We want to get to the Museum of Art and the Museum of Natural History on our next day off."

Seaver felt a natural intellectual curiosity, fueled by his surroundings. The literary nature of New York society did not escape him. He read books by John Steinbeck, who had written of the central California that they both grew up in. Steinbeck's vision of California was much different from Seaver's easy affluence, but Tom had an inquiring mind and absorbed all of it. He read books about politics, satire, and the classic baseball history book *The Glory of Their Times*, which allowed him to realize that he was part of something bigger than himself, that being a New York baseball star was special over and above playing in other cities. He had respect for the game and its traditions, and to Mets fans number 41 began to represent the sort of idol Whitey Ford and Mickey Mantle meant to Yankee supporters. They chanted "Seav-*uh*" as he mowed hitters down at Shea Stadium.

Seaver studied opponents and scouting reports. His dedication was total, but he also smiled and joked around. He was the quintessential "fan" living the fantasy of playing in the Major Leagues.

Almost all big leaguers were high school superstars who took their ability for granted, strutting around as if they owned the place. Seaver was still pinching himself. Not only was he privileged to wear the uniform, he was the ace of the staff! He was already the greatest player in Mets history. If he pitched well but lost for lack of support, he took the weight of defeat on his own shoulders.

"I just don't feel I'm pitching as well as I can," he lamented. "A mistake here . . . a mistake there . . . they add up. You wonder when you're going to come on and start eliminating the mistakes."

He was a perfectionist, a trait he inherited from his father. It applied to every aspect of his life—the way he dressed, the way he conducted his marriage, his life. He expressed admiration at brother Charles's sculptures, since he could attain a sense of perfection in the work that seemed impossible in the messy, up-and-down competition of baseball. Still, each game he came out hoping for a perfect game, something Sandy Koufax had done. Koufax once said that he wanted a perfect game until the first man reached base; a no-hitter until the first hit; a shutout until the first run . . .

He made no excuses just because he was a rookie. He handled every aspect of his business, not just pitching well but fielding his position, showing some pop with the bat, and cheerleading on days he did not pitch. The older Mets were replaced more and more by youngsters who emulated Seaver's professionalism.

Pitching coach Harvey Haddix marveled that Seaver absorbed his lessons, did not need to be told something twice, and analyzed his performances thoroughly.

"Yeah, I've helped him a bit," said Haddix. "But he's the sort of kid that doesn't need much help. I just watch him, make a suggestion once in a while, and he takes it from there. He's easy to work with and very quick to learn. He knows just how to use his pitching strength against a hitter's weakness. He's a helluva kid and is going to be one of the great ones."

On road trips, he sat with Mets broadcasters Lindsey Nelson and Ralph Kiner, figuring he someday would be doing that, too. He never tailed off, as so many young hotshots do when the league figures them out, or they lose the psychological edge. In fact, Seaver in 1967 established a trait he maintained throughout his career: a strong finish.

The Tom Seaver of 1967–1968 was still developing. In the beginning, he was considered a sinker-slider pitcher whose fastball was excellent but not nearly at the level of such heaterballers of the time as Sudden Sam McDowell or Bob Gibson. But the late maturation process that began when he entered the Marine Corps had not reached fruition. His hard work and weightlifting were paying off. Billy Williams of the Cubs told teammates "he brings it" after being set down by him.

On the season he was 16–13 with a 2.76 earned run average, easily garnering Rookie of the Year honors over Steve Carlton of St. Louis. Seaver pitched 18 complete games, striking out 170 hitters in 251 innings while walking just 78. His 16 victories came with little offensive or defensive support from the 10th-place Mets. He gave up four runs or fewer in 8 of his 13 losses. He easily could have won 20 games in a year in which the great pitching aces of the era—Koufax, Don Drysdale, Bob Gibson, Juan Marichal—were retired, hurt, or slumped. Mike McCormick, a journeyman southpaw with the Giants, won the Cy Young Award but in truth did not pitch better than Seaver.

After winning the Rookie of the Year Award, he said it was "nice" but added the unthinkable: "I want to pitch on a Mets' pennant winner, and I want to pitch the first game in the World Series. I want to change things . . . the Mets have been a joke long enough. It's time to start winning, to change the attitude, to move ahead to better things. I don't want the Mets to be laughed at anymore."

In the off-season Seaver continued his studies at Southern Cal. Years after achieving superstardom, wealth, and worldwide fame, he continued going to school in the fall. He was accorded celebrity status first by his hometown of Fresno, who gave him the "key to the city," then by the USC baseball program. Working out to stay in shape in the off-season with a team led by Bill Lee (which would win the College World Series), he was one of their own who had made it. The up-and-coming Trojans were eager to hear tall tales of big-league life. Seaver was good at weaving a yarn. Buoyed by a double in his rookie salary, courtesy of a $24,000 contract proffered by general manager Johnny Murphy for 1968, he was happily married, sitting on top of the world.

In 1968, Gil Hodges took over as manager, and the complexion of the Mets began to change. A hero of the famed Brooklyn Dodgers clubs of the 1950s, Hodges played for the original Mets, then became a respected manager of the Washington Senators. The old Mets were largely gone, veterans replaced by the youngsters who would a year later electrify baseball.

Some of those youngsters who Seaver first met during Spring Training in 1966 were breaking into the big leagues. Jerry Koosman, Tug McGraw, Bud Harrelson, and Nolan Ryan were the face of the "new Mets." Koosman was a hard-throwing farm boy out of Minnesota, his potential unlimited, but his was nothing compared to the Texan Ryan, already legendary for the monumental speed of his breathtaking fastball. McGraw was a flaky California southpaw but a potential star. Catcher Jerry Grote was a tough Texan, dead serious with no interest whatsoever in the old Mets legend.

Tommie Agee, a potential .300 hitter, came over from the Chicago White Sox. His childhood friend from Mobile, Alabama, Cleon Jones, had the makings of a star. Ron Swoboda and Ed Kranepool had been around a few years but were eager to shed the loser image. An incredible amount of optimism surrounded the club throughout the winter and then Spring Training. Considering how bad they had been, it seems to have been misplaced. Considering what they did just a year later, maybe not so much. The ultimate optimist was Seaver, but Hodges was a winner, a fan favorite, and one of those guys who earned status as a New York sports icon. He expected to win, too.

On the one hand the Mets were still the Mets, but their recent youth movement—led by Seaver—led many to believe that perhaps they could turn the corner. Nobody was expecting them to contend, but the prospect that they might play .500 ball, that they had a promising future, was very real indeed.

Seaver was at the cutting edge of major changes in the way baseball was played. First, starting at USC, he was one of the first to lift weights. Second, he was willing to admit when he was tired, almost unheard of before he came along. For a pitcher not to finish what he started was considered somehow unmanly, but Seaver worked so hard, with his drop-and-drive style and tremendous exertion, that he often was gassed late in games and was willing to turn it over to his bullpen. This began the full development of the closer in baseball, but a third major shift began in 1968 courtesy of manager Gil Hodges and pitching coach Rube Walker.

Pitchers always worked every four days. It was considered an article of faith, but Walker and Hodges started working their starters every fifth day. Seaver himself had to be convinced of the wisdom of this move. After all, over the course of the season it meant giving up five starts, probably more. However, he began to see the value in it. He was refreshed with the extra day's rest.

In 1968, Seaver's number one priority was to cut down on home runs. He threw hard and was around the plate, challenging hitters. Most of the long balls came with nobody on base, but he wanted to improve anyway.

"I learned that a Major League hitter capitalizes on every mistake a pitcher makes," he told Dave Anderson of the *New York Times* prior to the season. "I've got to cut down on my mistakes; 19 of my mistakes went over the fence for 19 home runs."

Rod Dedeaux's friend Casey Stengel "was always around in Spring Training, and I'd always enjoy talking with him," recalled Seaver. "He was one of the characters."

Once at St. Petersburg, Seaver, Koosman, and Casey sat in the stands together, but there was not "a drop of Stengelese. He was clear of mind about the game in progress, and we were really having a nice conversation. Then a writer from *Life* magazine came over and asked him if he could talk to Casey for a few minutes. Well, Casey went into this speech—you'd have to speak Arabic or something to understand him. And the writer left shaking his head, and Casey was laughing and laughing, and he turned to us and said, 'Do you think he has any idea what I was talking about?' He really enjoyed putting on that little show for us." Stengel was "an amazing character, really from another era of American history. I'm glad I had the opportunity to know him."

Charles Seaver often drove his large family to Los Angeles to watch a series of games at Dodger Stadium, as well as trips to San Francisco—the distance was about the same either way—to take in Giants games. Now on Opening Day at Candlestick Park, his son was on the mound against Willie Mays, Willie McCovey, Juan Marichal, and the San Francisco Giants. Seaver took a hard-earned 4–2 lead into the bottom of the ninth inning. Exhausted, he was removed and watched in despair as his bullpen blew the lead in a 5–4 loss.

Same old Mets. What good did it do to pitch his heart out, only to turn it over to a bullpen that could not hold the lead? "I thought we had it," he said despondently in the clubhouse afterward. "I thought we had it."

In his next start he shut out Houston for 10 innings but came away with a no-decision in a game lost by New York, 1–0 in 24 innings, when second baseman Al Weis let a groundball scoot under his glove.

Same old Mets.

In his first four starts, Seaver was as good as anybody in baseball. He was significantly better than he had been as a rookie, throwing harder and dominating the opposition. "Hitting against Seaver is like trying to drink coffee with a fork," said Pittsburgh slugger Willie Stargell. The Mets, however, simply gave him no backup. His record was 1–1 despite an earned run average of 1.59. It did not get better after that. Ten starts into the season his ERA was 1.91, but his record was 2–4.

After some early bumps in the road, however, the Mets rebounded and by mid-June were near the .500 mark, a remarkable record for this franchise. It was a reversal of 1967, when the club played well in Seaver's starts but failed when others pitched. In 1968 they gave better support to other Mets pitchers, in particular rookie left-hander Jerry Koosman. Seaver just plugged along, maintaining his professionalism, knowing that the breaks would even out over time.

Hodges and Seaver developed an excellent reputation based on mutual respect. Seaver's on-mound demeanor was very intense, but one game he was laughing and grinning with catcher Jerry Grote during a game he won. Hodges advised that he should maintain a more disciplined presence but was surprised to hear—and accept—Seaver's explanation that in a game he lost he was "too tight" and decided to loosen up in order to pitch better. Everything Seaver did had a method behind it. Hodges had seen many players over the years, and in Seaver he recognized a "new breed" of highly intelligent, motivated professionalism. The game was changing, and Seaver was changing it.

"He was a Marine," Seaver recalled of Hodges. "We were both Marines. He didn't take any guff. He was a man's man."

Once after almost blowing a 7–0 lead against the Giants but barely winning, he was called into Hodges's office.

"And that's *real bad,*" said Seaver. Hodges told him his approach was "miserable." He chewed him out for 10 minutes, then dismissed him with a summary, "You're done."

"I got that lesson in the middle of my second year in the big leagues—and never forgot it. Never," recalled Seaver.

But Seaver was in many ways an old-time baseball man. Despite his three-piece-suit, briefcase-carrying, *Wall Street Journal*–reading reputation, he was fun loving, chewed tobacco, and loved a few laughs over beers with the boys after the game. His teammates loved him. He was one of the guys, only more so.

The 1968 season was a strange one. Known as the Year of the Pitcher, it was a season in which the Most Valuable Player in both leagues was a moundsman. In the American League, Detroit's Denny McLain was the last 30-game winner. In the National League, Bob Gibson of St. Louis was even better, if that can be believed, hurling 13 shutouts and posting 48 straight scoreless innings and a record earned run average of 1.12, a mark that may never be broken. Gibson struck out 17 Tigers in the World Series, but Detroit's Mickey Lolich was the hero with three wins to earn the MVP. The National League won the All-Star Game, 1–0. Only one American Leaguer, Carl Yastrzemski of Boston (.301), batted over .300. Only five did it in the senior circuit. The combined ERA of both leagues was 2.99. Don Drysdale of Los Angeles set the all-time consecutive scoreless innings streak with 58. Oakland's Catfish Hunter hurled a perfect game. Gaylord Perry of the Giants and Ray Washburn of the Cardinals threw no-hitters against each other's teams on consecutive nights at Candlestick Park, a feat never accomplished before. With scoring and, by extension, attendance down, Major League Baseball decided to lower the height of the mound beginning in 1969. Baseball was dead, a casualty of pro football's sexy image. Or so it seemed.

"The more years go by, the more amazed I am when I look at Bob Gibson's record in 1968," Seaver recalled. "I don't know why people don't talk about that season more—it was just phenomenal. . . . Did you know he started out 3–5 that year?"

Gibson and San Francisco's Marichal both had huge years in 1968, conjuring memories of Koufax.

"When Koufax and Gibson stood on the mound, 'good heat' took on a new dimension," Seaver recalled. "Their fastball moved, defying gravity. . . . When Marichal stood there, he baffled 'em, with deceptive screwballs." Koufax "will remain the paradigm of a pitcher who is developed slowly by a patient management." Marichal was "entirely different, but just as much a master of the art of pitching."

For Tom Seaver, 1968 was another year of great success matched by frustration. Outside of the superhuman Gibson, he pitched as well as anybody else in the league, but if the 1967 Mets failed to support him, they looked like the Murderers' Row Yankees compared to the 1968 version. Seaver said they owed the rest of the staff as much as they had given him but did not mean that they metaphorically skip town on his day to pitch.

He again appeared in the All-Star Game.

"It's the 1968 All-Star Game, and we're off to Houston," Seaver remembered. "I take Nancy with me, but she won't go anywhere without our little French poodle, Slider. The name Slider had nothing to do with the pitch, only with the way the poodle walked.

"Anyway, we're staying at the Shamrock Hilton, and who gets to walk the dog—Nancy? Of course not! So I put the little poodle on a leash and sneak into the elevator, hoping nobody sees me. But the elevator stops, and who do you suppose gets on? Harmon Killebrew, this huge, massive slugger from the American League. 'Well,' I thought, 'maybe he won't recognize me.' But he looks up and says, 'Hi, Tom—your dog?' What am I going to say? 'No, I stole him'? So, I'm embarrassed, but I say it's my wife's. And Killebrew says, 'We've got one just like it at home. And if my wife were here, she'd have brought him, and I'd be walking him, too!'

"I got out of the elevator all shades of red, but I also learned what a nice guy Harmon was. And imagine that—he had a French poodle, too."

After having his photo taken before the game at the Houston Astrodome with Willie Mays, Seaver struck out five: Mickey Mantle, Carl Yastrzemski, Joe Azcue, Boog Powell, and Rick Monday. Challenging the superstar Mantle, then in his last year, he struck out the Mick, helping to preserve his league's victory.

"I said I wasn't ever much of a Yankees fan, but I admit that you had to make an exception for [Joe] DiMaggio. Well, Mantle's another one," recalled Seaver. "Mickey was everybody's hero in the 1950s and early 1960s." Mantle's "career was essentially over by the time I reached the Majors. I did get to face him once, in the 1968 All-Star Game in Houston. My parents were there, my wife was there, and believe me, it was quite a thrill just to stand on the mound and pitch to Mickey Mantle. I remember as he came up to bat thinking that I'd like to freeze this moment in time and tell my grandchildren about it. As luck would have it, I had a really good fastball that day, and I struck him out on three pitches. But it was his last year, and he wasn't the Mantle I grew up watching every fall in the World Series."

Seaver added this on Mantle: "No other player since then has captured the public fancy through that special combination of raw talent and inspiring life story. Nor has any player enjoyed such popularity at home or on the road as did the Mick in his final years as a player . . . His background had a Hollywood quality as well."

In August the Mets were challenging for second place. Seaver's desire for a perfect game almost came to fruition when the Cardinals' Orlando Cepeda broke up his bid in the seventh inning. It served to whet his appetite for one. After that, however, his team fell precipitously, finishing with 73 wins and a ninth-place spot. It was an improvement over previous Mets teams. The club was significantly more competent than any prior year.

After one victory Hodges said, "Seaver is Whitey Ford; younger, but he has more stuff than Ford."

"I think it's much too early in my career for any such comparisons," Seaver said modestly. "Wait until I've been around as long as

Whitey and have been as consistent as someone like Sandy Koufax or Don Drysdale."

He won 16 against 12 losses, with a sterling 2.20 ERA and 205 strikeouts. There was a distinct improvement in his velocity as his body grew in strength. Seaver dominated the opposition and could have won 20 or even 24 games in 1968, but the Mets were abysmal behind him.

They hit .228 as a team but gave Seaver even less. Over one 11-game stretch, his ERA was 1.91 but opposing pitchers were 1.72 against New York bats, when they scored a mere 19 runs overall. Seaver's record during that period was 2–5.

Off the field, Seaver visited Vietnam vets in the hospital. Nancy was a self-confessed "liberal," opposed to the war. Seaver still had the Marine experience drummed into his being, but he questioned America's involvement. On the one hand, he read enough and understood history, so he realized that appeasement fails. In 1968 the world did not quite realize the horrors of Communism, although they certainly knew enough. But Mao Tse-Tung's Cultural Revolution, then in its third year, and the 55 million murdered in Red China were not fully revealed yet. But for now, Seaver was aghast at the loss of American life, the suffering of the wounded.

He gave his time to disabled kids, leaving the hospital with tears streaming down his face. Seaver was a Christian but kept his religious views private. He had a deep social conscience, understood that he was a role model, and knew from having admired hero ballplayers himself what an impact he had on their young lives. Unlike Joe DiMaggio, a man of amoral self-interest, Seaver was happy to give of himself. Over the years, as he saw how those he thought were his friends really just wanted to get something from him, he would shut down somewhat, become wary, but in 1968 he was still a wide-eyed idealist who thought he could change the world.

Despite the Mets' batting woes, there were hopeful signs. "To understand the 1969 Mets, one must first take a look at the 1968 Mets," Seaver recalled. Rookie of the Year Jerry Koosman got the support Seaver did not. He also made the All-Star Game, winning 19 against 12 losses with a 2.08 ERA. The southpaw from Minnesota threw almost as hard as Seaver. Jerry Grote also made the All-Star team. With good young pitching, New York provided reason for celebration among their supporters. But Seaver, Hodges, and the young team found no reason to jump for joy over a below-.500 season. They had their hopes set on bigger and much better things. However, Hodges suffered a late-season heart attack in 1968. His availability was in doubt when the season ended. Somebody wished Seaver luck the next year and hopefully more run support.

"So much depends on number 14," Seaver said of 1969. Fourteen was Hodges's number.

5

THE HOPES AND DREAMS: SPRING 1969

"HIGH HOPES" WAS FRANK SINATRA'S CAMPAIGN SONG FOR JOHN F. Kennedy in 1960. Indeed, JFK's high hopes came true that year, but so much occurred in the star-crossed decade that followed; no pundit, prophet, or political scientist could possibly have painted a picture describing the changed, topsy-turvy, tragically beautiful world that followed. The cataclysmic differences between 1960 and 1969 mark the greatest social upheaval in American, and possibly world, history.

As 1969 dawned, there were high hopes that change was in the air. So much had gone wrong that it seemed there was no place to go but up. Richard Nixon was sworn in as president on January 20. He was a Californian, but like so many of New York's greatest sports stars over the years, he was also a bona fide New Yorker. He had taken a job with a "silk stocking" Wall Street law firm in 1963 and lived in a fancy East Side building that also housed Nelson Rockefeller.

New York had particularly high sports hopes for 1969. Something was in the air. Aside from having a quasi–New Yorker in the White House, the city was enthralled with the Jets. On January 12, Broadway Joe Namath engineered the seminal event in NFL history, a 16–7 upset of Baltimore. Mayor John Lindsay attached himself to the team, leading the over-the-top celebration when they returned from Miami. It had been such an upset, such a miracle, and was so full of magical serendipity that all things seemed possible.

Tom Seaver, who was always seemingly smarter than everybody else, had done his Marine stint in 1962–1963, before it got hot "in country," as they called Vietnam. He was done with his service commitment. Many Mets and Jets had to give up a weekend a month and two weeks a year, sometimes missing games in the process, at Reserve depots such as Camp Drum, New York.

"Seaver had done that bit," said Ron Swoboda. It gave him just a little more credibility than others. As Namath was shocking the world, Seaver was finishing up final exams at the University of Southern California. He told people later that the last thing on his mind was the Mets' accomplishing a similar feat. However, as he lifted weights and worked out with Rod Dedeaux's defending national champion Trojans in the winter sunshine of Los Angeles, the ever-optimistic Seaver could not help but have . . . high hopes.

"I always felt that New York fans were and are the greatest in the world," recalled first baseman Ed Kranepool. "They were always knowledgeable, and by 1967 last place wasn't fun anymore." When Hodges came on the scene, "It wasn't a matter of just showing up anymore . . . so many guys were used to losing that they had negative habits. It's contagious."

Ed Charles was an American League veteran, where he had seen Hodges operate. He had just a few good years left and had never been with a winner.

"Hodges changed the losing mind-set," Charles said in *Miracle Year: 1969 Amazing Mets and Super Jets* by Bill Gutman. "He was an upfront type of manager, very knowledgeable about the game, very firm in what he expected from the players. He told us when we were out there he expected 100 percent effort. If we couldn't give it because of a physical reason, he wanted us to tell him, because he wouldn't put us on the field."

Ron Swoboda later said he thought the 1969 Mets "could go out and play with anybody," but his limited expectations were the

.500 mark. "I don't think anyone came out of Spring Training aiming at the moon."

Bud Harrelson recalled Hodges holding Spring Training meetings in which he said New York had lost 36 one-run games the previous season and that "if you won half of them, you'd be in contention." Hodges put it in logical, easy-to-understand terms; if each pitcher won just one more game than he lost, this goal could be achieved. Since it seemed obvious that Seaver and Koosman would do much better than that, optimism soared.

Kranepool admitted that in other years he and his teammates "just showed up," but Gil "wanted us to learn how to win, to be able to find ways to win." This was the key: finding new, inventive ways to win, since in the past they had specialized in new, inventive ways to lose.

The Tom and Jerry Show reported to camp with raises; $10,000 (to $35,000) for Seaver and $15,000 (to $25,000) for Koosman.

"These are the two guys we call our untouchables, and they are worth the money," announced general manager Johnny Murphy.

"Seaver had Hall of Fame written on him when he walked into camp and pitched his first game in '67," Swoboda said. "He was a finished product when he came there. I don't ever recall the sense of him being a rookie. He came out of the box a big-league pitcher, and there was this golden glow about him. This was clearly *big* talent, intelligent, capable, controlled, and awesome stuff."

But he and Seaver were not "tight." Swoboda admitted he said some things he should not have, that he would have been smart had he "hung around Seaver." Seaver and Harrelson were "California guys" and Seaver came from "a different socioeconomic level," which apparently rankled the blue-collar Swoboda. Plus Seaver was "a younger, more aware person" than he was.

While few things are given less notice than big-league exhibition games, the Mets did beat the defending world champion Detroit Tigers, 12–0, and the defending National League pennant-winning Cardinals, 16–6. The thing most people watched that spring, however, was Hodges. He appeared to have made a complete recovery from his September heart attack, writing an open letter to sportswriter Red Foley stating, "I've never felt better."

"It was our catcher, Jerry Grote, who first thought we could be in the hunt," recalled Seaver. "He said so as early as Spring Training of '69. Few took him seriously. . . .

"That we were young and untested proved to be an asset. None of us were paid so much in those days before free agency that there was any jealousy. None of us had played for the stumbling Mets of the Stengel years, except Kranepool."

The Mets had pitching, always the name of the game.

"It was important that the Mets organization had always stressed pitching and shown great patience with young arms," assessed Seaver.

"Most of the guys had a philosophy similar to mine," Tom Seaver wrote of the club's mind-set going into 1969, in *The Perfect Game.* "Maybe they didn't articulate it, but deep down they shared my attitude. I wanted to be the best ballplayer, the best pitcher Tom Seaver could possibly be. Jerry Grote wanted to be the best catcher Jerry Grote could be, and Cleon Jones wanted to be the best outfielder Cleon Jones could be, and Bud Harrelson wanted to be the best shortstop Bud Harrelson could be.

"If each of us achieved his goals—a reachable, realistic goal—individually, then we could all reach our team goal, no matter how unrealistic, no matter how impossible it seems to outsiders."

That spring, Seaver, Grote, Harrelson, and Ryan bonded on regular fishing trips under Bayway Bridge in St. Petersburg, a retirement community and longtime home of Spring Training teams, which is adjacent to Tampa Bay. Occasionally they were joined by Hodges, who had been advised by doctors to lose weight and get more exercise, which he endeavored to do by trying to stop smoking and making the trek down to Bayway Bridge with a pole and some shrimp bait.

Sipping coffee or beer, the young Mets philosophized and predicted. There was bravado, perhaps unrealistic expectations of their own chances, and some put-downs of the competition. Pittsburgh, a perennial contender, had problems. Philadelphia was not strong. The Expos were the "old Mets," as far as they were concerned. Leo Durocher's Cubs were seen as the main competition . . . for second place. St. Louis was the prohibitive favorite.

"You know, we could win our division if we play up to our potential," Seaver dared to say.

Hodges began to talk about 85 wins. Seaver called himself "the Supreme Optimist with that touch of reality," almost an Age of Aquarius kind of attitude. "The Supreme Optimist thinks we'll finish second in the Eastern Division of the league," Seaver told Joe Durso of the *New York Times,* not wanting to overdo Hodges. "Maybe third, but more likely second. The only team we can't catch is St. Louis. The only team we have to fight off is Chicago. But we can beat Pittsburgh, Philadelphia and Montreal."

Optimism and "high hopes" were the order of the day with the New York Mets.

"We knew that our best days were in front of us," said Seaver.

Seaver the little boy, the baseball fan from Fresno, continued to marvel at the heroes he continued to meet. The year 1969 was the 100th anniversary of professional baseball. All-time teams were selected, and Joe DiMaggio made the rounds, anointed as the greatest living player.

"Do you think it's easy to just walk up to Joe DiMaggio and start a conversation?" Seaver recalled. "I've been around him at old-timers' games, and believe me, he's someone special. It's not easy to walk over and say, 'How ya doin', Joe, whaddaya say?' You really feel as though this is the one old-timer you have to call Mister."

6

THE ICON: SUMMER 1969

THE CONTRAST FROM THE FLORIDA SUN TO WINTRY CONDITIONS HAD its effect on Seaver, whose high 90s heat, exploding and moving, came in flat at around 88 miles per hour, perfect batting practice fodder for Montreal in the very first game in Expos history. The Expos went after the two-time All-Star like they were the 1961 Yankees. Hodges stuck with his ace in the opener, thinking each inning that the guy would settle down.

It was not all Tom's fault. When he needed a break to get out of a jam, he did not get it. Liners were misjudged in the windy sky, grounders booted by clunky gloves. "I think I've seen all this before," said veteran sportswriter Maury Allen. "Another bad ball club."

Then there were the Mets' bats, last in the league the previous year (.228), only today they made Shea look like a pinball arcade. It remains one of the ugliest games in New York Mets history, the antithesis of tight, taut baseball rhapsodized over by the likes of the *New Yorker's* Roger Angell.

There is an expression: "All's well that ends well." Or "A win's a win." In baseball, in all sports, coaches and managers take a win any way they can get it. Despite the ugliness, they could have been winners anyway. Seaver was ordinary, giving up two runs in the first inning. New York came back. Seaver struggled, throwing 105 pitches. He told Hodges he was done (as if it were not obvious) and departed with a 6–4 lead. He still could have gotten credit for the lackluster victory.

Al Jackson and Ron Taylor were roughed up. Rusty Staub went deep, and Montreal forged an 11–6 lead. The Mets still could have pulled it out, finally giving their fans an Opening Day win, and gotten 1969 off to a decent, even exciting start. Alas, they fell just short after Duffy Dyer's three-run pinch homer in the ninth, losing 11–10.

"My God, wasn't that awful?" Seaver said to the writers afterward. They agreed, and the next day's columns were negative, expressing little confidence that the high hopes of St. Pete would translate into a winning spring start, not to mention summer or fall. The most frustrating thing was to finally get real run support and waste it.

"You know Seaver is a better pitcher than that," Gil Hodges told the press. "The next time we get 10 runs when he's pitching, I think we'll win."

Shortly thereafter, the Mets took on the defending National League champion St. Louis Cardinals. The third game was a classic Bob Gibson-Tom Seaver duel. Lou Brock and Curt Flood manufactured two runs off Seaver in the first. The two settled down after that, but Gibson was untouchable in the 3–1 complete-game victory. It ran his lifetime record versus New York to 22–3. The Mets were 2–4, with Pittsburgh leading the East at 5–1.

"Early in the season we realized we had to win low-scoring games," Koosman said. If the Mets scored two runs, "then you *had* to win." This would be the formula eventually, but in the beginning the Mets were inconsistent. There was improvement over the 1968 offensive numbers, but the rest of the league was better with the bat, as well.

Seaver was their "stopper." He outdueled Gibson in their rematch, 2–1. Facing Gibson early in his career defined Seaver's legacy and view of himself. Speaking of a game against Gibby on an overwhelmingly hot day, Seaver "struggled to concentrate but held on to win by a run," adding that "such bracing competition is the lifeblood of our craft. All real pitchers thrive on it, live for it."

Ferguson Jenkins of the Chicago Cubs used nasty inside heat to defeat Tom, who was effective but got touched, losing 3–1. If Montreal thought they had Seaver's number after batting him around in the Shea Stadium opener, they saw the real Tom Terrific at Jarry Park. Seaver overpowered them 2–1.

On May 2 and 3, Chicago defeated New York, 6–4 and 3–2 before wild cheering at Wrigley Field. The Cubbies were the toast of the Northside. The whole early shaky Mets' season was seemingly always on the line, and Seaver would be asked to respond each time. On May 4 he came through with a 3–2 win over Billy Hands. In the second game of the doubleheader, the Mets made a statement, winning 3–2 again to split the series.

Seaver's game was key. It was a Sunday, the crowd loud and boisterous, drinking beer, the "bleacher bums" in full force, May weather starting to break the Chicago winter. Leo Durocher was in the other dugout. The Mets were the baseball image of *nice guys*, and everybody knew what Leo predicted for that. Hodges was a churchgoing fellow—quiet, unassuming.

Chump, thought Leo. Gil had a bunch of college guys, frat boys. Seaver, the preppie, faced Ron Santo. He was the face of the Cubs, the Italian guy, outspoken, a hard-ass. The time had come. No provocation really, other than Leo's *presence* in the home dugout. Seaver let one fly right at Santo's batting helmet. It flipped him. Santo stared out at Tommy Tom Tom.

So that's how it's gonna be, eh?

It was a baseball code, the way the game is played. The Cubs' star brushed himself off, the crowd booing. Did Leo scream obscenities at Seaver, at the home plate umpire, turn to Billy Hands and tell him to "Stick it in his ear"? No. He sat in stony silence. This situation required no words.

When Seaver stepped in against Hands, he got nicked on the arm. It was on. Hands got one in the leg. The benches looked to clear, players on the steps, ready to rumble. The umpire stepped halfway out to the mound. He warned Seaver, a $50 fine. Seaver knew he had reached the tolerance limit and could not afford another one lest he be thrown out. He needed to stay in to win.

Pitch after pitch. Cheese. Hard, hard sinkers, the kind that wore out Grote's hand, left him black and blue, broke bats, made the ball hit wood like shot-puts, induced grounders struck by noodles. Good old country hardball. Tom accepted the $50 fine as a small price to pay for victory and respect.

"That was my first really satisfying game," he told the media after the hard-won victory.

"I tried to brush him back in New York but I didn't do much of a job," Tom told Larry Merchant of the *New York Post* when asked about the Santo brushback. "He was hitting me well. Possibly he's taking the bread out of my mouth. I had to make sure he respects me. You can't let hitters dominate or intimidate you. The hitter shouldn't intimidate the pitcher, and the pitcher shouldn't intimidate the hitter, but there has to be respect. I had to let Santo know I knew what he was doing to me. Then Leo had Hands hit me. What do I do, throw a bat at Leo? I had to do what I did. It's a part of baseball. It's a good hard game."

"This is the code," wrote Merchant. "But the thing is someone can get hurt or maimed with a baseball. . . . The man who shoots back and kills may not know the first man was just issuing a warning. They are fooling with bullets."

"You would have thought it foolish to throw at us when we had Tom and myself and the other guys, who could throw hard, but we weren't that well known yet," Koosman recalled. "But they helped get the fire going. They generated a lot of energy. That was one club you loved to beat."

Seaver saw no ethical quandaries. "There's a fine dividing line between throwing at someone or brushing him back. It's the difference between good hard baseball and dirty baseball."

But the Mets would face Chicago again down the road, and Leo Durocher played "dirty baseball." Durocher "was a Chicago kind of guy: dapper, brash, and a night owl—perfect for day baseball" was how Seaver remembered him.

"Leo was a daring manager" was how Gil Hodges described him. "He'd take chances, and sometimes they'd work, and sometimes they wouldn't. But, more than any manager I ever knew, Leo was the guy that other managers managed against. I've seen managers who'd ignore Leo's team, trying to stay one jump ahead of Leo. It didn't work. One thing that I learned from Durocher is not to try to manage against the other guy. I try to concentrate on running my team and try to concentrate on stopping only the obvious moves that the other manager might make. If I try to figure out all the things he might possibly do, in every situation, I'm going to lose sight of my own job, and also I'm not giving enough credit to my players."

After a sloppy loss to Atlanta, Hodges dressed the team down. Seaver agreed, saying, "We needed that." When he shut out the Braves, 3–0, the Mets reached the .500 mark at 18–18. It was celebrated as a major accomplishment in the New York press. Seaver had the perfect reaction to it.

".500 is nothing to celebrate," he said. The tone was set.

Then the Mets got off to an 11-game winning streak in late May and early June, beating Los Angeles and San Francisco. Seaver beat San Francisco, 4–3, on May 30. The streak included victories over their old nemeses, the Giants and Dodgers, both in New York and on the West Coast, including a scintillating 1–0 win highlighted by an incredible defensive save by second baseman Al Weis. It was a seminal moment. It had been important beating the old New York teams, but now the ghosts of "Willie, Mickey and the Duke," as the song goes about former Big Apple icons Willie Mays, Mickey Mantle, and Duke Snider, were replaced by a new generation, a "new breed."

"We found ways to win games as opposed to finding ways to lose," wrote outfielder Art Shamsky in *The Magnificent Seasons.* "Don't get me wrong, at this point nobody thought about winning the East Division title or even visualized hopes of a pennant. But we were a better ball club than the Mets had ever been in our history. More important, we were starting to have faith in our own abilities. Positive things started to happen."

Shamsky had missed much of Spring Training with an injury. He spent the early part of the season at triple-A Tidewater before getting called up to the big leagues.

"We were learning how not to beat ourselves," recalled second baseman Ken Boswell, who was trying to debunk his reputation as a defensive liability.

"I thought if we could just start winning some close games you never know what could happen," said Grote. There was that computer analysis, and Gil's admonition too: 36 one-run losses in 1968. Win half of those, that is 18 wins added to the 73 of the previous year.

"I'm tired of the jokes about the old Mets," Seaver told Jack Lang and the assorted writers. "Let Rod Kanehl and Marvelous Marv laugh about the Mets."

After the Wichita Dreamliners had beaten Seaver in 1965, Rod told the young Goldpanner pitcher he was destined for the big leagues, and now here he was. When Seaver announced the "celebration" would come about only when a pennant was won, Maury Allen shrugged and said, "I'll be too old to enjoy it."

On July 8, the Cubs visited Shea Stadium. The press dubbed it the "first crucial series" in Mets history. At 45–34, New York trailed Chicago (52–31) by five games. A three-game Mets sweep could pull them to within two games. If the Cubs beat them three in a row all the air would be out of their tires.

Koosman squared off against Ferguson Jenkins in the first game. Jenkins looked unhittable, carrying a 3–1 lead into the ninth, but the Mets strung a few hits together, combined with a misplay by Chicago's rookie center fielder, Don Young. A bloop single by Ed Kranepool ignited wild enthusiasm, giving Koosman a complete-game 4–3 win.

The crowd, indeed the entire city, went crazy, but it was only the start. Tom Seaver was scheduled to start the next evening.

Just 29 hours and 45 minutes after Lindsey Nelson announced, "It's absolute bedlam. You could not believe it. It's absolute bedlam," when Ed Kranepool drove in Cleon Jones to beat Chicago 4–3, another event occurred that utterly eclipsed that one. It was at 9:55 p.m. on Wednesday, July 9, the Year of Our Lord 1969. In the pantheon of greatness reserved only for that most heroic of all heroes, the New York sports superstar, beyond that the *American* hero—"in the arena" as Theodore Roosevelt liked to call it, the bright lights of Broadway, the Great White Way . . . and Shea Stadium illuminating him in all his splendor; well, he is rare indeed and rarer still is his debut.

Olivier as *Othello*, the audience gasping in astonishment at his range.

MacArthur returned from the wars, our freedoms his gift, our thanks washing over him.

Gehrig telling a full house of sobbing mothers, kids, and grown men that he was the "luckiest man on the face of the Earth."

By 5:45 p.m., Shea Stadium's parking lot was full, and the stands were mostly full. The excitement and air of anticipation were at a fever pitch. It was a World Series atmosphere.

After batting practice, the Cubs held a players-only meeting in which Santo apologized to Young for comments he made about the outfielder's failure to catch a key ninth-inning fly ball the previous day. Many managers would have put Young back in the lineup to boost his confidence. Not so Leo. A little-known nobody named Jimmy Qualls was penciled in to start in center field. Durocher was Durocher, and he was back in New York, his old stomping grounds. Finally, he relented and gave some time to the reporters.

Qualls was a 22-year-old rookie who had just been called up from Tacoma of the Pacific Coast League. He was only now starting to get his swing down, having missed two weeks to serve with his Reserve unit in Stockton, California. In the Mets' clubhouse, Qualls's surprise start left Seaver, Grote, and pitching coach Rube Walker looking for a scouting report. Without any computer databases or Internet searches available, they had to rely on Bobby Pfeil, the only one to have seen him hit. Pfeil recommended "hard stuff"—fastballs and sliders—as opposed to curves and changeups.

"He can get his bat on the ball," he told Seaver.

At 7:48, Seaver began to get loose, but he was experiencing trouble. There was a twitch in his shoulder. He went through 103 pitches, trying to get the kinks out. "It still feels a little stiff," he told Rube Walker as he made his way to the dugout.

"Do the best you can," Walker replied.

Outside the stadium, a group of about 50 kids, described by a policeman as a "raving mob," managed to sneak into the park when Jerry Koosman's wife, Lavonne, arrived and the gate was opened for her. It was a portent of future events. The game was a sellout—59,083—with standing room only packed shoulder to shoulder, some fans having waited since 7:30 in the morning. Baseball was back.

Finally Tom Seaver, now stiffness-free and throwing easily, took the mound. His fastball simply exploded. The Cubs' hitters stared at it, or at what they *heard* of it, since they could not actually *see* the thing. They went down like the French Army circa 1940, one-two-three in the first inning.

Bobby Pfeil doubled into the left-field corner, giving Seaver a 1–0 lead.

"I have been to every ball game here, and I have never seen anything like this," broadcaster Lindsey Nelson told the hundreds of thousands tuned into the television broadcast. "People are everywhere."

Seaver retired Chicago one-two-three in the second inning, causing Rube Walker to tell Gil Hodges that he had "no-hit" stuff. Indeed, Mets fans were seeing something very, very rare.

Many a well-pitched game marks an average baseball season, but Seaver was out of his shoes, above and beyond even his best games over the course of his first two-and-a-half years. He was bringing it in the high 90s, maybe breaking 100 miles per hour, with perfect control and rhythm. What these fans were seeing was Koufax on his best night; Gibson in full domination mode; or any of the all-time legends, whether it be Walter Johnson, Lefty Grove, or Bob Feller. They say "good pitching beats good hitting." It does, but it has to be exceptional. Seaver was beyond exceptional. He was simply unhittable. His stuff could not be touched, merely waved at, gawked at, stunned by.

Seaver tomahawked a line drive between first and second base, scoring Jerry Grote. Then Agee doubled off the right-field fence, scoring Weis and moving Seaver to third. It was 3–0, New York. Shea was frantic. With Seaver knocking the eyelashes off flies from 60 feet, six inches, plus swinging the bat like he was Bobby Clemente, the outcome of the game was utterly without doubt. It was full-throttle momentum, and Chicago was as done as an overcooked Thanksgiving turkey.

"Break up the Mets!" began to be heard. It was a strange plea that fans occasionally chanted in Seaver's rookie year, when he for the first time demonstrated such unaccustomed excellence that the people conceived in jest that he had made them too good for the rest of the league.

Seaver mowed through Chicago in the third, one-two-three. In the fourth inning, Seaver faced the top of the Cubs' order—Don Kessinger, Glenn Beckert, and Billy Williams—for the second time. A strikeout and two easy grounders to Ed Charles made quick work of them. In the fifth, Santo, Banks, and Al Spangler went down—a fly ball, a grounder to the shortstop, and Seaver's eighth strikeout. In the sixth, as he went through the Cubs' order for the second time, Ed Kranepool said it: "He's got a perfect game." The tradition in the dugout of a pitcher with a no-hitter, much less a perfect game, is to say nothing, but it was obvious to every player and fan in Shea Stadium that evening.

At the offices of the Associated Press in midtown Manhattan, baseball writer Ed Schuyler was dispatched to Shea Stadium in case Seaver pitched a perfect game. Schuyler had done the same thing in 1968, arriving just as Orlando Cepeda of St. Louis broke it up.

On Long Island, Nelson Burbrink, the scout who signed Tom Seaver off of the USC campus a mere three years earlier, got in his car after scouting a prospect. As the car eased onto the Long Island Expressway, he heard Lindsey Nelson on WJRZ say, "Tom Seaver will get quite a hand when he comes up to bat here. He's faced 18 Cubs and retired them all."

Sitting in a box seat near first base, Nancy Seaver began to cry. Seaver glanced at her and saw the emotions start to spill out. The atmosphere was utterly electric, almost indescribable, a buzz of sound and anticipation bubbling to the surface, threatening to swallow up a stadium, a whole city.

Kessinger led off the seventh—the top of the order for the third time. Seaver had been pounding fastballs on Chicago all night, but thinking that he should give them a little wrinkle he curved the Cubs' shortstop, who sliced a liner to left field. At first Seaver thought it was their first hit, but the ball hung and Jones grabbed it easily. Beckert popped to Swoboda, sweating bullets of nerves in right. Williams bounced to Charles. Shea exploded.

With one out in the top of the seventh, Jones lined a homer, an "insurance" run on a night Tom Seaver did not need it. The score was 4–0. In the bottom half of the inning, Hodges sent Rod Gaspar to right field in place of Swoboda; Wayne Garrett went to second; and Bobby Pfeil moved to third, replacing Charles.

"You go into a game like this, cold and everything, and you're just hoping you can do the job if the ball is hit to you," Gaspar was quoted saying in *The Year the Mets Lost Last Place.* "It's a perfect game. We're going for first place. All the people in the park. It's frightening."

In the eighth, Seaver induced Santo to fly to Agee. Then, facing Banks and Spangler, he seemed to jet it up a half a notch. The middle innings were over, his pitch count low, the game in hand. There was no holding anything back. Incredibly, he started throwing *harder.* The Mets fans watched: loud, crazy, boisterous, yes, but by now in *awe.* They were observing a baseball Michelangelo, a sculptor of the mound. Seaver, who admired his brother the sculptor and wanted to somehow duplicate in baseball what he could do with clay, was now accomplishing this task.

"It was like having a magic wand that night, reaching out and touching the ball to a spot I had picked in my mind" was Seaver's description.

Old-timers who had seen it all over the past 50 years of baseball in the golden age of New York knew instinctively that the 24-year-old Californian was a new Koufax, a Ford, a Newcombe—maybe better than any of those guys! A "new breed." After Seaver rocketed a heater past Al Spangler to end the eighth, he walked off the mound to insane cheering. Announcer Bob Murphy then stated, "LADIES AND GENTLEMEN, AFTER EIGHT INNINGS, TOM SEAVER IS WALKING INTO THE DUGOUT WITH A PERFECT BALL GAME."

Grote grounded out but Weis singled. Seaver donned a batting helmet, undid the donut from his bat, and gave his warm-up jacket to the batboy. It was 9:55 p.m., Wednesday, July 9, 1969. The seminal moment in which George Thomas Seaver entered the pantheon.

The crowd rose; they had been continuously cheering all through Seaver's dominant eighth inning, building to a crescendo that rocked the five-year-old stadium to its very core. It was the sound Marilyn Monroe *wished* she heard when she gyrated before the boys in Korea. The sound Joe DiMaggio *had* heard when he was at his heroic best at Yankee Stadium, the knowledge of which he so contemptuously informed the breathless Marilyn when she tried to tell him, "Joe, Joe, you never *heard* such cheering."

This was the biggest of the big time, the ultimate stage, the winning over with the most impressive of all bravura performances of the most cynical, loud-mouthed, hard-core, hard-to-please sports aficionados on the face of the earth. In this we get to the heart of what made this different, what made this a *miracle.* The winning over of the crowd, the total childlike exuberance of the hard-bitten seen-it-alls, had a Pentecostal touch to it. They were *children,* all of them. The middle-aged men, who toiled for big bucks on Wall Street or union wages in a delivery truck; the grandmothers wondering what was happening to kids these days—all the drugs and sex and lack of respect—yet it all came together here, with Seaver a Pied Piper who did not quite know what was happening himself, so magical and mystical it was. The young man whom old folks related to, the sex symbol who was faithful to his wife, the sports hero who seven years earlier was 6–5 pitching for the Fresno High varsity.

"I know a thousand things were running through my mind," he recalled years later. "The fans were absolutely unbelievable. I grew up in Los Angeles where the fans clap softly when someone hits a home run or pitches a great game. Here the noise gets right into your system. You tingle all over. I could hear my heart pounding, feel the adrenaline flowing. My arm felt light as a feather. I know I thought about my wife and once looked over to where my father was sitting. And I remember sitting in the dugout and looking into the upper deck and seeing people standing, screaming in the aisles. I can't explain what that did to me. It was like being in a marvelous dream. . . .

"And I thought to myself, moments like these are reserved for other people; they're for the Sandy Koufaxes, the Mickey Mantles, the Willie Mayses of this world—not for the Tom Seavers and the New York Mets."

"If Woodstock was a happening, so were the Mets, game after every wonderful, energy-filled game," wrote sportswriter Peter Golenbock.

Swoboda said Shea "resonated in a way that you can't hardly describe. . . . It literally vibrated. It was awesome."

So the sound washed over Tom Seaver. As 9:55 passed into 9:56, it kept *coming* like baptismal firewaters, like a revival, like the Holy Spirit. Above the stadium, Christy Mathewson, John McGraw, Babe Ruth, Lou Gehrig, Branch Rickey, and Mel Ott formed a ghostly Hall of Fame, granting approval, imprimatur to the newest member. Ruth called Seaver "Keed." Matty told McGraw, "He reminds me of me." Rickey saw the perfect harmony of black and white teammates, the stands a diverse mix of New Yorkers, and nodded approval over that which he had wrought.

The latest true New York sports icon, the *savior* then laid down a perfect sacrifice bunt. The runner moved to second as he jogged off the field, cheered as if he had just moved a mountain.

An estimated two-and-a-half million New Yorkers were now watching Seaver trot off the field. "Housewives not the least interested in baseball have been dragged to the set by their husbands to watch history," wrote Dick Schaap and Paul Zimmerman.

Nancy Seaver wept as she watched her husband take the mound for the ninth. Next to her was Tom's father, Charles. Tom's body was floating with pure adrenaline. He had thrown a perfect game as a Little Leaguer, then had all his hopes and dreams for a baseball future seemingly dashed when he made the move to the "big diamond"; then there was high school, where the likes of Dick Selma—now a spectator sitting in the opposing team's dugout—had surpassed him by leaps and bounds.

The 59,000 fans chanted, "Seav-*uh,* Seav-*uh.*" It was beyond incredible, beyond heady. He later said his arm was light, as if detached from his body. He was in touch with his feelings. His heart pounded furiously, but the crowd noise was somehow so great as to be silent. He was in a zone. Few ever reach such a zenith.

But with all of this going on, Seaver still had a job to do, and it required concentration. Amid all the furor, he dropped, drove, and delivered furious heat to Randy Hundley. Hundley, as if acknowledging that to actually swing and hit Seaver was by now beyond conception, tried to bunt his way on. The ball came right back to Seaver, the easiest play in the world, except that under such intense pressure some people stiffen right up. Grote told him he had plenty of time, and Seaver threw out Hundley as if he did not have a care in the world.

Bud Harrelson, his best friend on the ball club, was watching the game at a restaurant called Giovanni's in Watertown, New York, where he was stationed for two weeks of summer training. Nobody knew who he was. Now, he was a fan like everybody else.

At seven minutes after 10, Jimmy Qualls strode to the plate. Qualls was the only Cub to get decent wood on a Seaver pitch all night, hitting a sharp line drive caught at the warning track, then a liner to first base. A left-handed batter, he had 47 Major League at-bats prior to his stepping in against Tom Seaver. Tommie Agee in center field was not sure where to play him. Seaver was throwing so hard that it seemed implausible that Qualls would pull him, but he seemed to be on Tom's pitches in a way no other Cub was on that night.

Bobby Pfeil's "scouting report"—hard stuff—was all Grote and Seaver had to go by. Seaver had dominated with the best fastball in the game, and that was what he and Grote agreed on. As he nodded yes to the sign, Ed Schuyler of the Associated Press arrived in the Shea Stadium press box.

Tom Seaver went into his windup, dropped, and delivered. Instead of a sinking action, down and away, the pitch came in waist high. He was just a quarter-inch off with his fastball. Qualls's bat connected, solidly, and the ball carried on a fly to deep left-center field. New York Mets center fielder Tommie Agee broke after the ball but quickly snuck a look at his boyhood pal from Mobile, Alabama, Cleon Jones, as if to say, "Hey man, you better get to it 'cause I ain't got it."

Jones just shook his head.

More than 59,000 people groaned as the ball dropped in for a single. Seaver, now a solitary figure on a mound of dirt surrounded by green grass, received another prolonged standing ovation. Seaver later called it the biggest disappointment of his life, "within my grasp," knowing he might not, probably would not, ever get another chance at something this close to perfection.

With a 4–0 lead, Seaver straightened up, took the mound, and worked to the next two Cubs hitters, retiring them easily. Seaver was immediately met by Nancy, still battling tears. "I guess a one-hit shutout is better than nothing," she told him. Tom Seaver's greatest triumph was a melancholy moment.

"After the game my wife, Nancy, met me in tears, but the fact that I kept my composure and got the last two outs showed we were a team of maturity—a team ready to win more 'big ones,'" was how he assessed the situation.

"I'm sure there was huge disappointment, but when you talk about Seaver, you're talking about someone whose emotion and skill were always under control," said Swoboda. "You had to pretty much go out and beat him. He wasn't going to give you much."

"There was no pressure on me at all," Qualls told reporters. "All I wanted to do was get a base hit and get something started."

When Tom returned to the clubhouse after appearing on *Kiner's Korner*, Dick Selma, his teammate at Fresno High, now with the Cubs, met him.

"Who were you pulling for?" Seaver asked him jokingly.

"I was pulling for us," Selma replied.

"Dear Diary, last night I sat in, with 60,000 other rabid believers, on the birth of a folk hero," wrote sportswriter Ray Robinson. "The folk hero . . . was Tom Seaver, a right-hander, possessing the virtues of Prince Valiant."

After the "imperfect game," Seaver was bidding to go beyond comparisons with other greats, such as Bob Gibson and Juan Marichal. Rather, he was now seen as a "sure" Hall of Famer already, his fastball and all-around ability comparable to Sandy Koufax, Bob

Feller, Lefty Grove, and a list so short it boggled the mind. His was a golden image that comes along once every century or so.

But as Seaver warmed up at Wrigley Field in his next start, a rematch with the Cubs, he felt a bothersome twinge in his shoulder. Wrigley Field was filled with placards and banners, fans singing and chanting. It had all the earmarks and regional pride of a World Cup soccer match. This being the summertime, a large contingent of New Yorkers was on hand, challenging the locals with signs of their own. The ushers and cops were all on edge.

The great Tom Seaver took the hill. Cubs fans booed, of course, but his appearance was a curious phenomenon. You could not help admiring this guy, his superlative ability. He was becoming a myth, a sighting. In the first, he was untouchable, appearing to be as unhittable as he had been at Shea Stadium. The first nine Cubs went down like doomed, blindfolded prisoners before a firing squad. In the sixth, Kessinger *bunted* for a hit and came around to score.

Seaver mowed Chicago down after that, but an almost unnoticeable problem, unseen by average fans, began to make its presence known. His fastball slowed down imperceptibly; his curve hung just that much; and worse, his shoulder was stiff. Billy Hands and the Chicago bullpen held the 1–0 lead—and Tom Seaver *had been beaten*! This concept seemed impossible, but here it was, right there at Wrigley Field in Chicago.

"I lost the battle and the game that day . . ." but "I have won a good share of the battles," Seaver recalled.

The next day the great Tom Seaver, the unhittable master, the superstar, the savior, was terribly distressed by severe stiffness, which became *actual pain* in his throwing shoulder. He lost a pedestrian 5–4 game to Montreal, and it was off to the All-Star Game in Washington, D.C. The proximity of his last start and shoulder stiffness, however, relegated him to the bench.

A black-tie dinner honoring the Greatest Team Ever in honor of professional baseball's 100th anniversary, along with a White House reception, highlighted the social calendar. President Richard Nixon was an enormous baseball fan who was reading the *Washington Post*

Sunday statistics of all big-league players when he was informed that President Dwight Eisenhower had suffered a heart attack in 1955, thus making him acting president. Seaver met the fellow Californian, whose wife was, like him, a USC alum (Nixon often courted her, sometimes even driving her when she dated *other guys*, at SC football games in the 1930s).

"Oh, you're the young man who won for the Mets when they were losing," President Nixon said to him.

Seaver told him it was great to finally be a winner.

Nixon smiled. He had lost the 1960 presidential election, had lost the 1962 California gubernatorial race, and was counted out by many before attaining the presidency the previous November.

"I know what you mean," he said to Seaver.

Doctors examined Seaver's shoulder. It was theorized that with all the adrenaline of the imperfecto against Chicago, he had simply thrown *too hard* for the human shoulder to endure. "It's only a muscle strain, maybe from throwing so hard in that one-hit game against Chicago," one doctor told him. "It's not a muscle tear, and there's nothing wrong with the joint. With proper treatment, it will be okay again."

He took Butazolidin pills and bathed the shoulder under heat lamps, but the pain would not go away. The unhittable master suddenly was very human, his record falling from 14–3 to 15–7. He lay awake at night, trying to convince himself it would be all right, but the harder he tried the more he worried. He used logic, refused to panic, thought it through, but came back to the basic question all athletes ask: *What do I do if I can't play anymore?*

One of his heroes growing up, Don Drysdale of Los Angeles, had been as healthy as an ox for years, never missing a start, even pitching victory after victory down the stretch in 1965 with broken ribs. Just last year, Big D had been as dominant as ever, throwing 58 straight shutout innings, but in 1969, without warning, a persistent pain in his arm forced him to retire years too soon.

After the Reds clobbered him, Seaver almost convinced himself he was done. He walked the streets of Cincinnati, reasoning that he would go back to college, that he had the intelligence to have success outside of baseball. Maybe he had earned enough notoriety in three years in New York to parlay that into broadcasting. But to have gone from the mountaintop of July 9, to be an *icon,* only to fall so perilously fast was mind-boggling.

Seaver contacted USC and told them to expect him to start classes in early October, as the Mets would not be in the postseason after all. Down by nine-and-a-half games, however, Gil Hodges still demanded professionalism.

On July 30 the Mets faced old nemesis Houston. Like the Mets, for the very first time the Astros were in contention, in the "wild, wild West" Division, with Atlanta, San Francisco, Cincinnati, and Los Angeles all neck and neck. During a terrible doubleheader loss to the Astros, Cleon Jones was perceived to have failed to hustle on a play in the outfield.

Hodges, seething, walked into the outfield grass, confronting Jones. After a few words, Hodges headed back to the dugout, a contrite left fielder a few steps behind him.

"Journalistically, it's conventional to want to look for turning points," said Ron Swoboda when asked if Hodges's move was just that. "In a 162-game season there's no single turning point. There is a collection of things that turn you in another direction, and for us the collection was [Don] Cardwell, Koosman, [Gary] Gentry, and even [Jim] McAndrew getting physically well. . . . They all had little things bothering them, and they didn't pitch very well in the first half of the year. Everyone but Seaver. Seaver was the same: dead steady."

After the post–All-Star Game slump, despite the Jones incident, Seaver felt "we never stopped hustling and never stopped believing in the miracle. After all, it was the same year man walked on the moon!"

Seaver felt the "key games" were played between August 16 and 19. They included two doubleheaders, all won by scores of 2–0, 2–1, 3–2, 3–2, and 1–0 (14 innings). On August 16, Seaver's arm, seemingly *touched* by an unseen hand and suddenly as strong as it had been on July 9, shut out San Diego, 2–0. In the second game, and in both of the next day's twin bill, New York pitching held up in tense one-run victories.

"As late as August 19, we were still nine-and-a-half games back, but then we started to make our move," Koosman said. "Seaver and I won our last 15 starts."

Koosman and Seaver challenged each other, acknowledging their one-upsmanship.

"We had so much confidence at that time," said Koosman. "Tom and I started to get cocky between ourselves. If Seaver struck out 10 the night before, and if I was pitching the next day, I tried to strike out 11. Or if he got a base hit, I tried to get two hits.

"We started making little bets as to who could get the side out with three pitches. And if we accomplished what we said we were going to do, I'd look into the dugout at Seaver, and he'd acknowledge me. If he said he was going to saw somebody off on a certain count and he did it, I'd acknowledge him. That's the confidence we had. At that point the press were calling us the Tom and Jerry Show—after the cartoon."

"The difference between the physical abilities of the players in the Major Leagues is not that great, and something going hand in hand with that, the difference between the teams is not that great," Tom Seaver surmised. "So what it comes down to is that the dividing factor between the one that wins and the one that loses is the mental attitude, the effort they give, the mental alertness that keeps them from making mental mistakes. The concentration and the dedication—the intangibles—are the deciding factors, I think, between who won and who lost. I firmly believe that. I really do."

This was Seaver's logical, reasoning mind at work, and of course each word of it is true. He once explained his motivation, his desire for perfection, the driving force separating him from so many others.

"It's why you run wind sprints in 104-degree heat in the middle of the afternoon in St. Louis in the summer," he said. "In the ninth inning with the game on the line, you draw strength from that."

But logic and hard work were not the only factors afoot in September of 1969.

On August 31, Chicago led the Mets by three-and-a-half games. New York had gone from nine-and-a-half back to three-and-a-half, and while those games obviously represented a mathematical advantage for the Cubs, the psychology of momentum worked in New York's favor.

With friends and family from Fresno in attendance, Tom tossed an 8–0 shutout at the powerful Giants, who were battling hard for the West Division crown. Over the next week, the Mets closed the gap every day. A crowd of 58,436 came out to see Seaver versus Jenkins in a game that defined why baseball still was and remains to this day our national pastime. The day-to-day tension, the spectacular hopes and expectations, the ebb and flow of a pennant chase cannot be duplicated—not by basketball with its fifth-place teams making the playoffs, not by soccer and its endless 0–0 scores, and obviously not by football and its need for a weekend climax followed by six days of wound licking and war preparation.

In baseball they *play for real* every day—not a press conference, not an injury report, not a practice in full pads. They strap it on, the fans pay real money to see 'em play real ball, and on September 9 they got it in spades.

Now, the score tells us New York won, 7–1 behind Seaver's dominant pitching. Despite the standings, the division was won on September 9. Furthermore, with Seaver at the full height of his powers, mowing Chicago down with the sheer velocity of a cannon mixed with the accuracy of a Special Forces sharpshooter, the crowd, the atmosphere at Shea Stadium, *surpassed* even the imperfecto of exactly two months earlier. Lastly, if on July 9 the crowd witnessed the birth of George Thomas Seaver as a true New York sports icon, then on September 9 he had his confirmation.

"Man for man, this was the best team in the National League in 1969," Seaver recalled of the Cubs. "The Cubs' day had come. The only problem was, they ran into a team of destiny, the Amazin' Mets, my club, and we wound up finishing eight games ahead of them in what should have been a magical summer for Cubs fans. The '69 Cubs are remembered in Chicago as the '69 Mets are in New York."

Miracle followed miracle. There was a doubleheader sweep of Pittsburgh, two 1–0 victories, the winning run in each game driven in by the Mets' pitcher. Not even a record-breaking 19-strikeout performance by Steve Carlton of St. Louis could stop them.

A series of "miraculous things were indeed happening to us, and everyone was expecting the unexpected every day," Seaver recalled. "We were as hot as any ball club could be. It was a rainy afternoon in the new Busch Memorial Stadium, and the Cardinals . . . faced elimination."

Carlton "served 152 pitches, and 150 of them stayed in the ballpark," except for two two-run homers by Swoboda in a 4–3 victory. The Mets took over first place and never looked back. After beating Carlton, New York led Chicago by four-and-a-half games. They had won 10 of 11 and were at .605.

"My God, the Mets have a 'magic number,'" said Tom Seaver. They beat the Cardinals again to clinch the East Division. The crowd descended upon the Shea Stadium playing field. A wild champagne celebration ensued in the clubhouse.

There was no letup after the clinching, as often occurs. In Philadelphia, Koosman, Seaver, and Gentry dominated the Phillies in a sweep. Koosman and Seaver tossed back-to-back shutouts.

"I think Tom and I won something like 18 of our last 19 starts that year," recalled Koosman.

Seaver pointed out that they outscored only San Diego, Montreal, and St. Louis but hit .360 with two outs and men in scoring position late in games. The Elias Sports Bureau said it was the best statistic in this category between 1957 and 1987.

Seaver finished 25–7, having won his last 10 decisions. He struck out 208 hitters in 273⅓ innings. Seaver's .781 winning percentage was the best in the National League, followed by San Francisco's Juan Marichal (.656). Marichal led the senior circuit with a sparkling 2.10 earned run average, with Steve Carlton at 2.17, Bob Gibson at 2.18, Seaver at 2.21, and Koosman at 2.28. Seaver's 25 wins were the best in baseball. Phil Niekro of the Braves won 23. Marichal and Fergie Jenkins won 21 each.

Considering all the factors, it goes down as one of the finest pitching performances in history. Others have had more dominant statistics. Sandy Koufax (1963, 1965, 1966) won more games, struck out more batters, and posted a lower ERA (he also did it pitching from a higher mound). Seaver won more than Gibson did in 1968 (22 victories). Denny McLain's 1968 record looks better, on paper at least (31–6, 1.96 ERA). Dean Chance won 20 games with 11 shutouts and a 1.65 ERA in 1964. Luis Tiant's earned run average was 1.60 in 1968. All of these pitchers benefited from the aforementioned higher mound.

In subsequent years, Seaver posted lower earned run averages in 1971 and 1973. He struck out more hitters in numerous seasons. Mainly due to a lack of run support, he never won 25 games again. If later Mets clubs scored for him the way the Tigers scored for McLain in 1968, to use one example, Seaver may have been a 30-game winner.

Steve Carlton (1972, when the last-place Phillies inextricably scored tons of runs when he pitched), Steve Stone (1980), Roger Clemens (1986), Orel Hershiser (1988), Greg Maddux (1995), Pedro Martinez (1999), and Randy Johnson (2001) enjoyed seasons comparable to what Seaver did in 1969. Jim Bagby won 31 for Cleveland in 1920. Philadelphia's Lefty Grove (31–4, 2.06 ERA) was spectacular in 1931 during an era of heavy offense. Detroit's Hal Newhouser won 29 games in 1944. Whitey Ford (25–4) dominated for the 1961 Yankees. The old-timers of the "dead ball era" (Christy Mathewson, Grover Alexander, Walter Johnson) of course must be viewed in light of statistical relevance. There were other pitchers who enjoyed individual seasons comparable on paper to Seaver's in 1969, but perhaps did not mean as much to their respective teams.

Seaver carried New York like the mythological figure on the cover of Ayn Rand's *Atlas Shrugged*, seemingly moving the world on his broad shoulders, honed under the hot Camp Pendleton sun doing "up-and-on shoulders." Few if any pitchers were so important, stood out so spectacularly as the single true star of a team, as did Seaver. Koufax and Gibson; a few others. The list is short. But not even these mound heroes were so singularly identified with their club's success, played such an overall role of leader and inspiration. Perhaps no baseball player, maybe no athlete in any team sport has ever had the image Seaver had in 1969. He was seen as a pure hero, on and off the field, a near-perfect human being as well as athlete. This was false, of course, since as Seaver pointed out, "I drink beer and I swear," and "There's only been one perfect man, and he lived 2,000 years ago." No human can maintain the kind of saintly stature of his hallowed, magical 1969 season. Others, such as UCLA basketball coach John Wooden, have lived lives of such decency and respect that the glow of near perfection resided with them until their passing, but Seaver never pretended to or sought such unattainable status.

Tom Seaver was seen as a modern Lancelot, riding a white steed to the rescue of a team, a city, and indeed a whole country. Subsequent reports of his ego, his human flaws, while few and far between, were magnified because in that one year he was seemingly flawless. There were some indications that his image was not quite what people perceived.

"Such a combination of Galahad-like virtues has caused some baseball old-timers to compare him to Christy Mathewson," wrote Roger Angell in the *New Yorker*. "Others, a minority, see an unpleasantly planned aspect to this golden image—planned, that is, by Tom Seaver, who is a student of public relations. However, his impact on his teammates can be suggested by something that happened to Bud Harrelson back in July. Harrelson was away on Army Reserve duty during that big home series with the Cubs, and he watched Seaver's near-no-hitter (which Seaver calls 'my imperfect game') on a television set in a restaurant in Watertown, New York."

"I was there with a couple of Army buddies who also play in the Majors, and we got all steamed up watching Tom work," Harrelson said. "Then—it was the strangest thing—I began feeling more and more like a little kid watching that game and that great performance, and I wanted to turn to the others and say, 'I *know* Tom Seaver. Tom Seaver is a friend of mine.'"

Koosman was lucky in that he was simply viewed as a fine pitcher. The weight of all the expectations Seaver carried never fell on him. He just went out and pitched. His first half was a mixture of spectacular success, a few nagging injuries, and some mediocrity mixed with a lack of support. In the second half, down the stretch, he was almost as good as Seaver, and this statement must be understood in its full meaning. *Almost as good* as Seaver was like an actor who was *almost as good* as Olivier, a writer who was *almost as good* as Hemingway, a political figure who was *almost as good* as Churchill.

Koosman finished 17–9 with a 2.28 earned run average, with 180 strikeouts in 241 innings pitched. Gary Gentry was 13–12, and everybody expected him to someday be a 20-game winner.

New York's 100–62 mark was the second-best regular season record in baseball (.617). Chicago (92–70) finished second in the East, eight games back,

Seaver was easily voted the Cy Young Award, but a major controversy came in the awarding of the National League MVP, which went to Willie McCovey. Tom Seaver was unquestionably the deserving winner of the 1969 MVP.

Two writers on the selection committee simply ignored Seaver on their ballots altogether. McCovey finished with 265 points, Seaver with 243. They both had 11 first-place votes. Had both of the writers voted Seaver second, or if other writers who penalized him for being a pitcher had voted him higher, he would have beaten McCovey.

It caused a howl in the New York press and made *The Sporting News* editorialize that pitchers were the "step-children in the MVP poll," reminding the Baseball Writers' Association of America members that indeed hurlers are eligible. It caused the rules to be changed so that the vote would no longer be kept secret; writers would face accountability. Seaver never complained, expressing only class and admiration for Stretch.

His only response, some years later, was "Obviously, I vote for the pitcher."

Seaver led the Mets to victory in a manner so heroic as to be compared only to very, very few athletic feats: Carl Yastrzemski of Boston in 1967 perhaps. Maybe Joe Namath and the Jets in 1968. DiMaggio in 1949 comes to mind. Bill Walton of the NBA's Portland Trailblazers cast a similar, singularly large shadow in 1977. Joe Montana's first Super Bowl title with the 1981 49ers is worthy of mention. Neither McCovey nor Willie Mays ever had that kind of take-the-team-on-my-shoulders season.

Seaver and the Mets revitalized the sport of baseball. They drew 2,175,373 fans to Shea Stadium and 1,197,206 on the road (3,372,579 in total). At the time, the 2 million mark in home attendance was what the 3 million mark became (inching toward 4 million as the new modern standard). However, as President Ronald Reagan later said, "You ain't seen nothin' yet."

7

THE MIRACLE: FALL 1969

"LET'S GET ONE THING STRAIGHT AT THE START," 79-YEAR-OLD Casey Stengel stated before the National League playoffs between the Mets and Atlanta. "The Mets will play all the way to the end of the World Series because they have more pitchers and they throw lightning. And you can look it up, that's best for a short series."

Stengel clarified his "all the way to the end of the World Series" statement. "Don't forget, I say it goes the limit to the World Series for the Mets."

A three-game sweep of Atlanta did not seem likely, but since New York had won 38 of 49, the heat of their momentum did not make that such an impossibility.

"Our attitude going in the series was that we just didn't want to get embarrassed," said Swoboda.

The opener in Atlanta was as unpredictable as snowfall in San Diego. Tom Seaver, fresh as a daisy, with Gil Hodges having lined up his rotation perfectly, took the mound. Was any pitcher, ever, hotter at that point in time than Tom Seaver? He had won 10 straight, but they were not just wins. They were masterpieces, artistic concepts, clinics. He threw blindingly hard with perfect control, a deadly combo. He was so devastating that Mets fans simply assumed he could throw his hat on the mound and two hours later another shutout was accomplished. Grote never moved his glove, Seaver's control was so good. His slider was wicked, his curve buckled knees, and his fastball broke bats. Measly grounders were gobbled up, "can o' corn" pop-ups gathered in like so many nuts at harvest. Umpires' arms shot up time after time: strike one, strike two, *strike three* . . . and you are outta there!

Batters gave up, as they had when Koufax was at his best, when Gibson took control. It was "Good night, Irene." See ya. Bye-bye time. Just avoid embarrassment. Take your strikeout, your oh-fer, and be glad not all the pitchers were such gods, such immortals. Seaver was not a pitcher, he was a Hall of Fame plaque built out of flesh and blood.

So what did this living embodiment of pitching dominance do in game one? He got hit around like a Little Leaguer, his mighty fastball reduced to straight batting-practice fodder. Instead of 99-mile-per-hour heat, it came in steady and straight around 87, or so it seemed. His breaking stuff didn't. Dennis Hopper had better control on the set of *Easy Rider*. The Braves teed off on him. He wound up, dropped, drove, and then strained his neck watching his fielders scramble for Braves line drives and home runs that traveled so far they needed a stewardess.

It was a perfect example of the very nature of unpredictability, the human element of sports, why athletics are so much darn fun. You just never know. It was just like the opener against the expansion Expos, when Seaver and his "high hopes" were batted about in a foul barrage of "bad feedback," in the form of well-hit shots off Montreal bats.

Oh, one more thing. Seaver was the winning pitcher. It was that kind of year.

Warming up he felt jerky and panicked. His mouth was dry. He could not spit. He had no plan, no stuff, nothin'. He tossed up batting-practice fastballs, hoping they would be over the plate by chance and that liners would be hit at somebody. By no reason other than luck, really, despite bouncing curves and throwing fastballs that had Grote leaping out of his crouch, he somehow retired the side. The Mets scored two runs, and Seaver thought maybe this would be the catalyst—he would recover and be *Tom Seaver*, for God's sake.

Instead, Seaver struggled, his body totally discombobulated, and gave runs back. Hank Aaron's double off the wall drove in a couple runs, but Atlanta ace Phil Niekro was no more effective. In the fourth Tom changed from the pitching motion that had earned him success at Fresno City College, Alaska, USC, Jacksonville, and New York City. Grote came out and said something like, "Are you out of your mind? What's the matter with you? Is this an act? Did gamblers pay you off?"

Gil Hodges turned to Rube Walker as if to say, "Do you see what I see?" Stunned, 24 Mets and 25 Braves just looked out at the car wreck that was Tom Seaver. It was not the beginning anymore, but he was choking from nerves. He was the embodiment of all that athletes despise the most, the man whose courage fails his team.

The game droned on. In the seventh, Seaver threw a slow "curveball" to Aaron. Aaron's homer landed in the middle of a Civil War battle reenactment somewhere. The score was 5–4. Seaver entered the dugout. If anybody still thought he was "perfect," he made sure the part about "swearing" when he had said, "I drink beer and swear," was made perfectly clear. But the Mets scored five runs. Seaver was mercifully removed for a pinch hitter, and by nothing less than a miracle, Seaver was the *winning pitcher*, 9–5.

"We got five runs off Tom Seaver," Hank Aaron, slumped before his cubicle, said disconsolately to the writers. "That should win it for us. There is something wrong."

"Could there really be 'Met magic'?" one writer asked him. Henry suggested an anatomical location for the "Met magic," but the Braves were stunned. Fate was not on their side.

Seaver spoke to the press as if he were the losing pitcher, trying to explain why he had pitched so poorly. Theories were propounded that he was rusty from not having pitched between September 27 and October 4. But Seaver had no excuses.

"I tried to control my nerves and I couldn't," he said in a frank confession. "I couldn't get my fastball and curve together. It is very hard to explain."

Seaver thought about it some more. "It rubs me, it frustrates me," he continued. "I know what I can do, but I just couldn't do it. It happens to me all the time, except that the tension dissipates itself after my first pitch usually. . . .

"I was more tense than usual and more nervous. It's a progressive thing that happens to me all the time . . . but today my state mentally led me to rush my pitching motion physically. My hips were more open when I was throwing the ball, and my arm dropped lower. Jerry came out to the mound several times and told me to get my arm back higher. It just seemed that I couldn't throw that many good pitches in a row. Some of them were good, and I guess that's what made me keep my sanity. The crux of the whole thing, though, was that I just felt more nervous than usual."

Then Seaver smiled. "Mind if I ask a question?" he said to a reporter.

"Feel free," was the reply.

"Who won?" Seaver asked rhetorically, and everybody chuckled. He had a point. Then Seaver stood up and announced, "I gave up five runs and still won the game. God truly is a Met." It was a variation on a theme gaining more support daily.

Atlanta was shakier than the Mets, making three costly errors in an 11–6 game two loss. Then Wayne Garrett homered and Nolan Ryan pitched the last seven innings, giving up just two runs on three hits in the 7–4 game three victory at Shea Stadium.

"What was going on here?" was Seaver's best Slim Pickens imitation of the light-hitting Mets scoring 27 runs in three playoff games.

Thousands of fans poured onto the field, tearing everything up, undoing all the work done by the grounds crew after the division clinching of September 24. It was absolutely out of control: a wild, chaotic, celebratory scene infused by an utter sense of disbelief. People grabbed each other, asked whether they could believe it, was it real, how did it happen? In bars and homes and schoolrooms all over the city, the state, and the nation, people cheered and expressed jubilation and total shock. It was unreal.

The clubhouse was a mad scene of champagne mixed with machismo and near-religious awe, grown men rendered unable to contemplate the glory of it all. Into this mix arrived Mayor John Lindsay, presumably wearing a suit he had chosen as one he could afford to get messy, because the bubbly was flowing and spurting in every direction.

"I poured the champagne on him, and Grote was scrubbing his head," recalled Rod Gaspar. "I got in the limelight doing it, and it helped get him reelected."

When the owner, Mrs. Joan Whitney Payson, entered the clubhouse, she was intimidated; she smiled and left before taking a champagne shower. Writers struggled to get quotes and protect their notepads amid the sea of champagne. The celebration lasted for three hours. It was a day game, so the press had enough time to delve into every story without being rushed by a deadline. When the players finally showered and dressed, 5,000 fans were waiting for them in the parking lot area beyond right field.

In Manhattan, mass hysteria was the order of the day. Churches were filled with people praying for miracles, because the Mets were living proof of such things. Men and women kissed each other on the streets as in those old V-J Day photos. Bars were filled, confetti dropped from office buildings, Wall Street was awash with people dancing in the streets. Busboys and corporate chieftains shared the glory equally. Probably because baseball is a game played daily, in which victory builds over time, each step on top of the other, the reaction by the city was even more spectacular and spread over a longer time than it had been for the Jets. It was a miracle. It was amazin'.

Mayor Lindsay's reelection probably could be traced to the next day's front-page pictures showing him doused in champagne by Grote and Gaspar. He attached himself to every public celebration of the team. Angst over racial strife, Vietnam, and New York's fiscal crisis faded in light of the Mets' victory. Union members found common ground with city negotiators.

The Baltimore Orioles were said to be one of the greatest baseball teams ever assembled. Worthy comparisons might be made with the 1909 Pittsburgh Pirates; the 1927, 1928, 1936, and 1961 New York Yankees; the 1929 Philadelphia Athletics; and the 1955 Brooklyn

Dodgers. The Mets, however, were hoping the comparisons would instead be made with the 1906 Chicago Cubs and the 1954 Cleveland Indians, two regular season juggernauts who stumbled in the Fall Classic.

Winners of 109 games, fresh off a three-game sweep of Minnesota, Baltimore had won the World Series in 1966 over Los Angeles. They were veterans, experienced, and seemingly unbeatable. They had the home field advantage. The 100-to-1 long-shot Mets were a fun story, but in October the magic would end. Right! Right?

Managed by Hall of Famer Earl Weaver, Baltimore featured three other Cooperstown-bound superstars: pitcher Jim Palmer, outfielder Frank Robinson, and third baseman Brooks Robinson. First baseman Boog Powell was one of the most feared sluggers in the game. The middle infielders—Davey Johnson and Mark Belanger—were defensive specialists. Center fielder Paul Blair was the best glove in the game. Pitcher Dave McNally was a 20-game winner. The man scheduled to face Tom Seaver in game one at Memorial Stadium was a Cuban-born "screwball" artist, the winner of 23 games and the Cy Young Award in 1969, named Mike Cuellar.

If the Mets had any chance, all hope rested on Seaver. He would get three starts in a seven-game Series. The concept of Seaver winning three games, Koosman one; or Seaver winning two and Koosman two . . . deep down inside baseball experts understood that this was not impossible. Seaver and Koosman *were* that good, but Cuellar, McNally, and Palmer were all aces, not likely to give up many runs. Could the Mets do it the way the Dodgers did it in 1963 and 1965, the way Baltimore did it in 1966: winning by shutouts, 1–0, and 2–1 games? They had won 100 games and swept a good Braves club, but this . . . ?

The headline in the Baltimore newspaper: "METS' MIRACLE STORY NEARS END."

"Even those who had come to believe in the Mets figured it was all over in the World Series," Seaver recalled. The Mets' ace was as nervous as he had been in Atlanta. The postseason forced him out of his usual routine. He was unable to get breakfast at the crowded coffee shop at the Chesapeake House, forced as were his teammates to come to the stadium on empty stomachs where the equipment manager supplied sandwiches picked up from a local eatery.

Trying to lighten the pressure before game one, Seaver and Gentry switched jerseys to fool the American League writers. Seaver wore Gentry's number 39. Gentry, wearing number 41, was asked, "What about Gentry?"

"I think Gentry is a horse—— pitcher," he replied just as Maury Allen wandered along and "informed" Tom, standing a few feet away, he was wearing Gentry's shirt.

Amid enormous press attention, he went out to warm up in the heat of Maryland's Indian summer, trying to convince himself the Orioles were just human beings, that he was a star, the ace, the best pitcher in baseball.

In the top of the first inning, Cuellar retired the Mets with little effort. Seaver removed his jacket and walked, plowboy-style, to the Memorial Stadium mound. He was again the "man in the arena." Up stepped Don Buford, a left-handed hitter and not a power threat. It was immediately apparent to Seaver, Buford, and the Trojan Nation that here were two USC players facing each other in the Fall Classic.

Seaver's first pitch was a ball, but as Grote returned it he suddenly felt himself again. He had the confidence to give Buford his best inside heat. He went into his windup and delivered just that, right where he wanted it, in on Buford's letters. Seaver was stunned to see Buford turn on the pitch, his rising bat meeting the ball and sending a drive to right field. An easy fly ball to Ron Swoboda, finally in the lineup against the left-hander Cuellar. Swoboda drifted back a couple of steps, pounded his glove, back a couple more, then his back was against the fence, and the baseball, as if driven by unseen forces, drifted over the fence for a home run. Not a homer by F. Robby, B. Robby, or Powell, but by *Buford.* One batter, two pitches, 1–0 Baltimore. Here we go. It was like fumbling the opening kickoff and watching the other team recover the ball in the end zone for six points.

Seaver on Buford: "On the second pitch I came inside with a fastball, a good fastball. Buford got his bat around and lifted a fly ball to right field, an easy fly ball, I thought at first.

"Then I saw Ron Swoboda fading back, and back, and back, and I wondered what in the world was going on. And then I saw Ron leap and saw the ball sail over his glove and saw it bounce on the far side of the fence. I couldn't believe it. I had faced one batter in my first World Series game, and I had given up one home run."

"Confirmation" of Baltimore superiority "seemed instantaneous when Don Buford, the miniature Baltimore left fielder" took Seaver deep, wrote Roger Angell. Swoboda said he could have caught the ball but did not time his leap, the ball touching his glove "at my apogee."

Cuellar was untouchable, mainly because he induced half the Mets to hit grounders gobbled up by Brooks Robinson. Seaver knew he needed to be at his best in order to give his team a chance. He settled into a rhythm and set Baltimore down in the second and third in the same fashion as he had dominated the National League all year. He was back. However, his legs, weakened by the inability to run between starts as usual (due to a muscle pull), were giving way. In the fourth, he got the first two men out but lost the hop on his fastball.

Everything fell apart. It was not the big boppers—Frank and Brooks, Powell—but Elrod Hendricks, Davey Johnson, Mark Belanger, Don Buford, even *Cuellar,* who slapped him around for three runs to put an end to his day. The crowd, as they say, "went wild."

"When Tom is pitching and giving up hits like this, I feel like a voodoo doll," Nancy Seaver explained. "I feel as if someone is sticking a needle in me with every hit."

In the Mets' fifth, Brooks Robinson retired Al Weis on a tough, deep chance. In the bottom of the fifth, Seaver felt like a man who had just finished a marathon after running a triathlon. He was completely jarred by the entire experience, the crushing blows of Oriole hits coming on the heels of such excitement and anticipation. Laboring, his knees buckling, the exhausted Mets' ace gave all he had to retire Baltimore, knowing he was done for the day via a pinch hitter in the next inning.

Cuellar was a mystery all afternoon. The game had no further excitement except for the seventh inning. New York scratched a run. With runners on first and second with two outs, Rod Gaspar pinch-hit, producing a "swinging bunt" roller toward third. Brooks

Robinson came swooping in, barehanded it, and threw the man out at first base. It was a spectacular play but as common in Baltimore as crab cakes and beer. That was that. Cuellar completed the 4–1 six-hitter, a dominant performance by Baltimore as a team with one small blip, not considered particularly noteworthy at the time. The two Robinsons and Powell were a combined 1 for 12. Mets fans had a difficult time finding much solace. If they were to have a chance, it had to be with Seaver, and now he was gone, a loser having pitched two straight underperforming games. The pipe dream of a Shea celebration was as distant as Apollo 11, which had landed on the moon on July 20.

Seaver was a stand-up guy in the postgame clubhouse, admitting that he "ran out of gas."

"Seaver couldn't blacken your eye with his fastball" in game one, said first baseman Donn Clendenon, "but we had Koosman" ready to go in the second contest.

"Two things came to my mind after the first game," said Seaver. "We were this group of so-called brash individuals that had no right to be in the World Series against the big, bad Baltimore Orioles with all the big names on that team. After we lost the first game I remembered here were these big, bad Orioles and they were jumping up and down in celebration. For some reason I expected them to be much more serene in victory. I was thinking, 'Why are they so jubilant?' Donn Clendenon came walking toward me, put his arm around me walking toward the clubhouse, and said, 'We're going to beat these guys.' It was the same thought I had in my mind. I pitched lousy relative to how I pitched during the regular season, yet Clendenon was feeling the same thing I was."

That night, Tom, Nancy, his parents, his brother and sisters, and their families went out to dinner at the Chesapeake House. His relatives were surprised at his cheerfulness. The fan in him could not be contained. He had *pitched in the World Series*!

As Tom made his way to the table, he saw the legendary Raoul "Rod" Dedeaux, his college coach at Southern Cal. His son, Justin, who roomed with Seaver at USC, was with him. They were dining with another Trojan . . . Don Buford.

"Front-runner," Seaver hissed. In jest.

* * *

Game two was a grim nail-biter. Inning after inning, Jerry Koosman set Baltimore down, carrying a no-hitter and a 1–0 lead into the late innings. When the Orioles managed to tie the game it looked even more grim, but in the ninth New York forged ahead on an RBI single by Al Weis. Reliever Ron Taylor got the last out in the bottom of the inning, and they were headed back to New York tied at a game apiece. They hoped they would not have to return to Baltimore, but the chances of winning three straight at home were still small.

The Mets gladly boarded a plane for New York City. Down deep, they knew something the Orioles only suspected. The reaction of the city would be as intimidating to the O's as their team had been to the Mets. Baltimore had heard about the crowds, the frenzy, the media, the pure adrenaline of 12 million people pumping as one—but they had not *experienced* it. Most of these Birds either could barely remember or had never experienced a truly meaningful baseball game in New York, what with the demise of the Yankees. A few—Brooks Robinson, Boog Powell, Dave McNally—had been on the team when they battled Mickey Mantle and Company down the stretch in 1964, but Yankee Stadium was *no comparison* to the noise chamber they were entering.

New York had gotten the split they needed. They had a 10th man, maybe even an 11th or 12th, at Shea in the form of the crowd. It was like putting an extra shortstop up the middle, an extra outfielder to guard the line. They were suddenly confident, almost ecstatic. On the plane they practically salivated at the prospect of playing for "their people" again. The Mets had clinched the division in their last home game of the regular season on September 24, then played a pennant-clinching home playoff game. New York had played nine games on the road and one at home beginning on September 26, yet the stars were aligned.

The city had watched on TV, listened on the radio, read in the papers, but now *they were here*, against the Baltimore Orioles in the World Series. It had all seemed like a myth, a rumor, but now it was for real.

On Monday, October 13, the town was in a state of utter frenzy. It was the most exciting sporting scene the city had ever known, and probably the most fevered sense of anticipation for an athletic event in American or even world history.

Game three broke every possible bit of conventional wisdom. The Mets touched the great Jim Palmer while rookie Gary Gentry had dominating stuff. Center fielder Tommie Agee made two of the greatest catches in baseball history to preserve a 6–0 victory. Now all bets were off. The city was off the hook. Seaver was scheduled for game four, with Koosman following him. *The Mets can win at home!*

According to *The Perfect Game,* Tom Seaver was reading the classic baseball book *The Glory of Their Times* during the 1969 World Series. He innately understood that he, too, was making history and wanted to understand what that history really was. Nancy called him Prince Valiant when inviting him to sit down for dinner in their apartment in Bayside, Queens. While Nancy did call him this—she also called him George, his given first name, not his middle name of Thomas—it was Seaver's way of saying without saying, "I really *am* Prince Valiant." At that point in time, he was. Terms such as Sir Galahad, Sir Lancelot, savior, "man on a white horse," Jack Armstrong, Frank Merriwell, "reincarnation of Christy Mathewson," and other appellations describing not merely a heroic but *perfect man* were routinely bandied about.

Seaver played to it by denying it, claiming the human faults of swearing, beer drinking, and chewing tobacco, while saying in so many words he was not Jesus Christ, who *was* perfect. In verbalizing a denial it was like saying he was, well, not *perfect,* you know, but pretty darn extraordinary, wink-wink. Seaver was in some ways setting himself up for a fall because his image was impossible to maintain throughout the bumps and grinds of life, certainly in the rough 'n' tumble world of the baseball clubhouse. So many things could go wrong, first and foremost the fact that he played a game in which people fail.

After 1969, it was Cooperstown or bust for Tom Seaver. Plus, there was this idyllic marriage he lived in public with his beautiful wife, and it is simply human nature to find something to criticize about *that.* Seaver was a great teammate, a clubhouse cutup, a funny fellow with an infectious laugh, but the high horse he rode, whether he mounted it or the public put him there—or both—made for natural carping from the Ron Swobodas, the Tug McGraws, and the rest of the all-too-human New York Mets, not to mention the New York press, which last anybody checked had a reputation for being . . . difficult.

Seaver described that Tuesday night before his start against Baltimore in *Ozzie and Harriet* terms. While the world around them was going insane with Mets fever, he and his wife were the most calm, composed people in the world. They splurged for some ice cream after a healthy dinner, despite the sense that the minute he showed his face anywhere in New York it had the effect of a John Lennon or Mick Jagger sighting. Aside from reading *The Glory of Their Times*, he managed to find what must have been the only TV channel not doing wall-to-wall Mets coverage, a serious news show about alleged Marine brutalities, stirring his liberal side while at the same time reminding him that, as a Marine, he was a lifelong brother of all those in the Corps.

Nancy wrote a column, a "diary" for the *New York Post*, revealing that Seaver was "reading" *The Grapes of Wrath*, not *The Glory of Their Times*, but in fact he was not really reading anything. He was turning the pages. "What's turning are all those little wheels and gears and sprockets in his head," she wrote, adding that once Seaver gets his game face, "from then on we speak in code."

After Aaron's home run in Atlanta, Nancy hatched a plan to take her husband's mind off the game. "As I vaguely remember it, it involved pouring myself into a super-sexy dress, breaking out a bottle of Lancers, and saying soft romantic things like, 'The umpire was an idiot, but let's forget about it.'"

The day of her husband's game four start versus Baltimore, Nancy wrote, "I'm not a losing pitcher's wife." She claimed neighbors came by their apartment to wish him well in "groups of 30s."

Wednesday, October 15, was a perfect day for baseball: a little cool, blue skies, what New Yorkers almost self-righteously call "World Series weather," the way Golden Domers make the environment part of the fall football ritual at Notre Dame.

When Seaver arrived at the Shea Stadium clubhouse, he found good-natured banter, the kind that, had it been expressed in *The Bronx Zoo* atmosphere of Billy Martin's 1977 Yankees, would have resulted in a fistfight. Donn Clendenon "warned" coach Joe

Pignatano that "our boys" (i.e., angry black militants) were coming to his house to "carve you up."

Piggy retorted that his guys, apparently a combined force of the Mafia and the KKK, were "just one" phone call away, and Clendenon would find himself strung up by his heels in Georgia with "machine gun bullets."

"And they both laughed," wrote Seaver. It was not the kind of conversation Elston Howard ever would have had with Yankees pitching coach Jim "the Colonel" Turner. It showed the times were definitely changing.

"When I was a kid, I was prejudiced," wrote Seaver, but his sports relationships with Mike Garrett at USC, and now with Jones, Agee, Clendenon, and Charles, led him to think of them not as "*black* Mets. Just plain Mets."

"Look who's here," Clendenon said when he saw Seaver. "It's the chubby right-hander, smiling and ready to go."

Clendenon had the natural, charming insouciance of a Jamaican Calypso singer. His first meeting with the lovely Nancy bordered on a seduction routine. It was not the kind of thing Vic Power, a black playboy who paid for it in the 1950s, could have gotten away with in *his* day.

A few cubicles down, Bud Harrelson was listening to a Johnny Cash tape. "Get a few hits today, Roomie," Seaver told him. Seaver's pregame routine was to casually get ready and included a trip to trainer Joe Deer. He applied tincture of benzoin and moleskin padding on the top of his foot, protecting it from scraping during his "drop and drive" deliveries.

Then Tug McGraw approached Seaver with a pamphlet. "Hey, have you seen this?" he asked him. "They're giving it out outside the park."

The front of the pamphlet showed Seaver with the legend "METS FANS FOR PEACE," with a reprint from a *New York Times* article headlined "Tom Seaver Says U.S. Should Leave Vietnam." It read:

> BALTIMORE, Oct. 10 (UPI)—Tom Seaver, the New York Mets' starting pitcher for the opening World Series game here tomorrow, believes the United States should get out of Vietnam. He

> says he plans to buy an advertisement in *The New York Times* saying: "If the Mets can win the World Series, then we can get out of Vietnam."
>
> The Mets would have to defeat the Baltimore Orioles before Seaver could place such an ad, but the 24-year-old Californian who electrified the baseball world by winning 25 games for the Mets, helping them to the National League pennant, thinks he can carry out the plan in any case.
>
> "I think it's perfectly ridiculous what we're doing about the Vietnam situation," he said. "It's absurd! When the Series is over, I'm going to have a talk with Ted Kennedy, convey some of my ideas to him and then take an ad in the paper. I feel very strongly about this."

According to Seaver, the UPI story "wasn't exactly accurate—but it did reflect my feelings." Prior to the playoffs, he was contacted by the antiwar Moratorium Day committee, asking if he would sign on to an ad stating if the Mets could win the Series, then "WE CAN GET OUT OF VIETNAM."

Seaver signed the ad. His opinion, at least at the time, was that the war was not helping the American image abroad, was splitting the country apart at home, and was not "adding much to our national security."

Seaver was not "opposed to all wars. I wasn't a confirmed pacifist," but Vietnam was in his view wrong. The Moratorium Day committee wanted to combine Seaver's star power with either Senator Kennedy (D.-Massachusetts) or Senator George McGovern (D.-South Dakota). Seaver was asked to wear a black armband in solidarity with the process but declined because it could disrupt his team. He felt a dual "obligation" to concentrate on baseball but also express his rights as a citizen.

Seaver was upset about the pamphlet because he had not authorized use of his name. The Moratorium Day committee had not issued it. The Chicago Conspiracy, the people on trial in Chicago for starting the 1968 DNC riots, were responsible. They were headed by self-described "Yippies" Abbie Hoffman and Jerry Rubin. The pamphlet also showed a B-52 and the Statue of Liberty in an attempt to paint the portrait of America as warmongers.

"It's terrible," said McGraw. Like many of the Mets he was a Reservist, but an impish one not likely to hold a hawkish attitude. Seaver certainly was viewed as a person who was "qualified" to speak since as an ex-Marine he had not dodged the draft, as so many of the protestors had. Even Senator Kennedy had served in the Army, and Senator McGovern was a respected World War II pilot.

Ray Robinson, the man who wrote that Seaver was the "24-year-old reincarnation of Christy Mathewson, Hobey Baker, and Jack Armstrong," stated that he came out "forcefully against" the Vietnam War. Oddly, when "Number 41, Tom Seaver," was announced, Robinson noted that the ovation was not quite as spectacular as it had been in other games. Seaver wondered whether his name on the pamphlet had anything to do with it.

In *Baseball Stars of 1970,* Robinson conjured the headline "TOM SEAVER, PITCHING FOR PEACE, BEATS ORIOLES." The writer said Seaver's less-than-thunderous ovation when his name was announced as the game four starter was because there were "too many hawks fluttering around in their expensive seats at Shea."

Robinson added: "By then the romantic notion, the quiet fantasy of an admirer, that a Tom Seaver victory would stop the killing and bring a half-million young men home from an unhappy land, was nothing more than a quixotic yearning," adding that Frank, Brooks, and Powell, he hoped, "wanted peace as much as Tom Seaver. And the dismal Vietnam War had absolutely nothing to do with the issue at hand."

Seaver's wife called herself a "liberal," but that term was a much different one than it is today. Seaver was probably a moderate Republican, although his desire to speak with Kennedy may lend to the belief he was not, at least in 1969. He was certainly not a "hawk" or conservative of the "bomb 'em back to the Stone Age" mentality. Kennedy was still reeling from his scandal at Chappaquiddick in July, just a few months earlier, but used the war as cover to regain public stature.

Among professional athletes, the GOP registration is probably between 60 and 70 percent, mostly because of the tax base. Among sports fans, it is likely to be about 55 percent, depending on the city in question. Team sports, discipline, family support, competitiveness, work ethic—these are among some of the traits identified with sports, to one degree or another with conservatism and, by extension, the GOP. They certainly described Tom Seaver.

The TV camera showed Nancy, wearing a tan tam o' shanter, almost as much as Tom during the Series. She was a sensation. It was like John Kennedy, who once introduced himself as "the man who accompanied Jacqueline Kennedy to Paris." A large banner was unfurled for television: "CORTLANT STATE LOVES NANCY SEAVER."

Warming up before game four, Seaver felt relaxed and smooth for the first time since beating Philadelphia in his last regular season start. His legs healed, he had been able to run since his game one start. He was working on four days' rest, not five, but had pitched only five innings in Baltimore.

"My timing, my rhythm, seemed perfect," was the way he described it. Seaver could tell Rube Walker was pleased. As was his style, Tom cracked a joke to break the tension. "Hey Rube, you think the Orioles are taking us seriously yet?" he asked.

Walker had a sense of humor. He told the oft-repeated joke about the weather being so hot, "I saw a dog chasing a cat this morning, and they were both walking." Once, when Seaver was too cocky, Walker said, "Seaver, you have as much chance today as a one-legged man in a butt-kicking contest."

Early on Seaver was throwing very hard, with excellent movement. He had his stuff. He was back. Donn Clendenon got hold of one for a second-inning homer, and it looked as if it might be enough to hold up. The crowd built in intensity, the pressure enormous.

Weaver, trying to kick-start his flailing team, got himself kicked out of the game by umpire Shag Crawford. Seaver pitched out of a few early jams but settled into dominance.

Seaver felt "nervous, apprehensive, and eager" as he took the mound in the ninth. The crowd was on edge. It was not a game of spectacular hits and catches, like the previous day. It was a typical Roger Angell–type of pitcher's duel: the slow, building tension of a 1–0 contest reaching a crescendo. The Mets were *so close.* Seaver could taste it, a 1–0 complete-game victory in the World Series. It was almost too good to be true. He began thinking of his near-perfect game on July 9 and the perfect game he tossed as a Little Leaguer. On July 9 Tom said he felt just as tense entering the ninth. Today even though he did not have a Don Larsen–style perfect game, the concept of winning 1–0, with his whole family in the stands, to give his club a nearly insurmountable 3–1 Series lead with Koosman pitching at home the next day; well, this could be *The Perfect Game*, the name of the book he wrote about it that off-season. Seaver glanced out at right field. He was surprised to see Swoboda still in there instead of his usual late-inning defensive replacement, Rod Gaspar.

"If Gil made a move, it was going to turn out right; if Gil didn't make a move, that was going to turn out right, too," Seaver assessed. "If, as some people said, God was a Mets fan, Gil was His prophet."

Paul Blair led off. Pitching carefully, Seaver induced a fly to Swoboda, the first action he saw in right field all day. Frank Robinson worked a two-two count, then fouled two outside fastballs. Seaver began to press a little. He was beginning to tire, but his adrenaline was pumping. Seaver decided to go with what had gotten him here—high, inside heat, attempting to overpower the slugger mano a mano, the style he made famous in numerous battles with National League sluggers over the years: Johnny Bench, Roberto Clemente, Willie Stargell, Willie McCovey, Hank Aaron, and so many others. It was good old country hardball, but with eight-plus innings behind him that extra mile or two per hour he needed to get it past the cat-quick F. Robby was missing. Seaver immediately second-guessed himself but was thankful Robinson missed by a fraction of an inch. Otherwise the game would have been tied.

"I was facing him in the ninth inning, leading 1–0," Seaver recalled. "I was young and could throw pretty hard, and I decided to bust the ball inside on him. He turned on it as quickly as you could turn on a ball and ripped a single to left." Frank Robinson, he added, "really made an impression on me that afternoon."

Powell came to the plate. Seaver decided on breaking stuff and jam pitches. He got what he wanted, a double-play grounder, but it had eyes: right field, base hit, Robinson racing to third. First and third, one out, grim tension gripping Shea.

With Ron Taylor and Tug McGraw warming up, Hodges came to the mound. In today's era, Seaver would have been gone; he probably would not even have started the ninth. Hodges trusted Seaver when he asked him how he felt. "All right," he said. "A little tired but nothing serious." Maybe he was, just this once, fudging a little, but Hodges had a hunch and stuck with him. He almost made his first serious managerial error in this year of infallibility.

They discussed the base to throw to on a double-play ball back to the mound. Brooks Robinson was quick, but not a fast runner. Hard stuff, in. They decided to pitch him. He had a .067 Series average but was clutch.

Then it happened. If it was possible that a better catch than Agee's two from the previous day could be made, better than Mays's in 1954, maybe the greatest catch in Series history, or some say in *all of baseball history*, it was about to happen. If Agee's catches defined the Series and the season, this would outdo them.

The crowd chanted "*DE-fense, DE-fense*," as if the Jets were making a goal-line stand, or the Knicks were trying to hold off Earl the Pearl Monroe with a minute left protecting a one-point lead.

After delivering the pitch, Seaver threw up his glove self-protectively when he saw Robinson's violent contact, in case he hit a shot back at him. Seaver jammed Robinson high, but he tomahawked a nasty, hard-sinking line drive toward right fight field. Swoboda raced toward it. He had no angle, no real place to turn his glove or his body to make a catch. He was like a matador trying to tackle a bull. This hit had all the earmarks of skidding past him, scoring Powell from first, putting B. Robby on third with a triple, making the score 2–1 Orioles. The third run would be 90 feet away with one out. Seaver would trudge into the dugout with his second loss of the Series. Baltimore would suddenly be very much alive, full of momentum after tying the Series at two games apiece, knowing they were going home no matter what. Seaver suddenly turned into a fan.

"I watched, fascinated by the race between Ron and the ball" was how he described it. His "fielding instincts, everything Rod Dedeaux had drummed into me, weren't working." Not sure what to do, whether the ball would go to the wall or be trapped, he did not know what base to back up, so went to none of them. From the mound he watched the ball start to sink, "and Ron left his feet and dove and jabbed out his glove backhanded. The ball hit the glove. It stuck."

In later years Tom said Swoboda was "no great outfielder," but he "made one of the all-time greatest catches ever recorded in World Series history."

Then, "even more remarkable than the catch, which was pretty remarkable," Swoboda rolled, displayed the glove to the umpire who made the out call, and in one motion came up throwing home to try to nab Frank Robinson, who had the wherewithal to tag up just in case. Robinson scored to tie the game. Powell—stunned—held at first. There were two outs.

Even though Baltimore had just tied the game, Shea went ballistic cheering for Swoboda. People asked themselves if they had seen what they just thought they saw. In the dugout, Gaspar just cheered, knowing that although he may have been a better fielder, he never would have made that play. Swoboda, despite his hard work, was *not* a good outfielder. He had bumbled around, letting Buford's fly land for a homer, Jose Canseco–style, in Baltimore. But Gil—hunch? intuition?—had done it again, to paraphrase from the Nicene Creed, "by what he had done and what he left undone."

Seaver was drained, mentally and physically. Realistically, he had no business staying in the game. His style, the opposite of the seemingly effortless grace of Jim Palmer, was one total exertion after another. There was a reason he worked so hard, ran so many wind sprints. He needed to in order to maintain the kind of physical condition necessary to sustain his "drop and drive" motion. In his head, he was disappointed—the shutout lost, victory now nebulous, momentum taken away.

But momentum was not with Baltimore, either. They had to be scratching their heads; first Agee, now *this guy*. What did they have to do to catch a break here? Hendricks took two balls. Seaver was losing it rapidly, feeding him an easy one that Hendricks hit for a two-run homer to put Baltimore ahead—that is, except for the fact that it barely curved foul.

God is a Mets fan.

Seaver gathered everything he had and delivered some heat to get Hendricks to fly out. Now the Mets would need to score in the bottom of the ninth for Seaver to get the win. The faulty memory of millions of New Yorkers is that they did just that. However, just as California tied the game *after* Dave Henderson's homer for Boston in the 1986 Championship Series, which they won in extra innings, the Mets did not win game four in the ninth.

In the bottom of the inning, the Mets threatened but did not score. Seaver sat in the dugout, not sure of his feelings. There was no logical way he should have been allowed to pitch the 10th. He was bushed. He knew it and half wanted, expected, to be pulled. But Hodges had his hunches, and this one said to stay with his ace. Seaver trudged out there, determined to draw his last reservoirs of strength.

The atmosphere was now a frenzy of pleading, begging, and cajoling the home team to victory, hope against hope. Seaver never looked at Hodges. He got up, took his jacket off, and crossed the foul line, "and I was safe." A whole city was with him, the hero, Prince Valiant; *don't lose, don't be the goat, not now, not after everything we've been through together.*

Seaver told himself not to let himself, Gil, the team, or the city down. He had thrown 135 pitches, but this was the World Series. They were all going to leave it out on the field, every piece of themselves, against the 109-win Baltimore Orioles. Things started out badly for Tom: a hard Johnson grounder to third, the difficult chance failed by defensive replacement Wayne Garrett. Belanger tried to bunt, but Seaver went with two-seam fastballs, throwing rising heat to induce a pop-up to Grote. Clay Dalrymple pinch-hit for Watt.

"He was no threat to anybody—except me" was Seaver's assessment of him. The Phillies beat Seaver twice in 1968, chiefly on a homer and another hard hit by Dalrymple. He singled, and there were runners on first and second. This was the bottom of the order, but they touched the Mets' ace. Now the top of the order came up.

Buford flied to Swoboda, but Johnson tagged and went to third. In the stands, 57,367 sweated it out; it was hold 'em Tom Seaver time. Hodges stayed in the dugout. Blair came up. Seaver knew he was the last man he would face, and he put all he had into getting him out. A hit would score a run and he would be lifted. An out would mean Seaver would be pinch-hit for. This was it. Seaver struck him out on two hard fastballs and a good curve. Relief, ecstasy, and hope mixed together.

In the bottom of the 10th, the Mets put a couple men on. Rod Gaspar went in to run for Grote. Seaver surmised that somehow Gil knew he would need Gaspar to pinch-run for Grote, which was why he did not use him to replace Swoboda, which was why Swoboda made the great catch, which was why the faster runner was now on second, which was . . .

J. C. Martin pinch-hit for Seaver. Kranepool was a better bunter than Martin, if that was the plan, but Hodges went with Martin. More mystery.

Southpaw Pete Richert, a two-time All-Star with the lowest ERA on the Baltimore staff, replaced Hall. Hodges stayed with Martin instead of right-hander Duffy Dyer against the lefty. On the first pitch, Martin laid down a perfect bunt about 10 feet in front of home plate. Richert picked it up and fired to first base. Martin was running about a foot inside the fair side of the base line! The ball struck him on the wrist and rolled down the outfield foul line beyond anybody's reach. Martin should have been called out for interference, as replays showed, but the umpires missed it. Gaspar was waved around third and headed home with the winning run.

Seaver: "I couldn't see his face. I could only see his legs. I saw them pounding up and down, kicking up dirt, and then, as Rod Gaspar's front foot stretched out and touched home plate, in the fraction of a second before I leaped out of the dugout to welcome him, my whole baseball life flashed in front of me, the perfect game I'd pitched when I was 12 years old, the grand slam home run I'd hit for the Alaska Goldpanners, the first game I'd won as a member of the New York Mets, the imperfect game I'd pitched against the Chicago Cubs, one after another, every minor miracle building toward that one magic day.

"I never realized before that a man's whole life could be encompassed in a single play, in a single game, in a single day."

Seaver burst out of the dugout and met Gaspar at home plate. A wild on-field celebration ensued. Afterward, Seaver and Swoboda were whisked into Hodges's office by PR man Harold Weissman, to be taken to a press conference. They were both itchy to celebrate with their teammates, who could be heard going "hog wild" next door.

It was strangely uncomfortable, the two players drinking beer. They were not friends. They were "different kinds of people," like George Patton and Omar Bradley, opposites brought together by fate and common purpose.

Later, Swoboda found much fault with Seaver, in their off-season activities, the way he "marketed" Nancy. He eventually admitted, more or less, that it was jealousy. But he was a young bull in those days—headstrong, saying things, teeing off on Hodges. He even expressed some remorse that some of his best plays in 1969 directly benefited Seaver more than Koosman or pitchers he liked more as people.

"Helluva catch," Seaver said to him.

"I was going after it all the way," he said. "I wasn't going to quit on it."

"If you have the right mental attitude, things go right," said Seaver.

"If you have the right mental attitude, you make a catch like that," replied Swoboda.

Eventually, they were taken by golf cart to what Seaver described as a "presidential press conference, dozens and dozens of reporters . . . television lights glaring, cameras clicking, microphones jammed against each other."

Oddly, Seaver recalled the celebrations, which had been piling up by then, as rote, "going through the motions . . . we had become public property," dealing with Howard Cosell, Dick Young, the national press, ABC, NBC. Gaspar was now a bigger celebrity than Jim Morrison. Each Met was a national figure, a hero.

Finally, the writers and camera crews left, leaving only Seaver and his teammates—exhausted warriors, having fended off a challenge to their manhood, their wives and children. He told Al Weis he would be "batting cleanup tomorrow, Babe."

Seaver told Koosman to wrap it up the next day. He had no desire to see Baltimore ever again. "That was the real Seaver today," Rube Walker said to him.

After the game, the Moratorium Day rally was held at Bryant Park in Manhattan. Mayor Lindsay and Senators Eugene McCarthy, Jacob Javits, and Charles Goodell delivered speeches. Seaver was there in spirit; his brother, Charles, was there in person.

The Seavers all went to the Holiday Inn, where his sister was staying. From there they went to Lums, their favorite Chinese restaurant, where the customers all rose and gave him a standing ovation. Nancy waved.

"Maybe the applause was for her," Tom recalled. "I'd already heard she'd been on camera during the game more than I had."

"All the Met wives were sitting together on one huge cheering section in Baltimore," she wrote in her *New York Post* diary. "But I have to confess something about the Series. It's an ordeal. Tom got beat Saturday and I guess I took it harder than he did. He was just thrilled about being in it. I forgot about being in it. I was just unhappy about his losing it.

"During the regular season I'm uptight when Tom is pitching and I'm having fun when he isn't. We [the wives] just sit there and chat about all sorts of silly things.

"But the World Series is something else. We probably had the loudest, wildest, kookiest cheering section in any ballpark. We were yelling ourselves hoarse." Nancy also added this: "I'm not a losing pitcher's wife."

Champagne was produced, toasted with, and drunk. Seaver did not mind getting a little high, adding a whiskey sour on this festive occasion. He would not have to work the next day, and maybe not again in 1969.

Finally, Tom and Nancy excused themselves and went home. Seaver was mentally and physically done. At their home in Bayside, a huge sign had been painted on their door: a picture of a Mets ballplayer next to the numbers four, three, two—only one left. The caption read, "Nice going, Tom, we knew you could do it."

Normally Seaver lay awake, replaying the game in his head. "But for once, on October 15, 1969, I had no trouble falling asleep," he recalled.

"I didn't want to change anything that had happened. The game was perfect."

The next day, Seaver's clarification of the antiwar pamphlet was printed. "The people are being misled, and I resent it," Seaver said of the Chicago Conspiracy. "I'm a ballplayer, not a politician. I did not give them permission to use me. I have certain feelings on Vietnam, and I will express them as a U.S. citizen after the Series is over."

Before game five, 57,397 fans jammed Shea, hawking with cries, shouts, and Pentecostal enthusiasm. Pearl Bailey, a big Mets fan and good friend of Mrs. Payson, sang the national anthem. While waiting to be introduced, she stood next to Koosman warming up. She told him she was into astrology or something and saw "the number eight" and "you're going to win the game." The contest started and the two pitchers settled into their work, which was to render bats quite useless. Then in the third, Baltimore made their move . . . finally. Belanger opened the inning with an opposite-field single, bringing up pitcher Dave McNally. A solo shot by Frank Robinson followed his improbable home run. It was 3–0, Baltimore, but nobody was dispirited.

"Seaver could win with bad stuff," said Ed Charles. "He was such a competitor with a gift for self-analysis. He always knew just what it would take to win on a given day. Koosman was so strong that he could struggle for the first part of a game then suddenly just start blowing you away."

Koosman settled down, untouchable after that. In the sixth, a controversial call revolved around shoe polish on Cleon Jones's shoes, leading umpire Lou DiMuro to order him to first base on a hit-by-pitch. Clendenon's two-run homer electrified the crowd. In the seventh Weis hit a homer to tie the game. In the bottom of the eighth, delirium built, people edging to their feet, anticipating a riotous on-field celebration. Cleon Jones met reliever Eddie Watt with a hard drive over Blair's head for a double. Weaver and his team looked like Napoleon when he saw the Prussians coming to Lord Wellington's aid in the late afternoon glare at Waterloo. The Orioles were the losers of history—at least this history.

Clendenon tried to bunt, but it was too hard. He was thrown out and Jones held. Swoboda took the stage again. He slammed a hard-sinking liner to left, not unlike the ball Brooks Robinson had hit to him the previous day. Buford got there but trapped it. Jones alertly waited halfway between second and third, then raced home with the go-ahead run when the catch was not made. The place was a madhouse. Charles flied out, but Grote hit a grounder to first. Powell bobbled it and threw late to Watt covering the base. Swoboda was hustling. He scored the insurance run that Koosman, now imitating Sandy Koufax, did not need anyway. Still, it electrified the audience. This was it. A done deal. The picture of Koosman hugging Swoboda as he scored appeared in *Life* magazine.

Koosman took the hill. The crowd was screaming, incomprehensibly noisy, edging toward the aisles. New York's finest nervously eyed this nascent South American revolution about to explode.

"It was so noisy at Shea you couldn't hear yourself think," said Koosman. "And the cops and the specials were already coming down the first row so people couldn't mob the field. It was so noisy you couldn't even hear the bat on the ball."

Leading 5–3 in the ninth Koosman walked Frank Robinson, induced a ground out by Powell and a fly out by Brooks Robinson, then a fly ball caught by Jones in left. Jones then sprinted for his life while the world exploded. The Mets quickly celebrated on the mound. Koosman jumped into Grote's arms like a little kid, and then "Here come the fans," he said. "They came right through the cops, and my mind immediately went from celebration to running for your life!"

Fans were coming over the top of the dugout, falling on top of each other. The Mets were surrounded like British soldiers in *Zulu.* Koosman tore one guy's leg with spikes stepping on and over him. The players quickly made for the dugout like youths running from bulls at Pamplona. Each member of the grounds crew was tasked with "saving" a base, but they quickly gave up. Jones never made it in. He jumped a fence! Fans were grabbing everything: hats, gloves, bats. It was sheer bedlam.

"I paced in the dugout, watching Jerry work," Seaver recalled. After the last out, "the place went wild.

"I don't think I've ever had another thrill as great."

"They did it with a full dose of the magic that had spiced their unthinkable climb from ninth place in the National League—100-to-one shots who scraped their way to the pinnacle as the waifs of Major League baseball," wrote Joseph Durso in the *New York Times.*

"Children, housewives, mature men, all swarmed onto the field where the Mets" had beaten "the avalanche by a split second."

"So, at last, we came to the final game, and I don't suppose many of us who had watched the Mets through this long and memorable season much doubted that they would win it, even when they fell behind, 0–3, on home runs by Dave McNally and Frank Robinson off Koosman in the third inning," wrote the redoubtable Roger Angell, perhaps the best of all Mets chroniclers. The Orioles, he added, suffered from "badly frayed nerves." One fan produced a sign that read, "WHAT NEXT?" Angell said he had no answer, describing Shea as "crazily leaping crowds, the showers of noise and paper, the vermilion smoke-bomb clouds, and the vanishing lawn signs." They won it with "the Irregulars" (Weis's first-ever homer at Shea, as if he had a plethora of long balls in other parks; Clendenon and Swoboda). They combined to hit .400 with four homers and eight RBIs. Powell and the Robbys were held to a .163 average, one homer, and a single RBI.

Defensive plays that "some of us would remember for the rest of our lives" gave the "evident conviction that the year should not be permitted to end in boredom" (Angell's chapter on the 1969 Mets in *The Summer Game* was called "Days and Nights with the Unbored").

He was prescient, too, acknowledging the "awareness of the accompanying sadness of the victory—the knowledge that adulation and money and winter disbanding of this true club would mean that the young Mets were now gone forever."

"This is the first time," said Swoboda (amid Moët & Chandon). "Nothing can ever be as sweet again."

Pearl Bailey came in the clubhouse and planted a big kiss on Koosman, which his teammates thought was more than just a little bit friendly on her part. She had predicted the "number eight." The score: 5–3. Supposedly, Jones gave the final-out ball to Koosman, but that has been an ongoing question over the years.

"It's beautiful! Beautiful! Beautiful! Beautiful!" Seaver shouted, over and over again, amid the crazy scene. "It's the biggest thrill in my life! We played to win. We never quit. We'd come from behind to win. We did it today! Beautiful! Beautiful! Beautiful!" He kept using the word *pleasure* in describing the experience, his teammates, everything. He also spoke of a serious topic.

"If the Mets can win the World Series, we can get out of Vietnam," Seaver said in the clubhouse. "I just decided to say it," he later told Shamsky. "History proved that they couldn't figure a way politically to get out." In fact, Richard Nixon's and Henry Kissinger's triangulation policy did end American involvement by 1973.

In the corridor outside the clubhouse, Seaver met with Nancy and the rest of his family. "We'll never forget this day," said Charles Seaver. "None of us will."

Somebody asked Mets coach Yogi Berra if it was "over now." Berra said he did not actually know how many World Series rings he now had. "Too many for my fingers," he said. Poor Ernie Banks, on the other hand, had never played meaningful October baseball! The postgame celebration was "the best in the history of baseball, and probably will never be duplicated," recalled Ralph Kiner.

"No team ever drank, spilled and wasted as much Champagne as the Mets who, within a space of little more than three weeks, had three clinchings to celebrate as they won first the East Division championship, then the National League championship, and finally the big one," wrote Jack Lang, who maintained that "through it all, the calmest man in all the world was Gil Hodges."

"I was able to bring a championship back to the greatest fans in the world," said Hodges.

Some of the most poignant moments, however, were captured in photos appearing in *The Sporting News Official Baseball Guide: 1970*. Hours after the game ended, as the celebration cooled a bit, a half-dressed Seaver and Gary Gentry inspected the field and the now-empty stadium. Clumps of sod covered almost every inch of the field, resembling Old Testament frogs.

"One of my fondest memories of 1969 is a photograph of Gary Gentry and me standing on the mound in an empty Shea, the field torn to shreds by the rabid Mets fans," recalled Seaver. "As we stood there in a moment of postcelebratory quiet, I realized for the first time that the ultimate joy is not in the clubhouse, spraying champagne, as I had thought growing up as a boy watching earlier World Series victories. No, the biggest thrill is on the field, in joining with one's teammates in the competition, in the application of all your training, coaching, education, and teamwork to achieve one common goal.

"That day I understood that the process in itself is the reward. It was also a lesson in maturity, a moment of personal growth. That is why as long as I live, whatever I accomplish, I will always be a '69 Met."

The city threw a ticker-tape parade, and in keeping with that theme, it surpassed previous such spectacles for Charles Lindbergh, Doug MacArthur, John Glenn, Namath's Jets, Neil Armstrong—astronauts, athletes, war heroes. In 1969, there were three ticker-tape parades: the Jets in January, Armstrong and the Apollo 11 astronauts after the July moon landing, and the Mets. The third totally eclipsed the other two. It was the biggest parade in New York City history. The motorcade went from Battery Park to Bryant Park behind the main library at 42nd Street. Banners and confetti were everywhere.

The players rode in open cars, fans held back by barricades. Girls threw themselves at them as if each were Joe Namath or Robert Redford. The cops, somehow sensing that it was joy, not a riot, restrained themselves. They instinctively realized this was the last of 1960s innocence. Later New York celebrations were like jailbreaks or the overthrow of dictators. There was very little vandalism in October of 1969. The people of this great metropolis were all like little children. They were in awe, like the saved entering the Kingdom of Heaven.

"It was bigger than the celebration of the end of World War II," wrote the *Wall Street Journal*. "It was bigger than the celebration of Lindbergh's solo flight, than the celebration of the Apollo astronauts.

"You could roll all these days together and it wouldn't compare to this."

At city hall, Mayor Lindsay presented them with keys to New York. Mrs. Payson and M. Donald Grant accepted on behalf of the players at Gracie Mansion. Lindsay announced that a street in Brooklyn was named after Hodges. It was declared "Mets Day." More than a million people lined the streets. Koosman and his wife were in the same car with Tom and Nancy. Gil and Joan Hodges were in the front car.

"The thought absolutely floors me—the world champion Mets," Nancy told reporters. "Six months ago the thought would have made me wonder if I should consult a psychiatrist."

"Below midtown office windows, scraps and streamers of torn paper still litter the surrounding rooftops, sometimes arranging and re-arranging themselves in an autumn breeze," wrote Angell. Four days after the Series he had to reassure himself that it was true, the Mets were world champs.

"The Mets," he wrote. "The New York *Mets*? . . . This kind of disbelief, this surrendering to the idea of a plain miracle, is tempting but derogatory. If in the end we remember only a marvelous, game-saving outfield catch, a key hit dropped in, an enemy fanned in the clutch, and the ridiculous, exalting joy of it all—the smoke bombs going off in the infield, and the clubhouse baptisms—we will have belittled the makers of this astonishment. To understand the achievement of these Mets, it is necessary to mount an expedition that will push the games themselves, beyond the skill and the luck. The journey will end in failure, for no victorious team is entirely understandable, even to itself, but the attempt must always be made, for winning is the ultimate mystery that gives sport its meaning."

Hodges was asked, "Gil, how did it all happen? Tell us what it all *proves*."

"Can't be done," said the Mets' skipper.

"Disbelief persists, then, and one can see now that disbelief itself was one of the Mets' most powerful assets all through the season," wrote Angell, who recounted that fans sitting next to him (his vantage point was usually as a fan in the stands, not a dispassionate sportswriter in a sterile press box) would fill out their scorecards and make a familiar refrain that there was "just *no* way" their lineup could be expected to beat whatever club of Clementes, McCoveys, Bankses, Aarons, or Robinsons opposed them on any given evening. What usually followed was another game won, a series swept. How they won it had a mystical quality to it, for even in the postseason, a review of lineups usually revealed that very disbelief. This somehow was their secret formula—underdogs, overlooked and underestimated time after time. Wars have been won and empires conquered based on such a formula.

Angell was no different in his praise of Seaver—"good looks, enthusiasm, seriousness, lack of affectation, good humor, intelligence"—even though the writer had a touch of the New York cynic in him, finding self-serving spin in the motivations of most.

Seaver the baseball fan appreciated the win perhaps more than the others. He knew just how good the Orioles were. He befriended most of them and wrote about them, too. On Brooks Robinson: "Yes, you can watch him here and there and see him make a great play, but to fully appreciate a player like Robinson, you've really got to see him for a full series, like from Thursday night to Sunday afternoon. Then you can understand the true value of Brooks Robinson. Of course, I had little chance to do that, except for seeing him in the World Series or league Championship Series, and it was truly watching genius at work."

Seaver also added this: "As great a thrill as winning that Series was, I remember hearing Brooks tell a reporter once that he considered the '69 Orioles to have been the best team he ever played on. That only added to the achievement of beating the Orioles that year."

Years later Seaver "had a very pleasant day with" Frank Robinson when he did the TV show *Greatest Sports Legends.* He was also on teams competing against clubs Frank managed. As a manager, "in many ways, he reminds me of Gil Hodges." Seaver would "look into the opposing dugout and see Frank managing" and could "still picture that quick bat lashing out at all kinds of pitches."

Then there was Earl Weaver, who was only in his second season at the helm in 1969 before a long Cooperstown career. "Earl can be mighty proud of his overall record, as I know he is," Seaver wrote. "Given the length of his career with one club and his scrappy approach to baseball, we may not see his kind for a long time."

8

THE DOWNFALL: 1969–1970

THE VICTORY SHARE OF THE SERIES WAS 18 GRAND. THE METS appeared on the *Ed Sullivan Show* and sang "You've Got to Have Heart." After that, things began to fray.

Shamsky, Seaver, Koosman, Clendenon, Jones, Agee, and Kranepool went to Las Vegas in the off-season. They did two shows per evening, dinner and midnight, with comedian Phil Foster. They sang "The Impossible Dream," the theme from *Man of La Mancha.* Each made $10,000 for the two weeks.

"We were stars wherever we went," said Koosman.

Things began to disintegrate in Vegas. They had been asked not to include their wives, to make it just about the players. Nancy came along anyway, annoying some of the guys who probably wanted to let their hair down and "let boys be boys." The faithful wife and the faithful husband were, to them, prying eyes looking over their shoulders. They had to answer to their own spouses who asked, "If Nancy Seaver was there how come I was not invited?" Nancy was always around the TV cameras, "honing in on their glory," according to sportswriter John Devaney. Criticism of her was not relegated to this group. Baltimore's Pete Richert said that her carrying that banner in Baltimore had been "bush" and that his wife stopped that stuff as a high school cheerleader.

"It went to our heads," said Swoboda. "Some stars thought they were superstars, some fringe guys thought they were stars, nobody worked hard, nobody really cared.

"Those guys [who performed at the Las Vegas club] made some extra dough, but they created jealousies. We won because we had been a one-for-all and all-for-one team. Now we were cashing in separately. That created problems. It even created problems among that group. Seaver wanted more money than the others got, and don't forget they had to play together again a few months later."

Most of the big-money offers came to Seaver, who was identified as the symbol of the team. The "all-for-one, one-for-all" concept of the season was lost in the glare of Seaver's larger-than-life persona. At 24, he was the youngest winner of the Cy Young Award and the youngest to win 25 games since Dizzy Dean 34 years earlier.

Seaver won the S. Rae Hickok Belt as the professional athlete of the year. *The Sporting News* named him Sportsman of the Year, the right-handed pitcher on the National League All-Star team, and the league's Pitcher of the Year. *Sports Illustrated* chose him as their cover story Sportsman of the Year, as well. Hodges was the Manager of the Year, Johnny Murphy the Executive of the Year.

The two publications featured flowery, overly flattering portrayals and fawning photos of the Mets' superstar with his luminous bride. Glowing terminology describing Seaver, his pitching prowess, and his wife filled these pages and more. The buildup of his personality, intelligence, and charm was over the top. He was a fictional character come to life, too good to be true.

Baseball Stars of 1970 had Seaver on its cover and as its feature story. Editor Ray Robinson repeated the Seaver quote that he was "not an All-American," that he could not be one because he drank beer and swore, but with a wink the pitcher added, "But I do keep my hair short, so I guess you could say I am an All-American boy."

"Tom is the greatest guy in the world," said Buddy Harrelson.

"Tom is as nice as everyone says he is . . . he's not just the product of an advertising campaign," said Dick Schaap.

Seaver, Robinson wrote, "contributed to the restoration of baseball glory in the battered, but unbowed, city of New York." He was a "Huck Finn of a pitcher."

"There are two things of primary importance to me, and they're both in this room—my marriage and baseball," Tom Seaver told the audience at the *Sports Illustrated* luncheon honoring him as Sportsman of the Year. The audience included Mets owner Joan Payson and baseball commissioner Bowie Kuhn. "I would not do anything to jeopardize either of them." Glancing toward Nancy, he said, "I wouldn't have had the success I've had without Nancy's help. I wish you'd thank her for me."

Hearing the applause, Nancy cried.

"Gee, I told you not to cry," said Seaver.

Seaver took out an ad in the *New York Times*: "Now available: Tom Seaver, America's top athlete and sports personality, plus Nancy Seaver, Tom's lovely wife, for those situations that call for Young Mrs. America or husband and wife sales appeal."

Some of his friends and teammates said it was in bad taste. His mother was "horrified." Tom spun it: "I won't take any offer that would interfere with my career."

Tom did not enroll in USC that fall. Instead, the Seavers bought a 90-year-old farmhouse in Greenwich, Connecticut, a suburban "bedroom community" of Manhattan business executives and socialites, located some 45 minutes from New York City. The choice of Greenwich was telling. It was and still is one of the wealthiest communities in the world, but not wealthy in the nouveau riche, Malibu sense of the term. It is the ultimate "old money, blue blood" town. President George Herbert Walker Bush, the nephew of Mets part owner Herbert Walker, grew up in its tony surroundings. Ethel Skakel, the wife of deceased Senator Robert Kennedy, was from a prominent Greenwich family.

Manufacturers offered free furnishings for the home if Tom would make a sales pitch. He built a winery, cultivating a lifelong love of the vintner's art. He was constantly on TV that winter and began to think seriously about a broadcasting career. Seaver appeared on the *Kraft Music Hall*, enduring a pie in his face. He appeared on many talk shows, including Alan Burke's. A pilot of his own show was discussed. He chatted with boxer Rocky Graziano.

"Would you believe this—here I am, an ex-middleweight champion of the world and a great actor, but it's dis kid and his wife who own their own TV show," said Graziano.

"That's because I'm better looking than you and I've got a lovely wife," Seaver joked.

"Oh, Tom," Nancy cooed.

"Visually, you appear to be the storybook version of Mr. and Mrs. America," said Burke. "Nancy, do you feel jealous about Tom's adoring female fans?"

"No, I want everybody to love him as much as I do," she replied.

"What is the most inspiring thing that's ever happened in your life?" Burke asked Tom.

"My wife," was the answer.

"Is that the key to your success?" he was asked.

"She gives me a reason for striving," said Seaver. "Without her, I wouldn't have been as successful in baseball."

The *Tom and Nancy Show* became, like the pilot discussed by Samuel L. Jackson's Jules in *Pulp Fiction*, one of those shows "that become nothing." Away from the cameras, the Seavers were "very tight," according to one writer. "They just want to be alone and walk on the beach."

The Seavers did commercial endorsements including a fawning advertisement for a gasoline company with Tom patiently explaining to his adoring blonde wife that they need not go to three different gas stations but rather could find all their needs at the local Phillips station. It still exists today at YouTube.com.

Sara Davidson of *McCall's* did a feature on them at their new home. In that article, which was based on several interviews with both Seavers in various locations, Tom's reputation for not bedding women on the road was first made public, at least in a wide-scale manner. This caused more than a little problem for other players. *Their* wives asked if Tom Seaver enjoyed his wife's company in Sin City, why did their husbands prefer . . . somebody else's company? They wanted to know what they *did* in Las Vegas. Tom Seaver's faithfulness toward Nancy could not help but imply that it was an exception to the rule—but an exception to what?

"I met Nancy for lunch on a day of incessant gray rain," wrote Davidson. "She was wearing a turtleneck sweater, a brown leather vest and mini-skirt, a scarf, cap, and chains, and Slider [their pet dog] was huddled at her feet. On television she appears hard and confident, but face to face she looks terribly young, trusting, all smiles and glistening eyelashes. We stood on a corner, shivering, trying to figure where to go, when Nancy called with childlike gaiety to a man passing by, as if he were on Main Street in Fresno, 'Where's a good restaurant?' The man recognized the face under the beige tam o' shanter, beamed and suggested Slates, a block away."

Nancy ordered a half bottle of rose wine and a Caesar salad, chattering in a California accent.

"He doesn't fool around on the road because he doesn't have to prove anything about himself," she told Davidson. "He's so honorable. We were both raised with the idea that you get married because that's the one person you want to spend your life with."

Athletes, she said "usually have good physiques. They're all male, well proportioned, they don't look like a librarian. When I was dating, I would usually go with guys on the swimming team or football or basketball team. We had common interests because I liked swimming, diving, gymnastics, and always cheerleading. I was a cheerleader seven years straight. Now I'm a professional cheerleader."

She said the players who chase on the road are the ones who get married too young, grow up in small towns, and cannot handle the big city. "You can't exactly blame them for that," she rationalized. "I'm not prudish about people going to bed with each other. It doesn't bother me at all. Just don't rain on *my* parade." Nancy said now that they had bought a house, "the baby's going to come next."

When Tom was on the road she "gets together with the wives" for pizza or movies. She said she liked all the Mets' wives, "and you would, too." Davidson felt she was a little flighty, waving good-bye to her salad, using words such as "baloney . . . zilch . . . icky," and talking to inanimate objects like the camera.

"I love to talk," Nancy continued. "Don't you love to climb in bed at night and just visit? Tom's trying to sleep and I'm talking. Weird. I got that from my old-day slumber parties."

"You know something?" Nancy later told a reporter. "When I first married Tom, I guess I didn't know him very well. During our dating period he was gone an awful lot of the time. He was either away at school or he went to play winter ball in Alaska [actually summer ball] or to summer camp with the Marines. You know, I knew he was an awfully nice guy. I mean, I loved him but I knew that he was just a nice guy. And I think that when you feel secure with somebody there must be a reason why. And I'll be frank, I really never thought we would ever, ever be where we are today. I never, well, for one thing, I didn't quite realize what professional baseball had to offer. And then when you do get to understand a little more about baseball, you consider the superstars the ultimate. They're not the same kind. They're rare gems. And you never consider yourself married to one.

"I guess I just didn't know that much about it to be able to see what Tom had. And the more I see him play, every year, I feel like I don't know him as well as I thought I did. I just learn something new about him every year. It's just situation after situation. To go to New York and do what he did, win 16 games with the Mets, a 10th place team, in his very first year—that amazed me. I thought he was the most wonderful miracle worker I'd ever encountered. Just incredible. It was like I didn't even know him.

"In the World Series games, God, it was like he was a total stranger. He's my own husband and I don't even know him. He's my own husband and I don't know what he can do. He amazes me."

When Sara Davidson sat down with the husband, she found him to be cautious, wary of journalists. He was "guarded and suspicious." Dismissing questions with a shrug, Seaver told her, "Shall we go round and round? I took journalism courses in college, so I know what most reporters are up to."

"Then he stood up abruptly, went to get a beer, read some papers, then dropped to all fours and crawled across the rug toward Slider," wrote Davidson.

He told her he was upset about the antiwar pamphlets because he had been "taken advantage of . . . I am against the war and want us to get out as quickly as possible without endangering lives," an interesting side comment, especially in light of what we know about "the Killing Fields," in which 1.5 million humans were murdered by the Communists after the U.S. finally did pull out. Seaver said he and Nancy were part of "the Silent Majority" that Nixon identified with so much success during the 1968 campaign: family people, Christians, patriots, traditionalists opposed to protest and immorality. He and his wife would never attend an antiwar rally, be "anti-President," or criticize Nixon. "You just don't get along that way." Seaver now more resembled Johnny Cash's famed description of himself as "a dove . . . with claws."

It was an era of changing moral codes reflected in entertainment at that time: the nude Broadway musical *Hair*, the homosexual-themed *Midnight Cowboy*, and the wife-swapping soft porn film *Bob & Carol & Ted & Alice*. In March of 1969, Doors lead singer Jim Morrison had been arrested for exposing himself at a concert in Miami. X-rated films were becoming popular. A few years later, *Deep Throat* became all the rage. The wife-swapping theme did not escape baseball. Athletes were always notorious for "sharing" girls, but Yankees pitchers Fritz Peterson and Mike Kekich took it another step when they scandalously exchanged wives. Seaver said he did not approve of X-rated movies or wife swapping. "I just could never live that way," he stated.

His success was based on "hard work, dedication, concentration, and God-given natural talents." He was charming and diplomatic with a "warm, hearty, sexy laugh." The couple was just overwhelmingly happy. "Nancy doesn't want to be treated as an equal, she wants to be treated as a woman," said Seaver. Nancy admitted to being "dominated," that "it's a man's world. I don't want to see Tom with an apron on. He's considerate and helps me when I need it. I'm not that enslaved. And as a woman I like being treated special—like I'm soft and round and shouldn't be knocked around."

"I like my wife," Tom said simply.

A few weeks later Davidson met the Seavers at Top of the Sixes for an event honoring Cliff Robertson and his socialite/actress wife

Dina Merrill (of the Merrill Lynch brokerage dynasty). "I don't know any of these people," Nancy whispered to the writer before being introduced to George Plimpton, Paul Anka, Estée Lauder, and assorted press agents.

"What's wrong with a backyard barbecue?" Seaver said to Davidson.

"At that moment, my heart went out to Tom Seaver," she wrote.

"We don't socialize much at all," Nancy said. "We don't like parties, they're too impersonal." Nancy liked books by Pearl Buck. Tom read about sports, politics, or the TV industry. At a signing in Manhattan, Seaver told somebody baseball "clings to the values of the past. I find myself very gun-shy watching football these days. Football has all the elements that certain segments of our society frown upon—violence, pain, collision. People go to football for ripping and things like that. Even the terminology upsets me. But baseball has maintained some of the principles that parts of our society have lost. Baseball has a sense of fair play; it's non-violent, wholesome, a clean-cut and clean-played game."

Seaver repeated he would not use his name to protest the war. His experience with the Moratorium Day organizers had soured him on the protest crowd. Suddenly rich and hoping to get much richer, he had more to lose and was cautious. Perhaps he now understood more, not just about his image but also what America stood for and protected. "Advertising Wheaties is not denouncing the war in Vietnam," he stated, clarifying why he pitched products but not political ideology.

Seventeen-year-old Vicki Curran, standing in a long line of people waiting to get Seaver's autograph, said the pitcher "typifies the youth of today. Not everybody our age has long hair. He seems interested in this country and he works hard for what he wants."

On December 31, 1969, Tom and Nancy Seaver placed an ad in the *New York Times*: "On the eve of 1970, please join us in a prayer for peace."

Johnny Murphy's sudden passing also caught the Mets by surprise.

"I knew Johnny Murphy personally," Seaver remembered. "He was my boss, my general manager when I joined the Mets. I didn't know a lot about his career when I first met him, but I learned, and I was impressed.

"Johnny was a man who spoke his mind. As an organizer of the players union, that was obvious . . . I'm glad he had a chance to see the Mets win the World Series in '69. He died only a few months later. I'm sure the thrill of that miracle win gave him as much pleasure as the days when he was pitching in the Series for the Yankees."

At some point, players started to complain that Seaver had become a "different guy . . . aloof," more concerned with outside things and TV appearances. The endorsements and attention lavished on all the Mets in the immediate aftermath of the glorious victory started to fade for most, but not for Seaver.

"He was somewhat more verbally polished than Jerry Koosman, his pitching partner, and considerably whiter than Donn Clendenon, the batting hero of the Series," wrote Robert Lipsyte in the *New York Times.*

Seaver signed a new contract for $80,000 and made it clear that his goal would be to someday be the first "$200,000 ballplayer," which was seen as money hungry.

"No one roots for Goliath," Wilt Chamberlain said and as the Orioles could attest. Seaver was no longer the peppy leader of a hungry band of underdogs. He was a superstar with all the trappings. "The cheering fades and the envy grows the nearer one is to the top," wrote Devaney.

Seaver told writer Milton Gross that he was trying to keep his "feet on the ground," admitting he was more "introverted." Everyday situations, restaurants, places where it was "fun to be recognized" were now problems. He had become a true New York icon. The things that made Joe DiMaggio a pain, Mickey Mantle prickly, now affected Seaver. This was the Apple, not Pittsburgh. He began to question whether people saw "a human being and not just a baseball player," adding that while he owed the fans full effort, off the field it was a two-way street.

In the spring of 1970, Ron Swoboda had a blowup with Tom Seaver. The players took up a collection for a clubhouse guy. Swoboda was not there, so somebody told Seaver to "get the money out of Ron's pants pockets." Swoboda had planned to give money to the man at Miller Huggins Field anyway. Seaver announced he had taken it out of Swoboda's pants, which were hanging in his cubicle. He implied that otherwise Ron would not have contributed. When Swoboda found out, the two had a screaming match in front of the writers.

"Then he was an apple guy," Maury Allen said, referring to Seaver. "Very bright, articulate, honest, if a little dull with his detailed description of pitching mechanics. From 1970 on Seaver really has been a different guy. He is bright, articulate, easy to talk to but still aloof."

"Following the winter of his great content, writers covering the Mets—and they are the closest that anyone could be outside of his own teammates—detected a certain aloofness in Seaver very early in Spring Training," wrote Jack Lang in *The Sporting News*. "Tom frequently did not have time to sit through long periods of questioning like he formerly did and there were many times he was in a hurry to get out of the club house."

Seaver set 30 victories as his goal for 1970. Denny McLain had done it pitching on a four-day rotation in 1968. It was not an outlandish prospect. Seaver had always been a late bloomer: nonprospect at Fresno High, coming into his own at Southern California, steady improvement in New York. He was one of the first to benefit from weightlifting. From his first year at triple-A Jacksonville until the 1970 season, he got better every year. He seemed to improve every month.

A look at photographs of the pitcher reveals distinct body changes over the years. He turned 25 in November of 1969 and by 1970 was finally losing his baby fat, the source of Donn Clendenon's humorous "chubby right-hander" remarks. His face hardened from its original boyishness. His work ethic was such that he simply continued to get better.

As good as Seaver was in 1969, he *had not yet reached his full potential*! It was a frightening, awe-inspiring notion that the best was still yet to come. Seaver probably did not reach his full, mature physical peak until 1970–1971.

"To win 30 games meant stepping back into another era and accomplishing something thought to be impossible under current playing conditions," Seaver recalled of the goal. "It was a landmark number that, like .400, seemed out of step with the times. For one thing, pitchers were usually only getting about 35 starts a year."

Sometime between 1968 and 1969, Seaver morphed from a hard sinkerball artist to a fastball/slider pitcher. In the first four-and-a-half months of 1970, Seaver threw much harder than he had in 1969. His fastball just *exploded.* Like Sandy Koufax in his prime, he was unhittable. Big-league hitters *feast* on fastballs, but Seaver threw with such blazing speed that, even knowing it was coming, the best batsmen in the National League could not catch up to it. He had reached the point where very few hurlers in the game's long and hallowed history ever were. Today, radar guns routinely read "100 miles per hour." It is a sham, as much for show and fan entertainment as anything. In Seaver's day, the radar gun was much more accurate, if not reading a little slow. He was consistently in the high 90s, occasionally around 99 or 100. The idea that any number of modern hurlers throw as hard now as Seaver did then is a joke.

Nolan Ryan threw as hard. Randy Johnson and perhaps Roger Clemens in the 1980s threw as hard. The list is that short, regardless of the oohs and aahs of fans reading inflated radar readings in the 2000s.

In 1970, Seaver's display had fans, writers, and opponents in awe, realizing that they were observing a once-in-a-lifetime talent. Between April of 1970 and August of that year, Seaver was as untouchable as any pitcher could be. He was on pace to have one of the best seasons any pitcher had ever achieved, if not the best. He struck out 19 versus San Diego on April 22 at Shea Stadium. That tied the big-league record set by Steve Carlton in a 4–3 loss to the Mets in 1969. He broke a record previously held by Johnny Podres for consecutive strikeouts, setting down the last 10 Padres he faced on strikes to win his game, 2–1.

"I had great control all afternoon and felt sharp, walking only two batters," Seaver recalled. "The 10 straight is a record of which I'm very proud," but he also added, "I think the more you play this game the more you find that the thrills come in the team efforts."

He began the year 6–0, running his regular season winning streak to 16 straight games. Seaver was so sharp early that he was "disappointed" with a one-hit, 15-strikeout shutout of Philadelphia. Seaver finally lost to Montreal, 3–0 on May 11. Later he lost again to Expos pitcher Carl Morton, 2–0 on May 20.

"We beat Seaver last week and maybe he was trying too hard to make up for it," Morton said.

"Is that what he said?" Seaver spouted when told in the heat of a postgame defeat. "It just shows how stupid he is."

"Losing appears to be getting to Seaver," Lang wrote in a biting *Sporting News* piece, shocking readers whose expectations of Seaver as a pitcher and man were sky high. Only perfection was expected of him, on and off the field. "He is not reacting to adversity as well as he did to success. He appeared in his first three seasons to be impervious to faults, but in his fourth season he is showing another side of Tom, a not-so-pleasant side."

Lang theorized he was on a pursuit of perfection since the imperfect Cubs game of July 9, 1969. Now he immediately became annoyed after walking his first hitter or giving up the first hit of a game. Still, losing two games in which he gave up an average of 2.5 runs in games his team was shut out certainly did not constitute any lack of effectiveness or "adversity."

But this was New York, the media swirl. He was an icon, "public property," living in a fishbowl at the height of his fame. It was a tabloid existence. Seaver gave the press none of the scandals they salivated over—drunk driving, strip club infidelities, criminality. They had to nit-pick, which certainly did not endear them to Seaver. Writers made caustic note of his reading material. Milton Gross mentioned that he publicly read *The Agony and the Ecstasy*, as if to insinuate that he took to such highbrow material in order to impress people.

Seaver's expectation level was impossible to maintain. He would strike out 15 but kick himself over a walk. He would pitch a shutout and call it an average game, what he expected. In his mind, he was not supposed to issue any walks or allow any hard-hit balls. He expected no-hitters and perfect games. Anything less was cause for self-analysis, a desire for improvement. Naturally, Seaver's drive for perfection wore on teammates because they could not relate to it nor come close to performing it themselves. Opponents were irritated that Seaver seemed to view them as bit players on a stage he starred on, as if any hit or run scored against the great Seaver was the result not of their skill but of Seaver's own temporary lack of concentration or a rare mistake.

His statistics piled up. He led the league in every category, dominating the NL with gaudy strikeout numbers on the way to the aforementioned 30-win plateau. He did it despite a disturbing trend, one that would, for the most part, dog his entire career in New York and, to a lesser extent, his years with the Cincinnati Reds. His team stopped scoring for him.

Many teammates have examined the psychology behind this phenomenon over the years. The Mets were never much of an offensive club in the Seaver years, not even in 1969, but they hit better for the rest of the staff than they did for him. The only explanation—Joe Morgan said as much in Cincinnati—was that with Seaver on the hill, they let down because, knowing he would give up one run at the most, they did not need to score. The result was that they did not. In 1970, Seaver was such an inexorable force that he kept winning anyway.

Hodges selected him to start the All-Star Game at Cincinnati's new Riverfront Stadium. The ace right-hander put on a power pitching display, dominating the best sluggers in the junior circuit with a scoreless three-inning, four-strikeout performance.

"Luis Aparicio always represents a very funny 'inside' joke for me," Seaver recalled of the night. "I was the starting pitcher in the 1970 All-Star Game in Cincinnati, and Aparicio was the first batter. I could see him going up and down the American League bench before he came up, asking everyone what I threw. He'd never faced me before. And, of course, everyone was telling him to look for hard stuff—the fastball.

"So, up he comes, and Johnny Bench gives me a sign, and I throw the game's first pitch—a great big looping slow curve. Well, Luis just broke out laughing, and we both looked at the American League bench, and they were all laughing, too. It was one of the inside things that happen on a field that no one ever really knows about."

The game allowed Seaver to get to know Bench better. There was a sense of rivalry between the two men, fellow superstars, but Bench heard whispers that Tom thought Jerry Grote was his defensive equal.

"Talk to Seaver, Koosman, McGraw, talk to them," Ron Swoboda said of Grote. "They will wave his flag. They will burnish his apple. And rightfully so."

After the All-Star Game, Hodges made the kind of mistake he never made in 1969. With the team struggling but still in a heated pennant race against Pittsburgh and Chicago, he decided to revert back to a four-day rotation. He asked Seaver to pitch with one day less of rest for each of his remaining starts in the 1970 season. Seaver agreed, for the good of the team and also because it would increase his opportunity to win 30 games. On August 14 his record stood at 17–6. He stood an excellent chance at winning those additional 13 games, and if so, the Mets would likely capture the East again.

On a hot, muggy night at Atlanta, Seaver led 2–1 in the ninth inning with two outs and runners at second and third. Jerry Grote called for a curveball against Bob Tillman, who could not touch breaking stuff. Seaver saw the sign and nodded, but his intensity level was such that, despite agreeing to the curve, his muscle memory told him to revert to the high, hard one. Seaver delivered an impossible-to-hit fastball, a blur to Tillman for strike three. It was a blur to Grote, too. Expecting a curve, the heat crossed him up, and it got away from him.

Seaver was so stunned and shocked at his own mental error, the strike-three passed ball, and the tying runner scoring from third that he stood like a spectator on the mound. The runner from second alertly raced past third and scored, too. It was the dumbest move Seaver ever made in a career of rare dumb moves. It was a terrible double whammy of defeat snatched from the jaws of victory; a sure 18–6 record on the road to 30 wins instead of now a 17–7 mark; and perhaps worst of all, a brutal, debilitating loss in the middle of a desperate pennant race. Combined with the intense heat of Atlanta, the recriminations from jealous teammates who felt Seaver had become too full of himself, it spelled doom for the 1970 Mets.

It was the very opposite of all that had happened in 1969. Hodges, the "infallible genius," had embarked on a disastrous four-days-of-rest pitching rotation after his five-day strategy had worked so well in the past. Seaver was unable to recover, mentally or physically, from the Atlanta game. The pressures in the clubhouse and his own strained relations with teammates were too big a burden to carry.

Perhaps the greatest evidence that the 1969 New York Mets were indeed the "last miracle," of a sort, came in examining the 1970 Mets. They were a pretty good baseball team. They were the natural progression of Gil Hodges's club, which had made strides in 1968, had been expected to be a .500 club in 1969, and had enough youth for a bright future.

The 1969 Mets probably were an 81–81 club, maybe an 84- or 85-win team, the numbers bandied about during the hopeful fishing trips at St. Pete. If all had played to form, the 1970 Mets probably were an 85- to 93-win team. They finished 83–79. Pittsburgh ultimately won the East with a pedestrian 89–73 record.

Inability to hit for Seaver; Seaver's September slump; and the team's personal failings after a winter of press clippings and idolatry probably account for their finishing somewhere between 5 and 10 games below their best expectations. However, after the 1969 campaign, the 1970 Mets were one of the most disappointing baseball teams in the game's history. The letdown could be heard from Long Beach, New York, to Long Beach, California.

New York, utterly and totally infatuated by the Mets in 1969, came out in droves, still watching meaningful pennant-contention baseball until the last few weeks. Their attendance of 2,697,479 was the second greatest in baseball history, just shy of the Dodger Stadium attendance mark of 1962.

The 1970 season was a cautionary tale about success and ego, but it also evened out the law of averages. If in 1969 the Mets were just lucky, over and over and over, then it stood to reason that in 1970 they could not continue to roll aces. If the 1969 team was a team of destiny, then the 1970 squad was God's way of demonstrating that the Good Lord giveth, and He taketh away.

Seaver won only once in his last 11 starts. His 17–6 record of August finished at 18–12 in October. He still led the league with a 2.83 earned run average, and his 283 strikeouts set the new league mark for right-handers. Late in the year, the Mets played a key series against Pittsburgh. Seaver started in the NBC Saturday *Game of the Week*, which in the days before cable and ESPN spotlighted a national contest in a manner modern fans cannot really understand.

Popular announcers Curt Gowdy and Tony Kubek broadcast these games. Prior to the game, Kubek spoke with Seaver. Tom was smiling and confident. If he could win this game, his team would be well positioned to pull it out, and he could still capture 20 victories. All would be well with the world. This was the kind of game he always won in the past. When the spotlight shone on him, Seaver was spectacular. Not on this afternoon. He was mediocre and his team lost. It was the last nail in the coffin, a game they desperately needed, a loss taking all the air out of their tires.

But the final symbolic indignity of the 1970 campaign came on the season's last day. Out of the race, New York played the Cubs for second place. A few thousand dollars were at stake in an age when a few thousand dollars meant something to big-league ballplayers. Seaver opted not to pitch, citing arm strain. The Mets lost to Ferguson Jenkins, 4–1. His teammates bitterly complained that had he pitched, they might have won and gotten the extra money. Seaver was seen as selfish. With his huge contract he already had his. Larry Merchant of the *Post* wrote that Seaver seemed more concerned with the "image of perfection that he has worked so hard to achieve in his professional and personal life" than he was concerned about the team. Many players were "disenchanted" with him.

"He has always tried hard, perhaps harder than most," wrote Milton Gross of the *Post*. "But things came so easily to him, within himself there may really have been the image of the perfect young man who finds it impossible to accept that he can be flawed with imperfection."

Gross's assessment had merit and perhaps accurately reflected Seaver's mind-set by 1970. However, things had not come "so easily to him" in his life. His high school struggles, Marine training, the tough test in Alaska just to earn a scholarship to USC, where

Seaver said, "I had to work hard just to be a starter," did not reflect any sense of "ease." On the other hand, the Tom Seaver of 1967 to August of 1970—in particular the Cooperstown-level superstardom of July 1969 and the 12 months that followed—may well have engendered in his mind a false sense of invulnerability in a very, very vulnerable profession.

"The 1970 season taught me a lesson, and out of everything negative that ever happens to me, I try to find something positive," he said to Jack Lang. "In this case I think I have. You shouldn't expect too much from yourself. You should remember at all times that you are a human being with certain limitations."

In the winter of 1970–1971, Tom decided to regenerate. Instead of returning to Los Angeles to pursue his studies at the University of Southern California, he and Nancy traveled across America, re-creating the adventures from one of his favorite books, *Travels with Charlie* by John Steinbeck. The author was, like the Seavers, a central Californian with an affinity for that rural, agrarian world. After visiting the Baseball Hall of Fame in Cooperstown, they traversed the highways and byways of the fruited plain like another traveler, Jack Kerouac (author of the seminal *On the Road*).

"I realize now that all of America doesn't live the way we do," Seaver told Joe Durso. "To them money isn't the biggest goal . . . I realize that there's no need to push myself. Instead of flowing downriver with the current I must sit back and evaluate things and I think I have that ability." He added, "You can't be greedy. You can't go out and beat everybody in the world pitching every other day."

Seaver did regenerate that off-season. After returning from the road trip, he got back to lifting weights, one of the keys to his success not just in terms of physical strength but for mental discipline as well. He signed a new $90,000 contract for 1971, and the couple's first baby, daughter Sarah Lynn, was born that early spring.

"Other things began to interfere with the way I physically went about pitching my game," Seaver recalled of that fateful season. "I just didn't function at all. The whole thing was like a gray fog, and nothing I did was right.

"Then I got to tampering with the way I was pitching, and that was a mistake. You just have to relax and rely on your own natural and learned abilities."

A young Tom Seaver talks with his father, Charles, who traveled from Fresno, California, to watch his son pitch during Seaver's first season as a Major League player.

The '69 Series program reflected the Mets' growth since 1962.
National Baseball Hall of Fame Library, Cooperstown, N.Y.

In 1969 Seaver felt manager Gil Hodges was virtually bulletproof in his decision making.
National Baseball Hall of Fame Library, Cooperstown, N.Y.

Jerry Koosman was the other half of a pitching combo that, in the second half of the 1969 campaign, was as great as any in history.
National Baseball Hall of Fame Library, Cooperstown, N.Y.

Seaver allowed only two hits in this 1973 game against the Pirates.
© Bettmann/CORBIS

Fellow Californian Bud Harrelson was admired by Seaver for his work ethic.
National Baseball Hall of Fame Library, Cooperstown, N.Y.

Mets fans were not happy about Seaver's trade to Cincinnati.
© Bettmann/CORBIS

Seaver, acting as player representative during the baseball strike, criticized the media for rumor mongering after talks broke down.
© Bettmann/CORBIS

The Reds' Johnny Bench ambushes Seaver with a kiss after getting wind of the compliments Seaver has been giving him.

Seaver celebrates his 300th career win with the Chicago White Sox in 1985.
© Bettmann/CORBIS

Seaver accepts Hall congratulations from his father, Charles.
National Baseball Hall of Fame Library, Cooperstown, N.Y.

Seaver with his wife, Nancy, and daughters, Sarah and Anne.
National Baseball Hall of Fame Library, Cooperstown, N.Y.

9

THE SUPERSTAR: 1971–1972

IF EVER AN ATHLETE WAS ON A MISSION, TOM SEAVER WAS IN 1971. The lessons of 1969–1970 had been learned—the hubris, the greed, the Vegas showcase, the adoration, the fan worship, the words of praise going to his head, the sense of invincibility. In 1969 Tom Seaver seemingly threw his hat on the mound and, two hours later, walked off it with an effortless complete-game shutout. For two-thirds of the 1970 season, he was even better! But in the last 50 games of 1970, this surefire Hall of Famer could not win no matter how hard he tried, pressed, and suffered.

So Seaver decided to get down to basics. His off-seasons would not be barnstorming tours anymore. He would return to USC over the course of several off-seasons until he graduated. He and Nancy would not pursue every marketing opportunity, every appearance, every endorsement.

"But all I needed was a 10-day vacation and I got it over the winter," he said.

But mostly, there was only one way Tom Seaver really knew to get back to where he was before: good old-fashioned hard work. So it was that he lifted weights and ran until he could no longer stand, getting in the best physical shape of his life.

"Actually you spend more time in Spring Training getting your legs ready," he explained. "The arm comes later." He also vowed never to pitch on three days' rest again, as he did when Hodges panicked in 1970, leading to disaster.

With Nancy giving birth in Connecticut, Seaver was alone during Spring Training for the first time since he was in the minor league facility at Homestead in 1966. Focused on baseball, he worked overtime to get ready. The prognosticators were predicting big things for him, and his team was expected to contend again.

That spring, Swoboda was traded to the Montreal Expos. At the time, he and Seaver were barely on speaking terms, and one of them had to go. The Mets certainly had no trouble deciding which one.

"Seaver and I have never been the best fans of each other," Swoboda told Milton Gross after the trade. "We come from different backgrounds. There are three or four people on the Mets I'm not sorry to be leaving. And they might not be sorry to see me go. I'm disappointed by one thing. Four of the greatest plays I ever made, he was pitching and three of them kept him in the game. In that respect, it bothered me a little bit.

"There were a lot of incidents after the Series that really sickened me. You can't like everybody in the world, and not everybody's going to like you. You can't get affection if you don't give affection. Tom has no such feeling for people. He's rather self-centered."

"That is spoken by one of the greatest self-analysts of our time, I imagine," Seaver said when informed of the remarks.

Swoboda was a young bull, in terms of appearance and headstrong demeanor, but it turned out that he *was* a man of "self-analysis," after all. In his candid remarks to Peter Golenbock, the author of *Amazin'*, a comprehensive oral narrative of Mets history, Swoboda freely admitted that the fault was at least half his, if not more. He said that he was young, that he basically blew his chance, not realizing the enormous advantages of playing in New York. He even said he would have been better off had he cultivated a relationship with Seaver, learning from him about politics and history, subjects Swoboda later became very interested in, particularly the Vietnam War. In Montreal he was a nobody going nowhere. In New York he enjoyed fleeting glory, but his name is still revered for moments of supreme Mets greatness. Swoboda admired Seaver's intelligence, gave him his due as an all-time pitching great, a tough mind and true pro, albeit a different personality type.

The Seavers were by 1971 well-entrenched residents of exclusive Greenwich. One of their neighbors was legendary *New York Times* sports columnist Arthur Daley. Tom Seaver and his lovely wife seemingly knew *everybody* of importance, not just fellow baseball stars but also Hall of Famers of the past, members of the media, Manhattan glitterati, legends of college baseball, actors, art patrons, opera stars, politicians: "I've had the help and benefit of meeting a lot of people who've been around baseball for a long time," recalled Seaver.

"You can't spend as much time playing ball as I have without picking up the stories that have made the game what it is. I love to sit back and listen to sportswriters, coaches, and broadcasters talk about old-time stars."

He used to commute to the ballpark with Daley and "listen to him tell tales of all the great ones.

"So, names like Ruth, Cobb, and Wagner became more to me than just names. I was able to create images in my mind of the things these men could do on a ball field. And at times, I've had the benefit of seeing old film and getting the thrill of really watching them perform."

Seaver said he was often asked how these players would do under today's conditions. "Certainly the changes would affect some more than others. But I think a star would be a star in any era, and it's hard to imagine any of these old-time All-Stars failing to produce today." Seaver would have been a star in any era, too.

Swoboda and Montreal came to Shea Stadium to open the season. It was freezing, a 40-mile-per-hour wind whipping rain across the field. Some 26,000 fans braved the conditions. Seaver struggled but held a 4–2 lead after five innings when the rain increased. The umpires called it an official game, and Seaver repaired to the warmth of the clubhouse a winner . . . again.

Seaver began to concentrate on consistency in 1971, creating a pattern of preparation that would overcome the vagaries of a baseball schedule. "Once every five days my husband stops speaking to me," said Nancy. Driving from Greenwich southwest down the broad-laned New England Thruway, crossing Whitestone Bridge, for 40 minutes Seaver created mental filing cabinets of his opponent.

Normally a jokester and prankster, on his pitching days Seaver was a "crank," according to Bud Harrelson. "Playing baseball to Tom is not a game," sportswriter Maury Allen said. "It is a job and he comes to the office prepared," telling Nancy as he left the house, "I have to go to work now."

Seaver's clubhouse routine usually meant sitting around half dressed; a little coffee; slowly, meticulously taking care of every little detail. He had ointments put on his feet, which took a beating from his "drop and drive" style, had the trainer massage his arm, and inch by inch buttoned up for battle.

His second start of the 1971 season convinced everybody he was "back," maybe better than ever. Calling it a "usual Tom Seaver game," he shut out the defending National League champion Reds, striking out 10 while allowing five hits and three walks. It was "usual," also, in that the Mets failed to score for him. Their 1–0 11-inning win was not credited to Tom's record. That was the way 1971 would play out.

The trials and tribulations of the disappointing 1970 campaign taught Seaver to be wary and also who his real friends were. Out of that emerged a strengthening of his relationship with his roommate, Bud Harrelson. Harrelson "snores too much," Seaver told people. "I can never get to sleep."

Harrelson told writers that because he played every five days he was more tired. Seaver stayed up late reading books, but the light never bothered Bud. They ate together and enjoyed window shopping. Seaver "always" beat his roommate in cribbage. Before leaving for the ballpark, Seaver further enjoyed reading. After games, the two enjoyed fine dining.

"Tom really knows fine food and wines," Harrelson told Maury Allen. "He's gotten me on everything, oysters, clams, shrimp dishes, everything. We go into all sorts of fancy restaurants. We eat a lot but Tom rarely gains any weight and I never do."

Tom regularly met with old USC friends who lived in towns the Mets visited. Harrelson would come back to the hotel and find a room full of Trojans, the air thick with cigar smoke, beer cans strewn about.

"We're not brothers," Harrelson said. "We are just roommates. We go our own way. . . . If not, we go our own way and there are no hard feelings. Tom is a real comfort to me when I'm going bad. He can really get me out of any depression with a quick laugh or a story. I do the same for him. I do it mostly by taking his mind off the game."

On game days Harrelson answered the phone, taking messages. Sometimes Harrelson would break him out of his funk by saying that he was "acting like an old woman," generating a laugh. Often Seaver would pretend to be Harrelson, or Harrelson would pretend to be Seaver, taking down messages from agents with business propositions.

During road trips, especially after the birth of baby Sarah Lynn, Nancy would drive over to Yvonne Harrelson's home for support and friendship. The two wives always met their husbands together at the airport upon their returns. Back home, Tom would play with his daughter while Nancy bugged him to make repairs on the 90-year-old farmhouse they moved into after the 1969 season.

But the 1971 campaign was not the complete return to glory many hoped it would be. The Mets slumped badly in June, and Seaver's run support was abysmal. He was easily the best pitcher in the National League, but his win-loss record did not reflect it. He was selected to his fifth All-Star Game in as many seasons, a memorable 6–4 American League win at Detroit's Tiger Stadium. Reggie Jackson hit a mammoth home run off the façade that is still impossible to believe.

"But sooner or later all modern players will talk about Reggie's homer in Detroit in the 1971 All-Star Game," recalled Seaver, the eyewitness to as much baseball history as almost any figure. "Not only was it hit a mile but, as seems typical of Reggie, under all the pressure of a national television audience and before all the great stars of the game."

In August, Jack Lang wrote a major story for *The Sporting News* headlined "MET IS NO LONGER TOM TERRIFIC." Lang was the first to write that Seaver's pristine reputation might have some chinks when he described his irritation after losing to Montreal in 1970, after a seemingly unbeatable run going back to 1969 or maybe even before that. But Lang's 1971 piece found no fault with Tom's personality; it was with his teammates' inability to back him up and perhaps a malady of undetermined origin.

"One thing is clear, it is not Tom Seaver's year," Lang wrote. "Regarded by many as the best pitcher in the league, Seaver was pitching well enough but not winning." At 11–8, he had lost by scores of 3–1, 3–2 (twice), 2–1, and 2–0. He had only one poor game. He was on pace to lead the league in strikeouts and earned run average. But an odd physical malaise reared its head.

Some time in 1968 Seaver progressed from the sinker-slider pitcher he had been in Alaska, at USC, and while breaking into the big leagues. He became a genuine power pitcher. In midseason 1969, specifically during his "imperfect game" against the Cubs, he jetted it up, the speed of his fastball increasing to close to 100 miles an hour. After a brief period of arm stiffness in August, he consistently maintained that level the rest of the regular season, and after two subpar postseason starts, he regained it in game four of the World Series against Baltimore. By that point his fastball was generally considered the best in baseball.

In 1970 he seemed to reach his physical peak, throwing even harder, which seemed impossible. Then in late August he inexplicably lost the edge. In 1971 he struggled to consistently find his maximum level.

"At times he has the old fastball," said Harrelson. "It's just that he doesn't have it as often. Sometimes it vanishes from game to game or during a game."

"There are games I don't have the fastball," Seaver admitted. "I have to fight to try to find it. But it happens every season."

But Seaver's hard work paid off, the wind sprints in 104-degree weather in St. Louis, the weight training. In early August, as if to answer Lang's article, Seaver found his stuff. Although he did not do it with the fanfare of 1969 or other seasons, he may well have been better the final two months of the 1971 campaign than at any time in his storied career. First he won seven straight games to up his record to 18–8. Pittsburgh was on a roll and captured the East, so Seaver did not have the motivation of a pennant race to spur him on.

When the Pirates beat him, 1–0, it set back his chances of 20 victories. "I pitched very well," he said dejectedly after the game. "I didn't win, though, did I? I didn't win. That's all that counts."

"It doesn't matter how good he pitches or how good things have been going for him," Harrelson said. "If he loses he just can't take it. He hates it. He really gets dejected when he loses."

In nine games he allowed six earned runs. In a rematch with Pittsburgh, the best-hitting team in baseball, the eventual World Series champions of 1971, Seaver dominated with a perfect game into the seventh, striking out 10 in a 3–1 victory. The key was a sinking fastball inducing Willie Stargell into a double play. Afterward Seaver admitted he sounded "egocentric" but explained to the writers that he achieved exactly what he had hoped to achieve with the pitch, adding it was "damn good pitching."

"The numbers come close to saying, yes, George Thomas Seaver is the best pitcher in baseball," wrote Vic Ziegel in the *New York Post.* "There is, Seaver understands, only one more number he must add to the list. Seaver will be trying for his 20th victory against St. Louis Thursday in the final game of the season."

There were whispers. He was pitching on three days' rest, which he swore not to do except in "extraordinary circumstances." In 1970 he chose not to pitch the last game of the season, when 20 wins was out of reach but second-place money was within reach for his teammates. In 1971 second-place money was out of reach, so was he pitching only for himself?

Columnist Larry Merchant of the *Post* wrote Seaver was an "intelligent fellow" but not particularly modest, often referring to his masterpieces as "a Tom Seaver game." Now he was about to pitch for his 20th victory, as if to announce, "Come see if I am a great pitcher, a pitcher for the ages, or just another 19-game winner."

A crowd of 42,000 showed up at Shea Stadium. Seaver told himself, "You're the best pitcher in baseball. And you're gonna win."

Then he struck out 13 Cardinals in a dominant 6–1 win. He was 20–10, leading the league in earned run average (1.76) and strikeouts for the second straight season. His 289 strikeouts broke his own 1970 single-season record for National League right-handers.

"It takes 20 victories for people to recognize you as a great pitcher," Seaver said. "I'd have been satisfied with my season even if I didn't win 20. But this proves something to all those people who may not know baseball as some of us do. All they do is look in the 'W' column. . . . I've been looking through the records, and I don't think I've had two bad days all year. I've been very consistent, and quite honestly, I feel I've pitched as well as anyone can pitch. I feel I'm the best pitcher in baseball. I really do." He added that winning 20 games was a goal "people set 100 years ago."

If Seaver was screwed out of the 1969 National League Most Valuable Player award, it is possible the decision to give Ferguson Jenkins of Chicago the 1971 Cy Young trophy is one of the worst awardings ever made. The Cubs right-hander was tremendous, but his 24–13 record was built on great offensive support. His 2.77 ERA was more than one whole earned run per game higher, and his team did not win the pennant.

As to whether Seaver was the "best pitcher in baseball," two American Leaguers challenged that notion. Oakland's Vida Blue enjoyed perhaps the greatest first half of any season ever (17–3) and finished with 24 wins, more than 300 strikeouts, and a 1.82 ERA, while earning both the Cy Young and MVP trophies. Detroit's Mickey Lolich won 25 games and also struck out more than 300 hitters. While both pitchers boasted statistics arguably superior in some respects to Seaver's, nobody was willing to say that in the pantheon of baseball—then or now—Jenkins, Blue, or Lolich was a better pitcher than he was.

While this may be difficult for some people to swallow, Seaver may actually have been significantly better in 1971 than even he was in 1969. Because the Mets were borderline mediocre overall and utterly hideous when he pitched, there were no postseason heroics with which to highlight Tom's season. Had he received the same support as Jenkins, Blue, or Lolich, not to mention Jim Palmer, Mike Cuellar, Dave McNally, or Catfish Hunter (all 20-game winners that season), Tom Seaver would have won 30 games, his stated goal during this period in his career. Considering Denny McLain had done it three years earlier, it was not an impossible feat.

It is also not an exaggeration to state that Seaver was every bit as dominant in 1971 as Cy Young (1901), Christy Mathewson (1905), Joe Wood (1912), Walter Johnson (1913), Grover Cleveland Alexander (1915), Lefty Grove (1931), Dizzy Dean (1934), Bob Feller (1946), Warren Spahn (1953), Sandy Koufax (1965), Bob Gibson or Denny McLain (1968), or subsequent hurlers such as Steve Carlton (1972), Ron Guidry (1978), Roger Clemens (1986), Orel Hershiser (1988), Greg Maddux (1995), and Randy Johnson (2001). Most of those aces pitched for World Series teams that supported them to the tune of well over 20 victories, and on higher mounds prior to their being lowered in 1969. In recent analysis, Pedro Martinez's 1999 performance has been credited as one season that may have been better, in large measure considering steroids and smaller ballparks. Perhaps Seaver's 1971 record would be better compared to two relatively obscure yet incredibly brilliant seasons: Dean Chance (1964) and Luis Tiant (1968).

It was a strange season. Seaver had periods in which he had to "search" for his best fastball, but all things considered, he was as consistently good from Opening Day to season's end as any pitcher could be. Tom Seaver's 1971 season remains one of the all-time underrated years ever—upon close examination, one of the greatest in history without question.

Jack Lang's recap of the 1971 campaign in *The Sporting News Official Baseball Guide* for 1972 was titled "Seaver Bridge Over Troubled Waters."

"Seaver was magnificent and might have enjoyed his best season ever if the Mets had gotten him a few runs," wrote Lang. "[General manager Bob] Scheffing figured that Tom might easily have won 30 games if the Mets had scored three or four every time he started."

Pat Jordan grew up in Connecticut, not far from the Greenwich home where Tom Seaver moved after the 1969 season. In the 1950s, he was a flame-throwing pitcher whose services were vied for by most Major League teams. He eventually signed a sizable bonus contract with the Milwaukee Braves.

Jordan pitched several years of minor league baseball but for various reasons failed to achieve any real success. He never made it to the big leagues. A few years later he wrote perhaps the greatest work describing minor league life, *A False Spring*. God had gifted him with the passion and talent to write.

In the early 1970s, he wrote a series of essays, much of which appeared in *Sports Illustrated*. Each concentrated on a particular pitcher. They included Cleveland fireballer Sudden Sam McDowell; former Angels playboy Bo Belinsky; the seemingly unlimited talents of the ultimately disappointing Dean Chance, a high school wunderkind from Connecticut who never made it; and Greenwich's own Tom Seaver. Eventually, the essays became a book called *The Suitors of Spring*. It remains a classic, probably one of the 10 best baseball books of all time.

The chapter on Seaver remains perhaps the most telling exposé of what made the superstar tick. By the time Jordan got together with Seaver, the angst of the 1970 disappointment had been replaced by the dominating 1971 campaign.

When Jordan's essay and book came out, Seaver was again well on his way to winning 20 games in 1972. His place in the pantheon of all-time greatness was completely secure. Any psychology attached to his "too much success too fast" performance of 1969 followed by the 1970 letdown was gone with the wind. Jordan found a man completely secure in every aspect of his life. Seaver knew precisely what made him perform at peak levels, consistently achieving the preparation and consequent result in machinelike fashion.

There was very little personality to his mound work. Seaver was a corporate pitching mechanism, like the formula for a blockbuster movie franchise that is guaranteed to succeed every time. A bulletproof movie/baseball star, a diamond John Wayne or Clint Eastwood. Asking Seaver why he was good was like asking a master architect why his bridges stood tall and sturdy. It was a matter of building blocks, a scientific approach resisting fallibility.

Seaver's personal life by this time had a similar master code to it. The problems with Nancy and teammates were by then mostly in the past. The way to avoid a repeat of those problems had been found, and that was that. End of problems. Seaver's perfections, his wine cellar, his house—every detail in his life—were expounded on by Jordan, who found a man who, after some tinkering, was seemingly at least, as close to *perfect* as someone other than Jesus Christ can get.

Jordan, the failed pitcher, a little bit scruffy and, to be frank, probably a tad insecure around such greatness, displayed just a touch of jealousy, but it was overshadowed by great writing, insight, wit, and the ability to capture what made Tom Seaver who he was . . . and is. Seaver never has been a colorful character, but as an example of a human being who endeavors to get the 100 percent most out of whatever he engages in—particularly pitching—Jordan discovered a personal goldmine and worked it for all it was worth.

The interview began during the dead of winter, prior to the 1972 season. Somehow the snow, the dark, and the cold lent the story personality: the Connecticut gentleman in repose (the interview later was picked up during Spring Training in Florida and early in the '72 campaign).

Seaver was not an "exciting" personality in the manner of a Joe Namath, Ken Harrelson, Reggie Jackson, Muhammad Ali, or any number of talkative, colorful, oft-controversial athletes of the day, but any sportswriter who covered him would freely admit he was as good an interview as any athlete who ever lived. His intelligence, great communication skills, and understanding of the game were nonpareil.

The *Sports Illustrated* essay came out on July 24, 1972. Titled "Tom Terrific and His Mystic Talent," it was a masterpiece that started: "The pitching wonders he works did not come swiftly or naturally to Seaver; in fact, the modesty of his skill was the making of the man," a reference to his rise from high school nobody to Major League superstar.

"I don't ever think about it," Seaver said about his talent. "Philosophically, that is. Why do I do it? What does it all mean? That doesn't interest me. I only know it excites me. It's the one thing I do in my life that excites me." As he admired the artistry of his sculptor brother, Charles, Seaver admired the grace and effort of seagulls flying above the Florida coastline.

"Aren't they fascinating!" he stated. "The way they work at it! I could watch them for hours. I'd love to fly like the gulls. But I can't. So I pitch. If I couldn't pitch I'd do something else. It wouldn't bother me much. But if I could pitch and I wasn't, that would bother me. That would bother me a lot.

"Pitching is what makes me happy. I've devoted my life to it. I live my life around the four days between starts. It determines what I eat, when I go to bed, what I do when I'm awake. It determines how I spend my life when I'm not pitching. If it means I have to come to Florida and can't get tanned because I might get a burn that would keep me from throwing for a few days, then I never go shirtless in the sun. If it means when I get up in the morning I have to read the box scores to see who got two hits off Bill Singer last night instead of reading a novel, then I do it. If it means I have to remind myself to pet dogs with my left hand or throw logs on the fire with my left hand, then I do that, too. If it means in the winter I eat cottage cheese instead of chocolate chip cookies in order to keep my weight down, then I eat cottage cheese. I might want those cookies but I won't ever eat them. That might bother some people but it doesn't bother me. I enjoy the cottage cheese. I enjoy it more than I would those cookies because I know it will help me do what makes me happy."

Jordan wrote that Seaver "has one of those smooth, boyish . . . middle American faces . . . so prized in the 1950s of Pat Boone and Tab Hunter." He described his great discipline, which included his adherence to a diet that kept his weight at 205 pounds from March to October; his use of weight training in developing his talent, his thick muscles, particularly his well-developed legs; and this telling passage: "Because he has worked so diligently in developing those parts of his body that relate to his talent, Seaver is highly critical—one might almost say contemptuous—of less conscientious players."

"Do you know he hit 20 balls to the warning track last year!" Seaver said of a teammate who, unlike him, did not hit the weights. "20! Another 10 feet and they would have been home runs. I know I'd find the strength to hit those balls another 10 feet."

"Treating one's talent carelessly is indicative of a weakness in character," according to Seaver. Jordan added that Seaver referred to a fellow pitcher of promise who wasted it as "a fool." Tom preferred the "company of people like Bud Harrelson and Jerry Grote, fellow Mets who have made the fullest use of their talents, no matter how meager."

"He seems to have no desire to call attention to himself, and if he is at all conscious of the image he presents in public, it is only up to, never beyond, the point when it offends his own sense of propriety," wrote Jordan. "The only attention he seeks is on a pitcher's mound, and even there he does not demand it for himself, but for his superb and unquestioned skill."

"After I won 25 games in 1969," Seaver said, "I got caught up in a lot of publicity. People who had never met me were making judgments about me, and things were happening that I had no control over. Then I had this fabulous realization—at least it was fabulous for me—that I had to cut this stuff out of my life. I had to return to myself, to what was most important to me, to be the best pitcher I could. Now, I don't care about publicity. I don't worry about what people say. I can relax and be what I am. And what I am, basically, is a dull guy. No one interviews me much anymore. Even my success is kind of dull, at least to everyone outside of myself. But to me it is fascinating.

"I used to think you could reach a point with success where it would become a bore. Too routine. But now I know that just as I'm refining my pitching, I'm refining the pleasure I get from it."

Sandy Koufax, wrote Jordan, was an example of an athlete born with amazing physical skills. Only when he learned how to harness his talent at the age of 25 did he become a great pitcher. "Because of the absence of any such raw talent, Tom Seaver was forced to start developing those same qualities at 14," Jordan observed.

By the time Seaver signed with the Mets in 1966 he "was as complete a pitcher as was possible for a man his age. He possessed not only superior speed, but stamina, control and self-discipline; unlike most young pitchers he would not have to spend valuable time in the future acquiring them. . . .

"Today, Seaver is generally acclaimed by baseball professionals as the best pitcher currently in the game. And some now say he is the best ever."

"I appreciate my talent more than most," said Seaver. "I had to put a lot of hard work into it. Some guys never know the gift they have."

"And because his talent is more conscious creation than gift, because it is his by acquisition, not inheritance, Seaver possesses it, rather than is possessed by it," wrote Jordan. "He has a greater understanding of what it is; of how he acquired it; of how he should retain it; and, most important, of how he should continue to refine it."

After beating Chicago's ballyhooed Burt Hooton, 2–0, early in the 1972 campaign, "His brilliant performance received less attention than did Hooton's, since it is of the kind one expects from him these days," wrote Jordan. "Yet, Seaver's fine performance was not surprising to those who knew the meticulousness with which he had prepared for it."

Jordan described how two nights earlier, following a rainout and late flight from Montreal to New York, after his teammates departed for family or the Manhattan bar scene, Seaver got a ride on the team bus to Shea Stadium, which was deserted and in darkness. He dressed and took a bucket of balls to the bullpen where, illuminated only by the lights from the parking lot, he threw baseball after baseball in the bullpen against a screen.

"He threw with great effort," wrote Jordan, describing his motion as "constricted, yet thoroughly planned, for Seaver has worked diligently to cut away 'all the excess crap my motion does not need.' He has excised no vital parts; his motion is a perfect compromise between flamboyance and deficiency. If it is not so esthetically pleasing as it could be; if it does not approach the grace of those gulls, still, it is mechanically perfect, and it is perfection, not grace, that Seaver seeks, since he long ago decided only this was within his grasp. It is a powerful motion, and there is a point in it when Seaver seems to pause for the barest of seconds before exploding toward the plate. He turns sideways, his left leg raised waist-high and bent, his glove and ball hand cupped close to his chest, his shoulders hunched about his ears. He seems to be withdrawing into himself, to be at that single moment in time and place where he and his talent come as close as they ever can to merging into one. He describes this pause as 'that point when I pull myself together, mentally and physically, to put everything I have into the pitch.' He needs that moment of intense concentration because—let it be stated once again—neither his delivery nor his pitches are a gift. They do not lie there, polished gems, waiting only to be dusted off for use. . . .

"To be a great pitcher, Seaver must be flawless in a way Sandy Koufax never had to be, and it was in the pursuit of perfection that Seaver felt he had to labor that April night in the dark Met bullpen. . . . When asked why he put himself through such an inconvenience, he said, 'It was my day to throw. I always throw on my day to throw.'"

"I don't have the stamina and mental concentration to live my life with the same intensity I do baseball," said Seaver. "I'm not a perfectionist in everything. For instance, a few years ago I built a wine cellar in the basement of my home. I used small fireplace flues as holders for the bottles. I laid out 20 flues in each row and 20 rows in all. It was repetitious work but it didn't bother me. Every flue was a victory, and every row was a 20-game season. The entire 20 rows was a career of 20-game seasons. I loved it. When I finished I began to panel the room. I'd paneled most of it when I came to a water pipe that stuck out of the wall. I couldn't focus on how to panel around that pipe. It was beyond my ability to comprehend. I got bored with it. Eventually, though, I did panel it all, but still, the wine cellar is far from perfect.

"But I can live with its imperfections. Some guys couldn't. They have to find out about themselves before they get on that train to New York in the morning. They're always digging deeper than things are. They dig so deep they forget to enjoy life. I enjoy my life. I don't live it at the same pace I do baseball. I can do nothing all day, and it's fabulous. I really could watch those gulls for hours, or just play dominoes with my wife, or watch Sarah, my daughter, play with her toys. In the winter I like to get up in the morning and sit by a fire. Sometimes I read the paper and sometimes I do nothing but sit by the fire. What do I think about? Ha, I think about how fabulous it is to watch wood burn. I don't have to pull every weed out of my garden. I don't have to win every basketball game at the YMCA. Maybe I deliberately don't tap this competitiveness in me. Maybe I'm saving it for baseball. It must be like an energy source that has its limits. If I use it up on too many things I'll have nothing left for baseball. Maybe I deliberately leave a few weeds in the garden. I really don't know though. I never think about such things."

In 1972, Seaver was the youngest pitcher in the history of baseball to sign a contract for more than $100,000 a season. He had averaged 19 victories a year. At 27, after five full seasons, he had won 95 games. Walter Johnson, winner of 417 games in his lifetime (more games than any pitcher in the 20th century), won only 80 in his first five seasons. Grover Cleveland Alexander, second to Johnson, won 70 games by the time he reached his 27th birthday; Sandy Koufax, 68; Bob Gibson, 34; Warren Spahn, 29.

As with Jordan, in 1972 the media wanted to address just who he was. The general theme: Will Tom Seaver be the best pitcher ever before he retires? Were they watching, day by day, something they would never see again? How good was he, really? Was he as good as they really thought he was? It was a subject the great Tom Seaver, baseball historian and fan who grew up unrecruited in Fresno, California, was willing to address.

The record said he might just be. It was estimated that Seaver could reach the magic 300 career wins within 10 years. Some felt that if his career ended at the time he would still make the Hall of Fame.

"Is there a pitcher in baseball [Bob] Scheffing would trade you for?" asked Milton Gross during Spring Training.

"Is there a player in baseball he'd trade me for?" Seaver replied.

"Scheffing says you're the best pitcher in baseball."

Seaver said that "it doesn't embarrass me if somebody says that about me," adding that his only goal was to be "the best possible pitcher Tom Seaver can be," which was different from saying, "I am the best pitcher in baseball. If you agree with Scheffing, fine. I say thank you. If it's not your opinion, that's fine, too."

Asked what a "superstar" was, Seaver replied that it was a player who performed at the highest level over a "certain period of time," an aspect of his eventually long career that, if pundits wished to use it to differentiate him from Sandy Koufax, would work to his credit. Seaver said Vida Blue was not a superstar yet after one year, adding that people thought Johnny Bench was, but after a subpar

1971, "can you be a superstar one season but not the next?" He did not say so, but it was obvious he did not think so. Consistency over a long career made a superstar, in his mind and no doubt in the minds of most.

Seaver had strung together four straight great seasons in his first four years. His 16-win seasons of 1967 and 1968 might not look "great," but with support he could have won 20 in 1967, 24 in 1968.

"Right now I throw harder than I ever did both in sheer velocity and action of the ball," he added. Most experts agree that age 27 to 29 is the peak age for athletic performance, but in Seaver's case he had been such a late bloomer, so unusual in his meteoric rise to a New York legend, that it seemed possible his best seasons truly were ahead of him. He certainly had not wasted the best years (and pitches) of his life in a pursuit of high school and American Legion glory, as so many others had.

Seaver's contract was $120,000, which was the most any pitcher ever received and made him either the highest-paid baseball player of 1972 or close to it. The whispers were gone by 1972, but they had said he was "money hungry" when in 1970 he openly spoke about becoming the first $200,000 player. He was on his way and would get there eventually, although thanks to George Steinbrenner and free agency would not be the first. That was a few years away.

"I had an idea what I thought I was worth after last season," he said. "I figured out exactly the number of games I'd won for the last five years, the percentage of the team's victories, attendance, and I came up with a value."

Asked about the goal of $200,000, he backtracked, saying he "never said it would be me," figuring it would be Reggie Jackson or Hank Aaron. He had asked for $125,000 and settled for $120,000. "If I go through my career and get $5,000 less than I think I'm worth every year, I'll be happy. It's good always to have something else to reach for," adding that "money is the name of the game" and "you play it for money, so you can pay your bills and feed your family." There was no question that Seaver was highly motivated by the almighty dollar.

At St. Petersburg, Seaver experienced arm soreness. Panicked, he shadowed doctors, pressing the acute pressure point and asking,

"But what is that?" Given medical jargon and terms such as "muscle trauma," he only wanted it to get better. Advised to rest, he did and he recovered. He had pitched 1,400 innings in five years.

"I can't proceed during the spring at the same pace I did at 23," he said. "I have to expect my body to break down a little with each year."

Gil Hodges once asked Tom if he looked at his wife in the stands during the game. Tom admitted he did, saying she was "an inspiration." He could not lie to Hodges and felt the manager did not approve, but the next day Gil showed him a photo of himself crossing home plate after a homer that broke a 0-for-30 slump, blowing a kiss to *his* wife.

The year 1972 was difficult on several levels. The baseball players briefly struck during the spring, a portent of the future. During the strike, Hodges suffered a fatal heart attack. It shocked the Mets, who never recovered.

"I was at my desk at home during the players' strike of 1972 when the phone rang," recalled Seaver, "and Buddy Harrelson said, 'Did you hear the news?' I thought the strike must be over, but Buddy just said, 'Gil died.' It was a very sad moment for all of us."

Nobody "had more impact on my career than Gil Hodges," Seaver added. "Playing for him was a learning experience, and he was a tower of strength. Not everybody liked him, but everybody respected him. He went about his job in a very professional manner, and he asked me to do the same with my job.

"I remember a game at Shea Stadium against Cincinnati. Gil had his way of playing the game and expected everyone to follow it. One of his rules was never to walk the tying run on base. Well, on this particular day, Lee May, a real power hitter, was up, representing that tying run, with Jimmy Stewart, whom I'd struck out twice, on deck. I walked May on four pitches, and before he reached first, Gil was on the mound."

"You pitched to him like you wanted to walk him," Gil said to him.

"I knew you never lied to Gil, so I said, 'Pretty much.' And he just turned right around and left," continued Seaver.

"Well, I struck out Stewart on three pitches to end the game, and after I had dressed and was ready to leave, I stuck my head in Gil's office and said, 'You don't agree with what I did, do you?' He smiled and said, 'If I'd known you were going to strike out Stewart, I wouldn't have wasted the trip to the mound.' But it was a worthwhile trip—he wanted to reinforce for me how he played the game."

Seaver, who loved his manager, was broken and had to adjust to Yogi Berra, whom he knew well but who was the complete opposite of Hodges. But when they returned, Seaver was at the top of his form.

Willie Mays came over in a trade with the Giants to finish his career where he started. New York briefly flirted with first place but quickly fell back into the pack.

"Willie Mays never hit a homer off me, and don't think I'm not proud of that one!" Seaver once stated.

Willie "would ask me before a game how I was going to pitch to each hitter. He'd write it down on a slip of paper and keep it in his uniform pants. When the hitters would come up, Willie would consult his list and play the outfield accordingly. Just the little extra edge he was always looking for.

"What a treat to have been his teammate!"

Seaver and Tug McGraw combined on a dominant 4–0 shutout of the world champion Pirates in the season opener and started 7–1. He and Mays quickly developed a friendship. Seaver always reached out to stars, particularly superstars. Seaver played practical jokes on the legend, which Mays sometimes was slow to pick up on, causing him to go into a high-pitched screech before realizing he was being had.

Seaver's quick, easy friendship with Mays was emblematic of his famous relationship with many black teammates and opponents over the years. So relaxed and easygoing was Seaver with blacks that the writers began to posit the notion that the young Californian, raised in suburban golf club comfort, actually preferred the company of blacks.

As the red-hot Mets began to fade, Seaver again suffered from lack of run support. He grimly delivered pure excellence every fifth day, but the writers noticed that he was not quite as tremendous as in the past. At 8–3, the man who completed 90 of 175 career starts entering the season had only two complete games in his first 10 starts.

"I've never been so screwed up as I am now," he said. He studied film but could not detect his flaw. "I was damned lousy." He did not think he was pressing. Rube Walker and Buddy Harrelson tried to pinpoint it. Joe Torre of St. Louis, the reigning league batting champion, said his "rhythm and motion aren't the same. I see the look on his face and I know he's bothered by it."

In June, Cincinnati knocked him around. The Big Red Machine, the great dynasty of the 1970s featuring Pete Rose, Johnny Bench, Tony Perez, and Joe Morgan, had gone to the 1970 World Series. After slumping in 1971 they were hot again in 1972 and would remain that way the rest of the decade. They were easily Seaver's toughest opponents for years.

Seaver settled down and held them but lost 5–3. His next start was also against Cincinnati. He regained his form, also hitting a homer off Ross Grimsley to power a 2–1 win.

"It's a wonderful feeling," he exulted afterward.

But the club suffered injuries, including Seaver's buttocks strain, which prevented him from running wind sprints at full speed. Predictably, this reduced his endurance. His record fell to 12–7, and Jim O'Brien's article in the *New York Post* glared "TOM NOT SO TERRIFIC." But "Seaver could sue the Mets for non-support and win the case without a jury trial." His ERA was still below 3.00, although his standards were closer to the astonishing 2.00 level. The club scored less than a run per game over his previous month's starts and seven runs in five starts.

"I've pitched for this team for six years and we've never been a team that scored a lot of runs," he told O'Brien. "I wasn't even aware that I got only seven runs in the last five games I've started." Asked what he thought about Ferguson Jenkins, his competition for the Cy Young Award, recently tossing a one-hitter, Seaver said, "That would be pitching from a negative aspect, trying to keep up with everybody else. I can't pitch like Ferguson Jenkins and Nolan Ryan or Mickey Lolich. Sometimes I even have trouble pitching like Tom Seaver. I'm in more competition with myself than I am with them. My incentives are internal. I don't feel I can perform my best thinking about such things. And I won't go away from what I feel is right. I got that watching Sandy Koufax pitch. You've got to pitch your own ball game."

As the season rounded into form and spring turned to summer, Seaver regained his form. Once his legs recovered and he could run sprints again, it got him back on track, sailing through the rest of the campaign. He went nine to beat Philadelphia, 3–2, overpowering Phillies bats in the late innings with his fastball.

"When you have a fastball late in the game . . . wow," he exclaimed. "I haven't been able to do that often. It's a luxury to have the good fastball late in the game."

On July 5 at Shea Stadium, Seaver ushered in a return, albeit briefly, of the Mets magic of 1969. Leading 2–0 over San Diego, he entered the ninth inning riding a no-hit game. He glanced behind the home dugout, looking for his "good luck charm." In the past that had been Nancy. Now it was his baby girl, Sarah Lynn, except that he could not spot her. Nancy was too busy keeping the toddler in order. Nancy herself was no longer as nervous.

Slightly discomfited by this, he set to work. He retired Dave Roberts on an easy grounder, and 40,000 fans roared. Then Leron Lee golfed a hard, low sinker, a broken-bat "banjo hit" that dropped beyond Harrelson's glove in medium center field to break up the no-no. After inducing Nate Colbert into a double-play grounder, however, Seaver had a one-hit shutout and, at 11–4, peace of mind.

Holding Sarah Lynn while speaking to reporters afterward, he told them, "I wasn't disappointed after the hit because I knew I had to get Colbert. Now, with the whole thing over, I do feel disappointed." Later, after identifying Colbert as the man in San Diego's lineup who needed to be dealt with, who could beat him with one swing of the bat, he told Jim O'Brien that others on the "list" included Pittsburgh's Al Oliver, Chicago's Billy Williams, St. Louis's Joe Torre, Montreal's Tim McCarver, Philadelphia's Greg Luzinski, Houston's Lee May, Los Angeles's Willie Davis, Atlanta's Henry Aaron, and San Francisco's Willie McCovey.

Seaver made his sixth straight All-Star Game, a 4–3 National League win at Atlanta. The winning pitcher was Tug McGraw. McGraw's win and overall excellent performance was a rare bright spot for the Mets beyond Seaver in 1972. They were a mediocre club, barely above the .500 mark. After Mays's early heroics and a spring winning streak, they slipped into a season-long funk. Their offense was abysmal, particularly when Seaver pitched. It was a terrible comedown from the 1969 miracle, now seemingly a distant memory, although attendance was still excellent at Shea Stadium. But the Yankees, after a long period of doldrums, were slowly rebuilding. George Steinbrenner bought the club from CBS in 1972, bound and determined to recapture Fun City. After 1969–1970, Tom Seaver's Mets, Joe Namath's Jets, and Walt Frazier's Knickerbockers owned the Big Apple.

By September, the only highlight was Seaver. "Consistency," he said of his performance. "That's the best way I know to measure if someone belongs in the category of greatness." But Seaver's greatness, contrasted with his teammates' mediocrity, again engendered jealousy. Berra pitched him every fifth day, regardless of rainouts or doubleheaders, sometimes usurping other starters in the rotation.

"If it rains, five guys get thrown out of rotation to keep one in it," remarked Nolan Ryan. In 1972 he was in his first season with the California Angels after being traded for Jim Fregosi.

Trading Ryan was "not the Mets' finest hour" but "those things are going to happen in baseball," Seaver recalled years later. "I suppose that now it would be considered one of the worst trades ever made." Reflecting on the ultimate result of the trade, Seaver said, "Jerry, Nolan, and I went on to win over 800 games in the Majors," but very few of Ryan's 324 came in a New York uniform.

Seaver's quest for 20 wins was again brought up as "proof" that he was not a team guy. His statistics were more important, but this was sophistry. He was their best pitcher. The more he pitched and won, the better for his club. There was no other way to logically look at it.

In the last weeks of the 1972 season, Seaver beat Philadelphia, 2–1, for his 19th win and shut out Pittsburgh, 1–0, for victory number 20. On the next-to-last day of the season he again beat the Pirates, a powerhouse offensive juggernaut heading to their third straight National League Championship Series, by a 5–2 score. The Pirates featured two longtime nemeses of Tom Seaver's: Roberto Clemente and Willie Stargell.

"In 1972, I faced Roberto on the next-to-last day of the season," Seaver recalled with a touch of melancholy, since Clemente died in a plane crash just a few months later. "He had 2,999 hits. I held him 0-for-3, thanks in large part to expert defensive positioning by Rusty Staub, who caught a wicked line shot down the line in right."

Stargell was "a bear of a man, with a simple warmth and kindness that made all players on his club look to him with respect." Seaver also spoke to Stargell about the Great One.

"I was talking to him one afternoon about Roberto, and he said something I found quite interesting," Seaver recalled. "I had mentioned the criticism that had been leveled at Clemente for not playing unless he felt 100 percent physically. Pops said Clemente was such a proud man—proud of his abilities and his ethnic background—that he never wanted to embarrass himself by playing below his standards. If it wasn't 100 percent, Roberto Clemente was too proud to take anything else on the field."

"But 1972 had not been what he would call 'a normal Tom Seaver year,'" wrote John Devaney, a magazine scribe planning to write his biography in 1972–1973. He was 21–12 with a 2.92 earned run average, significantly higher than his ERAs in 1968 (2.20), 1969 (2.21), and 1971 (1.76), the highest of his career. He struck out 249 batters, second in the league but far behind Philadelphia's Steve Carlton (310). He walked only 77 men in 262 innings but was "embarrassed" after completing only 13 of 35 starts, a statistic envied by any modern starter.

But on a third-place 83–73 team, featuring nary a single man with 100 hits and no power, it was obvious that only Seaver and two other talents, rookie hurler Jon Matlack and reliever Tug McGraw, kept the team above the .500 mark. While Seaver's 1971 performance was worthy of a 30-win season but yielded only 20, his 1972 21-win season was worthy of 21 (with great support he could have won 25). However, he was not in contention for the Cy Young Award, which rightfully should have gone to him instead of Jenkins in 1971. Carlton (27–10, 1.98 ERA) had a season for the ages on a last-place club that inexplicably played great on the days he pitched.

In 1972, Dodgers manager Walter Alston wrote a fabulous book for the benefit of coaches and aspiring players, detailing fundamentals, drills, practice tips, and a complete analysis of how to be a great baseball player or coach. In that book, coauthor Don Weiskopf interviewed Seaver, who provided a perfect description of his fundamental mound style.

"I studied my own anatomy and saw that I was heavy in the thighs and hips," said Seaver. "Therefore, I put myself on a weight lifting program designed to build up the bigger muscles along the thighs, back and shoulders, and take the strain of pitching off the smaller muscles in the arm. . . .

"The old school of thought was that the pitcher with a lot of waving arms would distract the hitter. I think that is a little passé now. I try to be compact and try to keep my balance forward, not getting back too far on my back leg when I go back, and there is a pivot on the right foot. . . .

"The 'drop and drive' is the biggest power element that a pitcher has, and he should try and utilize it to the fullest extent. . . .

"In my judgment, the good rising fastball is the best pitch in baseball. A pitcher has to be strong and be able to get that rotation—get that ball going up."

Seaver credited his running regimen for his excellent control and concluded, "I never pitch a game that I do not expect to win."

In the off-season that followed the 1972 campaign, Devaney endeavored to research what eventually became his 1974 unauthorized *Tom Seaver: An Intimate Biography*. It may not go down as the greatest of all sports books, but it was remarkably telling anyway. One of the most telling aspects was what was *not* in it, namely a sit-down interview with the subject himself.

Devaney detailed his dealings with Seaver, Nancy, and his agent. Nancy was "sweet" over the phone, always helpful, but there is no way to describe Tom's approach other than to say he gave the writer the "runaround." That is putting it kindly.

Devaney reached Seaver at his Greenwich home by phone after several tries, mainly leaving messages with Nancy. Finally he was told Seaver was too busy. Devaney was asked to call back in a month. When he finally spoke to the pitcher exactly a month later, they had a very businesslike conversation. Devaney asked to arrange an interview. After suggesting the Seaver home, Tom hesitated and said no, he would rather do it at an empty Shea Stadium in the winter. He was very protective of his family and personal life, especially now that he was a dad. Devaney agreed and a date was set. The writer bought a book, *Complete Pictorial History of the World Series*, as a gift for the pitcher.

The day of the interview, Devaney had a dental appointment in New York, but it was early enough to make an 11 a.m. interview at Shea. He left the dentist's number with Seaver and, just before leaving for Shea, received a call canceling it. Excuses were made about the lack of a babysitter.

Reaching Seaver at home later to reschedule, Devaney discovered that everything had changed. Seaver hemmed and hawed, "wondering if there would be a conflict in talking to you." He was contracted to do some other books, mainly treatises on pitching mechanics ghostwritten by others. Devaney saw where it was going. Try as he might to explain he just wanted to get Seaver's views on his career and particularly things written about him in the press, he was referred to his agent. That was a "no man's land."

Describing a voice on the phone that sounded like a man speaking "out of one side of his mouth while a cigar projects out of the other," the scribe described the agent's attitude as "if you want to talk to Tom, why don't you pay good money like everyone else?"

Devaney was left to his own devices, but in so doing very well may have gotten closer to the real Seaver than he would have speaking to . . . the real Seaver! That off-season he approached most of the major writers who covered the Mets and dealt with the pitcher up close for years. Numerous writers spoke openly about Seaver and his wife. Incredibly, none were quoted by name. Apparently, they would only honestly open up if given a cloak of anonymity. This from the opinionated New York press corps, shrinking violets none of them. None of this made Tom Seaver look good.

In summarizing the overall attitude about Seaver, Devaney said that "to a man" the media acknowledged Seaver's pitching greatness was up there with the all-time greats and that he was as intelligent an athlete as any of them ever covered. But he was a not a nice guy. Not a bad guy, but not a nice guy. A little selfish, money hungry, a bit plastic. Loyal to his friends, yes, but a closed fellow. This view, first placed forth by Roger Angell of the *New Yorker* as early as the second half of the 1969 season, was the general consensus by 1972–1973.

This was a rather strange transformation. The Seaver of 1967, 1968, and the first half, if not all, of 1969, seemed to be a completely different person than the subsequent Seaver. As a rookie and young rising star, Seaver was an ebullient man, the life of the party. He was pure joy to be around. But after winning the 1969 World Series, something happened in the off-season. There was the ill-fated Las Vegas show, the move to tony Greenwich, the fawning publicity, the naked aggrandizement and endorsements, the big money and contracts, then the argument with Swoboda. This was followed by Jack Lang's biting article, Seaver's first negative publicity, and eventually his first pitching failures. In the off-season of 1969–1970 he took a Steinbeckian road trip, claiming it gave him a new perspective, but it did not seem to result in character improvement.

Yes, he pitched in the pressure cooker of tabloid New York, but Seaver's attitude was now said to go far beyond normal guardianship of his privacy. One anonymous writer said Seaver's talent was universally admired but his decision not to pitch with a few thousand dollars on the line the last day of 1970 angered his teammates (stirred further when he did pitch on three days' rest for victory number 20, a personal goal, a year later). It was speculated that Hodges's death affected the pitcher. The two got along very well, but Yogi Berra "doesn't pay the same homage Hodges did."

Another writer told Devaney, "Tom thinks he's smarter than 90 percent of the people he meets. That may be so, but it rubs people the wrong way because you can sense he feels smarter." Another said, "Maybe because of our own chemistry, I have never been able to get close to him. I find him slightly suspicious of my motives" beyond hits, runs, and errors. Tom did not get angry and was "easy to interview," was "bright, but there is something slightly phony about him, something money-hungry, slightly calculating."

Another said Seaver appeared to be more into his endorsements than his team. Another said he was "loose" at the stadium but emphasized batting-cage friendship with superstars on other teams (Aaron, Clemente, Stargell, Mays, Santo) more than lower-tier members of his own, but the writer acknowledged Seaver was as good a competitor and hard a worker as there was, a pitcher who left nothing on the field.

Even his work ethic was questioned, although this did not seem fair. He was said to run and work so hard in order to avoid injuries that would cost him money and his "historic place in the game," that he was obsessed with goals such as 30 wins in a season, the Cy Young Award, 300 career wins, being the first $200,000 player, and eventually the Hall of Fame.

Another admired Seaver's friendship with blacks, particularly Tommie Agee. Regarding speculation that he actually liked blacks more than whites, this was probably not an entirely accurate observation. He was an absolutely race-neutral, fair Californian, but he had a falling out with Cleon Jones, a "carouser and drinker" who was caught nude in a van near Shea Stadium "with a woman, not his wife," according to an embarrassing news report. Jones, it was said, was "taking bread out of Tom's mouth."

Another example of Tom's friendship with blacks was his association with Jackie Robinson, who tragically died shortly after making an appearance in the 1972 World Series.

"Two of his former teammates, Gil Hodges and Rube Walker, were with me on the Mets, and they'd often talk about the type of man Jackie was," Seaver recalled. "There was a great caring among all of those close to Robinson. Whenever I'd see Jackie, which I'm happy to say was frequently, he'd always ask me how Gil and Rube were doing. . . .

"Anyway, I had the good fortune to live near Jackie in Connecticut, and the times I'd be with him, at the ballpark, on the golf course, at banquets, he was always complimentary to me and always good-natured. I remember fondly that funny, crackling voice of his and how regal he looked to me—a man of great stature, on and off the field. . . .

"Sadly, there are probably some young players who don't recognize the name Jackie Robinson, much less understand his significance in the history of the game. A player is cheating himself if he doesn't develop an appreciation for the accomplishments of his ancestors of the diamond."

The Mets pitchers, particularly those on the club over several seasons, universally "treat him with hero worship," emulating his work ethic and admiring his skill (which they all acknowledged was impossible to match) and "especially his salary. It is what makes ballplayers heroes to each other." His friendship with Harrelson was sincere, perhaps his only really close one. Seaver "likes making the All-Star team and needling other stars, and can both give and take a needle."

Koosman and Seaver were closely aligned because of the 1969 Tom and Jerry Show but were "not really friends. Seaver is an intellectual, interested in politics, art, music, good books, lots of money," while Koosman was a country boy.

Seaver wanted a future in broadcasting and cultivated relationships with Mets broadcasters Lindsey Nelson, Jack Murphy, and Ralph Kiner, a form of preparation. He seemed to enjoy radio and TV people more than the scruffy writers and made himself most accessible when in Los Angeles. He "seems extremely close to his family" and was a good family man. Seaver had a great relationship with his parents and siblings and was called by one scribe a "moderate drinker . . . and probably still the last of the non-adulterous ballplayers."

Nancy's role in his career was undoubtedly the most divisive aspect of his relationship with teammates and even writers. This went back to the 1969 postseason, when Nancy was so publicly associated with the Amazin' Mets, exacerbated by the Vegas incident and too-blatant pursuit of endorsements. It still lingered. In this respect, it is important to put oneself in Tom Seaver's shoes. He wanted to protect his wife and family. He was very displeased with public criticism of her. He was a huge celebrity, one of the biggest in the world, and operated on the biggest of all stages. Unlike an actor or singer, who can compartmentalize public appearances and access to the press, he was surrounded every working day by writers watching his every move, his every flaw, almost hearing his every word.

Nancy was criticized for being "around too much," but this was unfair. Would the writers or anybody prefer he keep his wife at arm's length, hanging instead with the mistresses, groupies, and strippers who occupy so much of a pro athlete's attention? If Seaver thought the birth of his child might soften attitudes, it did not quite work out that way. Some players resented the way he characterized Sarah Lynn as his "good luck charm," saying, "So is everybody's kid, but it's reaching and other players don't go for that."

Another added: "A little on Nancy. She is all Hollywood, very pretty girl—uses Tom's stature on the team as her own status-getter. Dresses in Hollywood style, loud colors, flashy clothes, overdresses I believe." Another writer noted that interviews with the ace always took place at the stadium, never his home. "He guards his home life very well," he said. "He keeps it separate from baseball."

The commentary about Tom Seaver's personal side must be judged with several things in mind. For one thing, criticism was limited to a few aspects of his character. Much of Seaver's stance, especially in light of the New York bubble, was understandable. There was even a sense that the criticism was stretching it a bit, that since real and actual fault was hard to find in Tom Seaver's life, something had to be discovered. After all, the man was not perfect . . . was he?

His well-known fidelity to Nancy, in particular, was a case of people's finding fault with a man for being morally better than they were. Many of Seaver's teammates were said to admire him so much that they actually refrained from road trip groupies in order to emulate him, but others probably wished he would cheat on her so their own failures would not engender such guilt.

Jealousy on the part of the writers (in the 1970s the economic and social gap between athletes and media grew rapidly from the old days when a Bud Furillo was a drinking buddy of a Bo Belinsky) and the players was only human nature. The print journalists of the era, in particular, were a peculiar crew. In New York they tended to be a little scruffy, their hair growing longer, their appearance a bit unkempt. They probably differed in religious and political persuasion from Tom Seaver, the All-American boy from California; the son of an executive; a product of a conservative, traditional school (USC); married to a shiny "Hollywood" blonde, both dressed to the nines. Both Christians, probably Republicans, certainly not the McGovernites many in the media were at the time. Regardless of anybody's personal quibbles with the man, there was no denying Seaver was a superstar on the verge of ascending to an even higher plane.

10

THE FRANCHISE: 1973

SEAVER SPENT ANOTHER OFF-SEASON STUDYING IN HIS QUEST FOR a degree from the University of Southern California. The Trojans were in the middle of a remarkable run of College World Series championships, winning five straight between 1970 and 1974. Rod Dedeaux's team included such stalwarts as Fred Lynn and a football-baseball star named Anthony Davis.

When Spring Training began in 1973, labor strife again reared its ugly head. Locked out of camp, Seaver organized a quasi–Spring Training, taking on unofficial "managerial" duties that included supervising the workout routines of Mets pitchers and "ordering" Buddy Harrelson to get a haircut. For 10 days players went through the paces in what came to be called "Seaver's underground camp."

"One of the most organized camps I've ever seen was Seaver's Underground," wrote the *New York Post*'s venerable sports columnist Dick Young, a veteran of some 30 Spring Trainings. "He ran it with precision and efficiency. No doubt if he chooses, Tom Terrific will be a manager of the future."

When the dispute ended, Seaver's Guerrillas were in top shape. Seaver kept detailed charts of their conditioning progress, handing them to the coaches. Jerry Koosman and Jon Matlack were both in the camp. Each was highly influenced by Seaver, on and off the field.

"Tom Seaver was . . . a friend," Koosman said. "He's younger than me. We came up to the big leagues the first year in '67, and we made a little pact between us that our goal was to win 20 games each year and get five years in the big leagues so we could qualify for the pension plan. He was a college graduate, well-spoken, well-read, a man who handled himself well with the press."

"I learned an awful lot from having my locker stuck between Koosman and Seaver," said Matlack. "It was a very, very good location to be in. For the first two, three years Tom, Jerry, and I had a competition among ourselves as to who would get the most hits during the course of the season. The losers bought dinner for the winner. There was some friendly competition plus a whole lot of help for me early on from those guys."

Relieved of the responsibility of the camp, Tom settled down with general manager Bob Scheffing for contract negotiations. Steve Carlton and Bob Gibson were both being paid $160,000. Seaver felt he was worth as much as either of them.

Scheffing offered two years at $150,000 each, a $30,000 raise, but Seaver wanted more. He agreed to a one-year deal at $140,000 with the proviso that if he came through with a "normal Tom Seaver year" in 1973, he would get a raise that might go as high as $200,000 for 1974. Aaron was the only $200,000-a-year player. That was the figure Seaver talked about after the 1969 season, the nice round number he made as his goal. Seaver saw salary as a validation of his worth and place in the baseball hierarchy. To be paid more than Gibson, Carlton, even Aaron, meant he was *better* than they were. He wanted to be the best pitcher, maybe even the best player, the most important, valuable player in the game. Certainly on a team that hardly hit, there was not a performer in the game more important to his team than Seaver was to the Mets.

Mays was in his last year, an ancient. Roberto Clemente died tragically on New Year's Eve in a plane crash. Aaron was awesome but winding down. Reggie Jackson and Dick Allen were sluggers but had flaws. National League MVP Johnny Bench was a superstar . . . again. Pete Rose, Joe Morgan, Rod Carew, Gaylord Perry, Catfish Hunter were all in their primes, but was anybody really a bigger baseball star than George Thomas Seaver?

Scheffing, an old-school baseball man, seemed dismayed by the amount of dollars at stake in the modern game. Seaver told the writers he did not like negotiating contracts. Adding what he got was "a little shy" of his asking price, he said despite being a 21-game winner in 1972 it was a subpar year because of a muscle strain he endured in his buttocks. "I don't see any reason I can't improve on my record of last season and the club can't improve," he added. Jim Fregosi and Cleon Jones, he said, were the keys. Yogi Berra predicted that with Pittsburgh weakened after Clemente's loss, the National League East could be won with only 90 wins.

"Yogi was a man who didn't look like a ballplayer," Seaver recalled. "He was stumpy and kind of waddled when he walked, but he had the Midas touch—he was a winner. Everywhere he went, he was the bearer of good tidings, and pennants just seemed to follow him around. As a player he was in the World Series almost every year. When he was a coach, the Mets became an outstanding team, and then the Yankees won a string of pennants, depending on where he happened to be working. It's a truly amazing record.

"Yogi was also one of the kindest, nicest men I've ever met. You could always go to him to talk. And, of course, all those funny sayings he's credited with, well, there was always a ring of truth to them. Like the time Kenny Boswell of the Mets was in a slump. He went to Yogi and said, 'What should I do? I'm swinging up at everything.' Yogi said, 'Swing down.' Beautiful."

First baseman John Milner was expected to provide much-needed power. Felix Millan was a good second baseman and line drive hitter acquired from Atlanta for Gary Gentry, who never lived up to the promise of his 1969 rookie year. Outfielders Rusty Staub and Cleon Jones could both hit. Harrelson anchored the infield. Mays was going on 42, but nobody was willing to tell him to sit down or retire, even though it was obvious. Duffy Dyer and Jerry Grote had been Mets catchers for years. Pitching, as usual, was the club's keystone. Could Koosman return to the glory days of 1968–1969, when he like Seaver appeared to be Cooperstown bound? Matlack was a left-handed talent. Veterans included George Stone and Ray

Sadecki. Jim McAndrew was still around from the glory days, as was Tug McGraw, now rounded into one of the best relief specialists in the Major Leagues.

The opener was a classic for the ages: 27,326 fans at Shea Stadium on hand to see Seaver versus Carlton and Philadelphia. It took Seaver, with closing help from McGraw, an hour and 56 minutes to shut out the Phillies, 3–0. That season, Mike Schmidt emerged as a budding star.

"When Mike Schmidt first came up, the talk of the league was generally that he wouldn't last," Seaver recalled. "He had hit a lot of home runs at Eugene, but I remember people saying it was a small park. Then he went through a season of education at the Major League level, and bang—in his second year he's a star."

Then it was on to St. Louis and another classic matchup, the kind of pitching duel that seemed to mark this golden era in baseball history: Seaver versus Gibson. In Spring Training Gibby drilled Milner. In a legendary exchange of brushback pitches, Seaver retaliated, spinning Gibson with a heater that seemingly split the difference between Gibson's skull and his batting helmet.

"I know you got better control than that, Tommie," Gibson said to the glaring, unsmiling Seaver.

"Remember the one you put under my helmet last year?" said Seaver. He was not exchanging screechy, high-pitched needles with a fellow superstar during batting practice. Respect had been earned.

Both pitchers brushed each other back with wicked fastballs that, if landed in the wrong place, could kill a man. Seaver threw a 99-mile-per-hour fastball. Gibson's fastball was slightly less but still tremendous.

"He wasn't digging in after that," remarked St. Louis catcher Ted Simmons after Seaver gingerly struck out.

Seaver won the war in the end, a 2–1 masterpiece that defines our national pastime. Asked about the dangerous exchange of good old country hardball, Seaver said, "The message was relayed. He got it. He isn't going to intimidate me or my team. We can't let an opposing pitcher run us off the field. It's a hard part of the game . . . I feel even now, but if it goes on all season, we'll remember."

"Tom knew what to do," remarked Berra.

Gibby hid in the Cardinals trainer's room. He finally emerged and said, "I don't want to make a big thing out of this." The next time they faced each other, both pitchers had pinpoint control.

"As for Bob Gibson, he had about him a mystique of fearlessness and indestructibility. . . . Gibson was more intimidating than Koufax or Marichal, because hitters thought he was more apt to knock them down" was Seaver's recollection. "This gave him a tremendous psychological edge. As a fast worker who liked to get the ball back and fire it again, he never seemed to weaken, never seemed to tire. If he looked tough in the first inning, you figured he had you."

Early-season hope was quickly replaced by a constant Mets nemesis: injuries and anemic offensive production. Seaver fell to Chicago by a 1–0 score. Five days later he departed after nine innings tied with the Braves, 1–1. Atlanta won in extra innings. In his next start the Braves beat him, 2–0. In 40 innings he allowed five earned runs but was only 2–2. The Reds, juggernauts in 1973, racked him around, 6–1, but he beat Atlanta in a complete-game, 7–2 effort to even his record at 3–3. He should have been 5–1.

As the season headed into June, Seaver was arguably pitching better than ever in his career. He shut out Pittsburgh, 6–0, and then won 4–3 in a complete-game effort. He pitched well in a 7–3 win at Los Angeles, then struck out 16 in a 5–2 win at San Francisco.

"Two of the toughest hitters I had to face over the years were Willie McCovey and Willie Stargell, and of course, Steve Garvey has always been a great player," Seaver recalled of San Francisco's great slugger, still a major threat in 1973.

"But McCovey is my choice" as the best first baseman he ever played against. "All I can think about is that big, arching swing and the constant threat of the long ball . . . Off the field he wasn't fearsome at all. He was kind and soft spoken."

After beating the Padres, 9–2, he was 7–3 with a 1.74 earned run average. He had six complete games and led the league in strikeouts.

Los Angeles, a young, remarkably talented club at the beginning of a great run in the decade, defeated Seaver in New York, but after a complete-game, 3–1 triumph over San Francisco he was 8–4. In a rematch with the Dodgers Seaver pitched his heart out until almost collapsing in a game that ended up going 19 innings. Over 21 days the only four games New York won were Seaver's starts. More of their players were on the disabled list than the roster. They simply *could not hit.*

"I don't know where we'd be without Tom," said Berra.

"In last place with a 17-game losing streak," Jack Lang told him. They were playing .500 ball, in third place, six-and-a-half games behind Chicago. After beating Pittsburgh, 5–2, on June 24 for win number nine, Seaver started three times, yielding eight runs in 21 innings, but was rewarded with three no-decisions. He pitched on a rare three days of rest but lost to Cincinnati, 2–1. The team fell apart. McGraw, after compiling back-to-back 1.70 earned run averages in 1971 and 1972, was roughed up and his ERA was 6.07. The overall New York bullpen had a 5.15 earned run average.

Harrelson, recovering from a minor injury, sat behind home plate one game and tried to analyze McGraw's problems. He noticed that his motion had changed, causing him to "aim" his fastball. Tug was completely flummoxed, standing on the mound, head bowed, while the scoreboard lit up. He told the press he had pitched since age seven but now felt as if "I had never played baseball before." His arm did not hurt. He was in the prime of his life yet had what golfers called "the yips."

Starters Harry Parker and the surprising George Stone were pitching effectively, however. Jon Matlack recovered from a frightening line drive off his skull and pitched well. Then there was Jerry Koosman. He was a shell of his old self, the fastball artist of 1968–1969, but by 1973 was learning how to pitch. He had grown up with the gift of a great fastball, relying on it as he rose through the minor leagues and in his first two seasons in the Show. When he lost his heat, he lost his ability to win.

Seaver, on the other hand, grew up a "junk ball artist" who learned how to pitch with control, setting up hitters. When God seemingly touched him with the best fastball in the National League, he was a complete package. On days—and there were a fair number of them—in which for whatever reason the fastball was not quite there, he still knew how to compete, often with little or no drop in his winning success.

By 1973 Koosman, out of necessity really—which is often the best motivator—was finally pitching well again, using breaking pitches and control. In the meantime, Seaver was at the peak of his marvelous career. His fastball was consistently outstanding, his stuff virtually untouchable. Runs and hits were usually the result of luck, bat meeting ball by accident. He was in his prime, better than he had been in 1969. "Seaver was holding them afloat like a 10-armed lifeguard," wrote Larry Merchant in the *New York Post.*

On July 18 Seaver, given a rare horde of runs, beat Atlanta, 12–2. On July 24 he pitched a scoreless inning in the Nationals' 7–1 shellacking of the Americans in the All-Star Game at Royals Stadium in Kansas City. It was his seventh All-Star Game in seven years. He had yet to give up a single run. He struck out nine in defeating Houston, 3–2, then triumphed against St. Louis, 2–1. On August 1 he shut out the Pirates, 3–0. On August 5 he again tried pitching after three days instead of four and again lost, 3–2 against the Cardinals. He was 13–6.

On August 10 the power-hitting Giants fell like Eastern Europe under Joe Stalin, 7–1 at Candlestick Park. On August 12 Seaver battled the Big Red Machine for 12 excruciating innings, Goliath versus David armed with a 99-mile-per-hour slingshot, but he was finally removed without a decision, the score 2–2 in a game New York lost, 8–3. Over nine starts he was 6–2, with losses by 2–1 and 3–2 scores and no-decision in an extra-inning 2–2 effort.

On August 25 San Francisco bested him, 1–0. On August 30 he lost in the 10th inning, 1–0, against St. Louis. Heading into September he should have been closing in on the 30 wins he publicly expressed as a realistic goal back in 1970. Instead, winning 20 looked to be an uphill battle. Pundits who saw the great Sandy Koufax in the 1960s argued whether Seaver was even better than the Dodgers ace. He was doing it on a lower mound than Dandy Sandy had, and as anemic as the Dodgers' offense had been, the Mets were even worse. Old-timers tried to recall a better pitcher. Bob Feller? Lefty Grove? Walter Johnson? Could anybody really argue these guys were better?

Recent mound heroes such as Bob Gibson, Juan Marichal, and Don Drysdale were great, but none were as brilliant as Tom Terrific.

There was no question Seaver was now the best pitcher in the game. Steve Carlton, Jim Palmer, Catfish Hunter, Gaylord Perry—all great hurlers, none at Seaver's level. His decision to play under a one-year contract was now viewed as a brilliant maneuver. The economics of baseball was changing in 1973–1974. Curt Flood's challenge to the reserve clause was opening the game up to free agency. A star like Tom Seaver was about to cash in on new financial realities, his goal of $200,000 suddenly not just attainable but maybe, considering the marketplace, a lowball figure.

At 15–8 he could have been 25–3. His ERA was a microscopic 1.70. He had a league-leading 15 complete games and was first in the senior circuit in strikeouts. Meanwhile, a chubby left-hander with the Giants named Ron Bryant benefited from a San Francisco lineup consisting of Bobby Bonds, Gary Matthews, Gary Maddox, Dave Kingman, and Willie McCovey in their primes, most having the best years of their careers. He was on pace to win 24 games or so with an ERA approaching 4.00. Oh, the injustice!

The Mets were 61–71, but 1973 was a year like no other. In the wake of Roberto Clemente's death, nobody seemed willing or able to win the East Division. St. Louis held a tenuous lead, but New York trailed by only six-and-a-half games.

"We could be out of first place by 25 games the way things have gone for us," remarked Harrelson. "But Tom and the other pitchers have kept us close. We still have a chance."

By September, Staub and Milner were healthy and hitting. Cleon Jones was back in form. Jerry Grote returned and immediately—mysteriously—McGraw became "lights out." Over 10 games McGraw saved six games and won three. The club was now two-and-a-half games behind. Seaver beat Philadelphia, 7–1, and lost to Montreal, 3–1. He struck out 12 in an 11-inning win over the Phillies, 4–2. If he had not learned the lesson of three days' rest yet, he should have when he tried again, only to get battered around by the Pirates, 10–3, to go to 17–10. If not for the Pittsburgh loss, his ERA threatened to be among the greatest of all time.

Still back by two-and-a-half games, club chairman M. Donald Grant told the players they needed to believe in themselves. "You gotta bee-lieve!" McGraw shouted. He began repeating the phrase, pounding his glove and yelling it during games, and especially after saving game after game down the stretch. The players and the fans began to repeat, "Ya gotta believe!" Soon Shea—always filled with banners and placards—was adorned with signs with the phrase on them.

The atmosphere became electric, a re-creation of the 1969 magic. The intensity of emotion affected the players and also opponents, most of whom were around four years earlier and realized when a team and a place become infused with that sort of Pentecostal energy, they are all but unbeatable.

"It's beginning to feel like 1969 again," said Koosman. "We've got that pennant feeling." The veterans of '69 were jubilant in recapturing the magic, passing on stories of it to younger players as if it were a Biblical tradition, a charismatic religious awakening. The club caught fire and won night after night.

"We might be the first club in last place on August 20 to win a pennant," McGraw told his teammates. "Last place to first place in six weeks—wouldn't that be something?" Talk started: Had this been seen before? The 1914 Miracle Braves, the 1951 Giants . . . the 1969 Mets. Wow!

Berra, who saw it all, seemed to be pressing when he started Seaver on short rest *again*, but this time his ace, given runs, won easily by a 10–2 score over the flailing Pirates. It was a Friday night at Shea, September 21, the first day of fall. It was so similar to 1969 it was eerie. The scoreboard lit up with the glittering words "Look Who's Number One!" The "sign man of Shea," Karl Ehrhardt, held up a sign proclaiming the same thing. History was not repeating itself, it was rhyming!

New York, Pittsburgh, St. Louis, Montreal, and Chicago all crawled toward the finish line, each around the .500 mark. At 79–77 the Mets were indeed "number one," but at 75–80 both the Cubs and Expos were a mere three-and-a-half back, not eliminated by any stretch. Only Philadelphia was eliminated. Many have asked whether the great Steve Carlton might have been better than Seaver. One of the best reasons the answer to that question is "no" can be found, among other reasons, in the 1973 campaign. The perfectly healthy 28-year-old southpaw was 13–20 with a 3.90 earned run average, allowing 29 home runs. Never in Tom Seaver's entire career, not toward the end, not when injuries curtailed his effectiveness, did he approach such an abysmal record.

Now, as the horses approached the stretch run, Tom Seaver, veteran of more than 3,000 career innings, a complete-game pitcher often asked to pitch on short rest, carrying his team like a figure out of Greek mythology, was exhausted, and he stumbled.

The weight of the New York Mets fell with him, his fastball coming in flat, even, and average in speed in an 8–5 loss to the Expos. His ERA, around 1.70 all year, now threatened to break the 2.00 mark. His chances of winning 20 in a year he could have won 27, maybe even 30 games, seemed gone.

"The ball felt like a shot-put," he told reporters. It was a remarkably candid statement, one rarely uttered by the modern athlete, the warrior willing to admit he was fallible. He was frustrated. He did not say it but he wanted, *needed*, his teammates—his fellow pitchers and especially the offense—to pick him up.

As Bobby Kennedy so fatefully once said, "It's on to Chicago and let's win there." Seaver and his teammates hoped their fate would be kinder than the one RFK met after uttering those words in the Ambassador Hotel, 1968. Chicago was . . . Chicago: blustery, cold, rainy. Doubleheaders were scheduled for Sunday and Monday. If the race was still tied after that, a playoff scheduled for Tuesday would be held.

Naturally New York bats fell silent in a 1–0 loss to Rick Reuschel on Sunday, Jon Matlack pitching brilliantly yet in vain. But then they won 9–2, and Seaver was scheduled for Monday. The way it played out, if he could win the Mets clinched. If he lost, there would be further exhaustion, more resembling a marathon than baseball, before the East was decided. Waiting and watching, rested and raring to go, were the Cincinnati Reds, one of the great dynasties ever. The Mets, it seemed, were always just inches from futility.

"Tom Seaver had reached a level only a few pitchers ever reach, a level reached by a Christy Mathewson, a Lefty Grove, a Carl Hubbell, a Sandy Koufax, a Bob Gibson," wrote John Devaney, but Seaver was too tired to contemplate such loftiness.

"When you get to where Tom Seaver is, it doesn't only matter how many you win but which ones you win," wrote Larry Merchant. "In short, you must win the games that win pennants, you must win the big ones," continued Devaney.

Tom Seaver had done precisely that in 1969—down the stretch, shakily but victoriously versus Atlanta, in "the perfect game" against Baltimore. All season he did that, the load heavy, his shoulders strong enough to withstand the weight, but now . . . now it was different. His teammates said things rarely heard today. Jon Matlack flat said, "I don't want to be negative but I'm leery." Harrelson already made excuses for his roommate, all but explaining that he was so tired he could not be expected to reach such superhuman levels, and that when he ultimately failed, "I got to sympathize with him."

So what did the great Tom Seaver say? That he was feeling fine, that he was confident, that he was born for this sort of challenge? "I'm happy to try it." But down deep Seaver, the historian, knew that Gibson was tired in 1964, Koufax worked on two days' rest in '65, Yaz was on fumes down the stretch in '67. Was he one of those guys? He already had his moment in the sun, back in 1969, and that could not be taken from him, but he was in a business, and in a town, that asks, "What have you done for me lately?"

"In baseball you have to re-prove yourself over and over," commented NBC baseball broadcaster Tony Kubek. "Tom Seaver is discovering that this year."

The philosopher-pitcher added, "You feel almost like an artist creating something in pitching. Then you get to Pittsburgh and, boom, you make a mistake. Those two lousy games kind of soured the season for me. Coming back and winning after the Pirates game washed out the bad taste for me. Winning this one would wash out the bad taste of the Expos game."

The next day the weather at Wrigley Field looked more like a Bears game than a Cubs game. It was cold, the field slick. The crowd was tiny, not interested in a makeup game played after the rest of baseball had closed its doors. It was not the wild scene Seaver was used to, the winner of big games played in front of capacity crowds in a tent revival atmosphere. The desultory surroundings were foreboding, seeming to say that this was the day Tom Seaver got his comeuppance. The day God humbled him.

It looked as if it would be that way early. Seaver had nothing and knew it warming up. The cold stiffened him. His fingers had no feel. The game started. Seaver had nothin'. Well, not quite nothin'. He had the gift of concentration, drummed into him since youth by Charles Seaver, reinforced by Rod Dedeaux and Gil Hodges and Seaver himself. The Cubs had nothing on the line but were belligerent, forced to play an extra day instead of heading off for the winter. There were still remnants from '69 who wanted revenge. Whatever fans were there wanted some payback, too.

Seaver slogged through two innings, untouched. Cleon Jones went deep against Burt Hooton. Grote guided Seaver. He had no heat so Grote went to the slow curve, using the "fastball" as a changeup. In the fourth New York added two more. "Come on, baby!" a few Mets fans in the crowd were imploring them. "Ya gotta believe!"

New York added two more. In the fifth Seaver led 5–0 but was shaky. Was it enough? Nerves, nerves, nerves. Then came the inevitable. A drip-drip-drip of Chicago bloopers dropping in and two runs scored. But Seaver was not walking hitters. He was forcing the Cubs to swing and earn their way on. In the seventh, he gave up a single, and Rick Monday, his old teammate with the Alaska Goldpanners, homered to right field. Berra came up to get his aching, tired ace. He led 6–4, having given up 11 hits and four earned runs. Monday's shot pushed his ERA on the season above 2.00, to 2.08. It was a crying shame but not at the forefront of anybody's mind.

The best possible man in baseball for this situation was called on. Tug "Ya Gotta Believe!" McGraw was everything Seaver was not: "lights out." He closed the door on the Cubs, and that was it; the 1973 New York Mets, at 82–79, were East Division champions. It was not pretty. Much of the season was ugly, but for pure baseball excitement it was one of the most memorable years ever.

Amid a champagne shower, Seaver and McGraw went wild (the oft-businesslike Seaver was easily one of the most exuberant championship clubhouse champagne celebrators of all time), shouting, "*Ya gotta believe!*"

"I'm the eternal optimist, but this summer strained even my eternal optimism," Seaver said. "If you had told me in August we would make the playoffs and have a chance to be in the Series, I would have said you were crazy."

Seaver finished 19–10 to go along with his league-leading 2.08 earned run average (the third time in four seasons he led the league in this category). He pitched 18 complete games, posted three shutouts, struck out 251 (also the third time in four seasons he led the league), and allowed a mere 64 bases on balls, 219 hits, and 23 homers. In 36 starts he pitched well enough to win at least 30 times. In a modern statistic called "earned run average adjusted to the player's ballpark," Seaver's was 175 (according to Baseball -Reference.com). This was also the third of four seasons his was the best in the senior circuit in this statistic. He fashioned a 0.976 walks plus hits per nine innings average, another league best; gave up less than seven hits per nine innings, walking two per complete game; and struck out almost eight a game, while fashioning 3.92 strikeouts for every walk.

He did not win as many as in 1969, but he was better. He threw harder. He might have been significantly better than he had been that season. It is difficult to ultimately argue he was better than he had been in 1971, and all things considered the Seaver from April to mid-August of 1970 might have been on his greatest stretch, but considering the pressure of the pennant race, he may have reached his apogee in 1973. It is this writer and historian's humble opinion that Seaver's 1973 season was the best non-20-game-winning performance ever (Greg Maddux, 1995, and Pedro Martinez, 2000, are certainly worthy of comparison, but both pitchers received good support from their respective clubs).

Considering how little support *he* received, one began to see why Seaver placed so much emphasis on winning 300 in his career. If he went for years with so few runs it would be a tremendous feat, albeit a wearing, jarring one, but it would ultimately validate him and make up for years such as this in which he did not get to 20 victories.

The powers that be in baseball, in all their wisdom, made a wise choice, which was to schedule the playoffs beginning on Saturday after several days of rest following the regular season. Seaver pitched the day *after* the season ended, but Saturday still fell on his usual fifth-day start. The pressure valve finally opened up, leaving chilly Chicago; the weight removed for a few days at least, Seaver was refreshed and looking forward to game one of the National League Championship Series at Cincinnati.

The press, however, questioned whether Matlack should start. Matlack was dominant late in the season. Seaver more resembled Don Drysdale at the end of the wearing 1962 campaign, a 25-game winner but fatigued, undependable in crunch time. But a "great" 12-minute side session at Shea, along with a heavy lobbying job by Seaver, in addition to a clean bill of health pronounced by Dr. Peter LaMotte, convinced Berra to start his ace in the opener.

In the history of Major League baseball, there may never have been a bigger postseason underdog than the 1973 New York Mets going up against the Cincinnati Reds. Managed by George "Sparky" Anderson, Cincinnati was a team for the ages. Winners of the 1970 and 1972 National League pennants, they were hungry to win the World Series, which had eluded them. In 1973 they were itching to get at the Oakland Athletics, winners of an improbable seven-game title bout over them the previous season, or the Baltimore Orioles—Oakland's AL playoff opponent—the team that knocked them out in 1970. (A New York-Baltimore rematch offered an unlikely but intriguing scenario, further play on the rivalry between the two cities that also included the Jets and Colts.)

The Reds featured Johnny Bench, the greatest catcher in Major League history; first baseman Tony Perez, a clutch RBI man of the first order; Joe Morgan, who some have said might be the best second baseman; Dave Concepcion, the best fielding shortstop of the era; and left fielder Pete Rose, the league batting champion (.338, with 230 hits) and MVP at the height of his storied career. Early in the season, the Los Angeles Dodgers captured the imagination of baseball with the young infield that would form their 1970s glory years—Steve Garvey, Davey Lopes, Bill Russell, Ron Cey—along with a powerhouse pitching rotation including Don Sutton, Andy Messersmith, Claude Osteen, and Tommy John. Manager Walt Alston's club won 95 games, but the Reds clawed away, eventually passing them to win with 99 victories. It was felt, with a certain amount of arrogance, that in winning the rugged National League West, they were the best team in baseball and a shoo-in to go all the way. The A's world championship in 1972 was viewed as a slight aberration, unlikely to be repeated. Manager Earl Weaver's Baltimore Orioles rebounded after an off year in 1971, recalibrated with speed, and seemed to be Cincinnati's stiffest obstacle.

The New York Mets were little more than a bump in Cincinnati's glory road, an 82-win collection of stiffs. Yet, yet . . . there was something there. In the back of minds was this uncomfortable notion, this memory of what they had done four seasons earlier, but more specifically, there was Tom Seaver, Jon Matlack, and Tug McGraw. The old saws were still good saws: "Pitching is 90 percent of baseball; . . . good pitching beats good hitting."

The Reds had mediocre pitching. Anderson, known as Captain Hook, lifted his so-so starters early and won with a bullpen by committee and an offense that bludgeoned opponents to death. It was a regular season formula for success, but they would potentially have to face *Tom Seaver* twice in a short five-game series. *Tom Seaver*! Energized by another postseason, on five days' rest after beating Chicago. If that guy was on his game, any time he pitched he was favored. All other records meant nothing. The entire series rested on the opener. If Seaver could be beaten, the Mets were done.

Dave Anderson of the *New York Times* asked Seaver if his late-season drop-off could be attributed to pressure, and if so, would the pressure of the playoffs affect his performance?

"If somebody wants to feel that way, that's up to them," Seaver replied. "In my own mind I know what kind of job I've done. If an athlete went up and down with what fans say, he'd be on a seesaw of emotions. One day you'd think you were great because the fans gave you an ovation, the next time you'd think you were lousy because they booed you. After a while you wouldn't know what you were."

Seaver, who had never heard boos at home, put aside a crossword puzzle he was working on in the plane from New York to Cincinnati. "Concentration and effort, that's what pitching is, no matter what the situation. I don't pitch harder against one team than another team. If a person buys that theory, he's looking at it from the wrong angle. By that theory the most important item is the team you're pitching against. To me, the most important item is that it's a game to be won.

"I'm like a kangaroo court. I am my own judge and jury. Every time I go out to the mound I expect an awful lot of myself. I expect to win. Some people may have forgotten that down the stretch in 1969 when we won the pennant, I won my last 10 in a row."

The Tom Seaver of 1973 was a different man than in 1969. He was mature, possibly tempered by parenthood, certainly by money, expectations, and responsibilities, as a team leader and husband. But perhaps most different was his view of himself, his expectations. A transition had started and now was a fully formed psychology. Seaver was once like a guy plucked out of the stands, magically touched with extraordinary powers, like Joe Boyd, transformed into the powerful 22-year-old Joe Hardy in *Damn Yankees.* But by 1973 he expected to be the best because he was. It was not a question, as if it ever had been. The fantasy was indeed reality, and he worked too hard to maintain that reality. He, like Paul in his letter to the Corinthians, had "put away childish things" and was a deadly serious baseball marksman. His aim now was on the Cincinnati Reds.

In Tom Seaver's entire career, the first game of the 1973 National League Championship Series, played before 53,000 fans at Cincinnati's Riverfront Stadium, may rank as both his best and his most frustrating. What happened that crisp October day was mind-boggling to the extreme, on both ends of the emotional spectrum. It was all part of a crazy postseason that had not yet played to form and would continue to do so.

Tom Seaver pitched the greatest game of his life that day. Tom Seaver lost. For Seaver aficionados, true fans, and followers, what he did on the artificial turf of Riverfront Stadium was more dominant even than his 1969 "imperfect game," his 19 strikeouts against San Diego in 1970, or any of his near-no-hitters, shutouts, and masterpieces. First, it was the Reds, not San Diego or the Cardinals or the Cubs, normally good teams that more often than not were mere fodder for the Seaver cannon. Seaver rendered the most dangerous team in the game, maybe the most dangerous collection of bats since . . . since . . . since when? The 1936 Yankees maybe? He rendered them a collection of Little Leaguers flailing away in ineptitude, spectators forced to watch him, his unreal fastball buzzing past them, unseen really, and as unhittable as a howitzer. Use any war metaphor—he was the Romans seizing Gaul, Patton on the march. A juggernaut. To those who saw it, it was as great a pitching performance as ever witnessed . . . for all of 8⅓ innings.

The game started with Rose, Morgan, and the Reds going down with nary a peep. In the second, New York nicked Cincinnati starter Jack Billingham for a run, *Seaver's double plating Harrelson.* This was a joke in and of itself. Billingham was a 19-game winner, the same as Tom Seaver. The idea, the concept, the very theory that in this world Jack Billingham could win as many baseball games, playing by the very same rules as Tom Seaver, was ludicrous, but on a team that scored six or seven runs most of his starts, there it was: Jack Billingham, 19–10. The unfairness of it was startling. Nothing against Billingham, a nice enough guy, competent, but his fastball was so ordinary Bench once caught it with his bare hand to get him to amp it up a little.

But that was it, 1–0. Billingham holding down the Mets (Seaver apparently New York's strongest threat), an act that did not differentiate him from a large number of National League hurlers throughout the decade. Seaver was completely holding Cincinnati down, an act unheard of at the time. Certainly nobody did it the way he was doing it. The old tired Seaver in Chicago, the man trudging through his last three starts, was replaced by a man at the very apex of his powers, his double a do-it-yourself addendum to his shining greatness, an all-encompassing baseball figure dominating in a way seemingly unseen since Babe Ruth was both the best pitcher and hitter in the game.

It all seemed preordained, a kind of Calvinistic diamond excursion, with Heaven waiting for the New York Mets courtesy of their savior, mowing down the forces of evil inning after inning. In the fourth with a runner on second, he struck out Bench and Ken Griffey, making them look like children. With a man in scoring position in the fifth, Rose, the contact hitter and a career nemesis of Tom Terrific's, went down, overmatched, on strikes. Sparky Anderson did not come out and say it, but he told himself Seaver was "the best in the league" and did not expect he could be beaten. He was strategizing about game two.

In the seventh Seaver tied a playoff record with his 10th strikeout and broke it with his 11th. Hal King opened the eighth with strikeout number 12. Seaver was throwing harder than ever. He was not tired. The Mets' bullpen was silent. Then Seaver walked into the Mets' dugout. The crowd looked on, wondering at this oddity. The camera showed that he removed his shoe. He had the trainer apply a new pressure pad. He trudged back out, and there was Rose.

The count went to two-and-two. The crowd, silent for two hours, cheered a little but expected less. Seaver worked him inside, but the crafty Rose was guessing inside. It was a good pitch, on the hands, but Rose adjusted and muscled his bat in a tight semicircle, meeting the pitch with the barrel out front. "When I get out in front with the bat, I can hit the ball as far as anyone," he later said. His high liner disappeared over the right-field fence, he sprinted around the bases, the crowd went crazy, and it was 1–1.

All the air was out of the Mets' tires now. Their offense was nonexistent. There was little expectation they would score. Seaver, it seemed, would have to grimly pitch well into extra innings if the club had any shot here. Morgan went down on strikes for number 13 and Seaver finished the eighth, but the Reds' second baseman thought Seaver's fastball lost just a fraction of hop. Johnny Bench took notice.

Naturally New York went down without a fight in the ninth, so Seaver trudged out, a lonely hero. Tony Perez tapped out, and it was Bench. He knew Seaver's diet: low fastballs, in and out. Seaver wore him out, ate him alive. He could not get around on his heat, but he was so powerful sometimes he got hold of one. Tom rammed him inside, and on 1-and-0 Bench got around, smacking a liner that disappeared over the left-field fence—and that was it, just like that. 2–1, Reds.

Seaver walked off the field and paced the clubhouse. His teammates murmured in soft tones with newsmen. Seaver was approached but could not speak. He disappeared. The most engaging and honest of all players, he was beside himself. This may have been the low moment of his entire career, before and after that day. The writers tried again. Seaver left again. Finally he reappeared with a can of beer. He fielded ginger questions, trying to explain it but could not, mostly repeating phrases such as "So what? We lost, 2–1."

The Mets entered the series a profound underdog, but at this moment their prospects were as low as any Major League baseball team's in any postseason series going back to the turn of the century. Nobody gave them a chance. So what happened after that? The New York Mets dominated the Cincinnati Reds, outplaying them in every way one team can outplay another: offensively, defensively, and especially on the pitcher's mound.

The next day Jon Matlack was not as dominating as Seaver but ultimately more effective in a masterful 5–0 shutout. Now the series shifted to Shea Stadium and all the craziness thus entailed. In one Sunday afternoon the complexion of the game was completely changed. The crowds at Shea in 1973 were even more rabid than in 1969, to the point of ugliness. It was a bad time in the history of New York City. It was a period of dirtiness, corruption, crime, and strife in the Big Apple, depicted in gritty movies such as *The French Connection*, *Serpico*, *Taxi Driver*, and *Marathon Man*. Whereas in 1969 the scene was joyous, almost childlike, the fans in a state of innocent euphoria, the 1970s—a period of long hair, drug abuse, sexual immorality, and a lack of patriotism unmatched in American history—resulted in sporting scenes more resembling a Latin American soccer mob. The Reds were literally frightened at Shea Stadium. All bets were off.

In game three, New York blasted Ross Grimsley out of the box, and Jerry Koosman found lost glory in a 9–2 win. The scene became downright dangerous when Rose took out little Buddy Harrelson in a hard slide at second base.

"Oh, how I remember that day," recalled Tom. "It was not unlike the 1934 World Series, when the commissioner of baseball had to remove Joe Medwick of the Cardinals from the game for his own protection after Tigers fans pelted him with garbage. At Shea, the fans threw so many objects at Rose in left field that a small contingent of Mets players, myself included, walked out there and asked them to stop, lest we forfeit the game. Did I mention that Pete reminded us all of old-time baseball?"

In game four George Stone appeared to be in control, the Mets leading 1–0. It looked to be enough to hold up, but Cincinnati tied the game. The Reds, one of the grittiest teams in ages, somehow pulled out a 2–1, 12-inning game, and so it was Tom Seaver in game five with everything on the line: $6,000 for the losers, $14,000 for the winners, then World Series money beyond that.

Rose was the first hitter. The crowd was in bad form. The future Hall of Famer's homer the previous day was a poke in the eye to the Shea faithful, but he was retired on an easy grounder. But Seaver struggled. He did not have the fastball he showed in Cincinnati and was forced to pitch out of a bases-loaded jam. Unwilling to challenge Bench, he walked him intentionally to fill the bases, a dangerous first-inning move, but induced Ken Griffey to fly out.

The Mets jumped out to a 2–0 lead, and Grote guided his pitcher, focusing on his slider, curve, and good control. The Reds touched him for single runs in the third and fifth to tie it, 2–2. Willie Mays's high chop for an improbable infield hit highlighted a two-run bottom of the fifth, and New York added two more in the sixth to take a 6–2 lead. Shea was rocking, and Rose's health was seemingly always in danger in the outfield, the threat of a bottle flying out of the stands always palpable, especially on any fly at the warning track. Toilet paper littered the field. Seaver himself lined one down the line. Rose dove but missed, and Seaver had a double, the crowd in ecstasy. Cleon Jones drove the pitcher home, and it was 7–2.

Buoyed by the lead, Seaver began to pump his fastball in there with more vim, mixing it with slow stuff. He worked through the eighth and entered the last inning amid the threat of violence in the air. It was improbable, really. Seaver was the game's ultimate gentleman, the All-American boy, but now he was the darling of a mob, of anarchists.

As Seaver struggled, loading the bases with one out, play had to be stopped as fans ran onto the field, the special police barely able to hold back the crazies. Berra replaced Seaver, and McGraw's appearance only exacerbated the situation when he whipped his glove—McGraw easily got two outs. The Mets desperately tried to avoid the swarm as they ran off the field. Cincinnati's players were forced to hold off the mob with baseball bats. The "fans" turned the Shea Stadium field into something more resembling Flanders or the Somme within minutes, only days before it would have to be ready for World Series play.

In some ways it was Tom's greatest victory. It was vindication after the loss in Cincinnati, victory in "the big one" that the greats must attain. He did it without his best stuff in the most pressurized of atmospheres with all on the line. But his teammates had stepped up, giving him the chance to gain this baseball redemption. In the clubhouse Seaver was ecstatic, swigging champagne and yelling, "Whoopee!" over and over again.

"It's been a long uphill fight, and by God it's good to get here," he exclaimed. "I feel . . . I feel like somebody pulled a cork off the top of my head and it's all pouring out." Then he poured champagne all over Mayor John Lindsay, whom he called "buddy." Seaver gave full credit to Grote, a great, undervalued catcher who Seaver always insisted was as good as Johnny Bench.

"I never worked so hard in my life," he said. "I feel like there's a load off my back." Standing on a platform with Ralph Kiner, Seaver caught Tug McGraw's gaze from across the room. "*Ya gotta believe!*"

"*Ya gotta believe!*"

That night Manhattan went wild, millions trying to recapture the magic of 1969.

Waiting for the Mets in a hot, hazy Bay Area were the defending world champion Oakland Athletics. The A's beat Cincinnati themselves in 1972 and rallied to fend off Jim Palmer and Baltimore in a tense five-game American League Championship Series. Their legend was not yet made, but ultimately they would prove themselves to be one of the greatest dynasties ever assembled.

They had everything: a complete ball club, both stars and role players with no weaknesses. Third baseman Sal Bando was their anchor, a clutch hitter with power. Left fielder Joe Rudi was the best in the game, a line drive hitter. Right fielder Reggie Jackson was his league's MVP, a superstar at the height of his powers, as was Tom Seaver. They broke into baseball the same year, 1967, contemporary faces of the new game, the present and future of baseball as the likes of Hank Aaron and Willie Mays neared retirement.

The Mets' advantage was always pitching, pitching, pitching, but now suddenly they faced a club with *better pitching*! Seaver may have been the best in the game, but Oakland ace Jim "Catfish" Hunter (21–5), while less spectacular, was just as effective. Left-handers Ken Holtzman and Vida Blue were power pitchers, also 20-game winners. Then there was their bullpen, one of the deepest in baseball history. Darold Knowles and Horacio Pina were "lights out," but closer Rollie Fingers was off the charts, the winner of seven games with 22 saves and a 1.92 earned run average. No relief pitcher had ever won the Most Valuable Player award, but many argued that it was Fingers, not Jackson, who deserved the honor. Fingers had "the perfect temperament for a relief pitcher" was Seaver's view. "All the great ones are like that—Sparky Lyle had it, Tug McGraw had it." All in all the 1973 Athletics featured four future Hall of Famers (Hunter, Fingers, Jackson, and manager Dick Williams).

One of Oakland's secret weapons was heavy emphasis on advance scouting. Their people had a thorough report on New York's staff, and it was so daunting it almost had the effect of discouraging them. "They raved about Seaver," recalled Jackson, as well as the other Mets' hurlers. But it got so over the top that Jackson started to laugh, wondering why they were not all 25-game winners. The scouts basically painted a picture in which Seaver, if he was on, was unbeatable. Only some lucky bounces and a shutout by Oakland could hope to stop him. Jackson came up with one of the great quotes of all time.

"Seriously," he stated, "there isn't a person in the world who hasn't heard about Seaver. He's so good blind people come out to hear him pitch." It was similar to a line writer John Underwood uttered about Ted Williams when he interviewed a blind man at Fenway Park who said he came to the games to "listen to Williams hit."

Seaver was asked about Hodges's death. "I lost a great manager . . . a great friend, and I think about him," he replied. "I miss him. He was so much an inspiration to me. I think about him now and it gives me a tremendous feeling about this [the Series]."

The creation of the tense best-three-of-five playoff format, started in 1969, created a new dynamic in which players, particularly winners of a five-game series, felt relatively relaxed in the first couple games of the World Series. They were just happy to be there, at least until a game or two were played and the tension mounted once again. Both Oakland and New York came in having survived fierce competition.

The first two games at the Oakland-Alameda County Coliseum were off form to one degree or another. An error by Felix Millan gave Ken Holtzman and the A's a 2–1 win in the opener. With a tired Seaver unable to pitch until game three in New York, Oakland desperately wanted to get two wins under their belt before heading east. Instead, they played one of the all-time sloppiest games. Their airtight pitching and defense completely fell apart. The light-hitting Mets tagged Vida Blue and his successors in a 10–7 extra-inning victory.

Suddenly, as with the Cincinnati series, all bets were off. Now it was anybody's to win. Oakland's confidence was shaken, the specter of Seaver and his 99-mile-per-hour fastball in a night game at Shea Stadium staring them in the face. After weather approaching 90 degrees on the West Coast, the chilly 50-degree temperatures seemed to favor the home club. It was a classic matchup for the ages, Seaver versus Hunter.

"It is generally conceded that Seaver is the best pitcher in baseball," wrote Maury Allen of the *New York Post* ("Who's King of the Hill?"). "It is generally conceded that, except by some Jim Palmer die hards, that Hunter is the best pitcher in the American League."

Game three remains one of the strangest games of Tom Seaver's career. Like game one in Cincinnati, it was a game in which he was as good as he has ever been, at the height of his great talents. Staked to a 2–0 first-inning lead, he dominated Oakland. The poor A's had never seen anything remotely close to Seaver—not Palmer, not Bert Blyleven, not even Nolan Ryan of California, a fastball artist par excellence they usually beat because of his control troubles.

New York had Hunter on the ropes in the first, but after allowing two runs he pitched out of a jam. Through five innings they left nine men on base. Meanwhile, Seaver threw so hard blind people could hear him pitch, striking out five straight A's (one short of the World Series record) and nine overall over the same time. Mets fans were seemingly not worried about victory, which looked to be in the bag. They wanted to know what the all-time Series strikeout record was (Bob Gibson's 17 in 1968 broke Sandy Koufax's 1963 record of 15).

In the sixth Seaver blew heat past Jackson for his 10th strikeout, but Gene Tenace's double plated Bando and it was a game, 2–1. Hunter held the line and turned it over to his bullpen. In the eighth Bert Campaneris singled and stole second. Rudi's off-field hit scored him, and it was 2–2. Jackson hit one hard, but outfielder Don Hahn ran it down. Seaver got Tenace for his 12th strikeout and trudged into the dugout, but Berra and pitching coach Rube Walker decided to lift him for a pinch hitter after 112 pitches.

Tenace was stunned when the Mets' ace did not come out in the ninth, telling writers Seaver looked as strong in the eighth as he had in the first. In the 11th Oakland touched the New York bullpen and held for a 3–2 win. It was similar to the loss at Cincinnati, the ace "losing" (Seaver had a no-decision), his club now in a hole against a highly favored team. Would his teammates pick him up again? They would.

Matlack and Koosman were absolutely spectacular in 6–1 and 2–0 victories, pushing the Series back to Oakland with the Mets leading, three games to two. Reggie Jackson: "Seaver's the best pitcher in baseball."

The sixth game, played under warm, blue skies on a Saturday afternoon, was a Seaver-Hunter rematch. With champagne packed on ice in the visitors' clubhouse, Seaver went out on three days of rest. Hunter retired the Mets in the first. In the bottom half, Seaver had good stuff but was a notch below his usual level. After Joe Rudi singled, up came Reggie. The A's slugger hardly touched the ball in New York, overmatched, but he found one he could hit and smacked a run-scoring double to the wall. It was 1–0.

In the third, Bando reached on an infield hit and Jackson got a slider, driving it for another double. Outfielder Rusty Staub had a sore arm and could not make the throw. Bando scored to up the lead to 2–0. Hunter heard the incessant East Coast talk, insisting

Seaver was better, the best, number one, all superior. He was determined to show his considerable worth, retiring 11 straight and breezing through the Mets' lineup. Seaver had the best at-bat of the day against him, driving one to the wall where Rudi made the catch.

Trailing 2–0 in the eighth, Seaver was removed for a pinch hitter. New York managed a run, but McGraw gave it back. Leading 3–1, the Oakland bullpen shut the door and won the game.

Afterward Tony Kubek interviewed Reggie Jackson. Kubek said he felt Seaver's shoulder was sore. "That wasn't the real Tom Seaver we saw today," Jackson said. "He ate me up in New York with those fastballs. They were by me before I could say hello. Today he didn't throw near that hard. And he didn't have that good curve he had the other night. That wasn't the real Tom Seaver today but that was a gutsy Tom Seaver we saw today."

Seaver and Jackson always maintained a mutual admiration society. "Nobody in our game has been able to generate headlines like Reggie Jackson," the pitcher recalled of the slugger, eventually like himself an iconic member of the New York pantheon.

"Now, there will be those who don't take what Reggie says seriously, or those who think he goes after those headlines too much, but Reggie Jackson has been great for our profession by getting publicity. So, in a sense, we all owe a debt to him for drawing fans who might otherwise never have come to notice baseball."

Seaver munched on a chili dog in the other clubhouse. He was oddly relaxed, not pacing about in sheer frustration as after most losses. His season was over. It was up to Matlack in game seven. Seaver had done all he could do. He had allowed two runs courtesy of the best hitter in baseball in a strong start. Again, his team failed to support him. He fought the good fight.

He said he "didn't pitch badly," just "badly enough to lose," a wry comment. He added he did not have his good fastball and concluded, "When you pitch for the Mets there are no easy games, there are no easy innings." He was 0–1 in the 1973 World Series after giving up a mere four runs in 15 innings of work (2.48 ERA). The next day the dream died. Jackson took Oakland on his back, carrying them past Matlack in a 5–2 triumph, the second of their three consecutive world championships.

After game seven, "Rudi came into our clubhouse and sat down with Seaver, myself, and Cleon Jones, and we talked about the various plays, the pitch sequences, just talking baseball," said Jerry Koosman. "He must have spent 15 or 20 minutes before he went back to his locker room to celebrate, which I thought was a class act."

After the World Series, the media focused their attention on Seaver's chances at the Cy Young Award. San Francisco's Ron Bryant, winner of 24 games, and Montreal reliever Mike Marshall were his main competition. Seaver was 19–10, but three losses were by 1–0, two by 2–1.

"I don't think I'll win it," Tom told friends, adding that 20 victories was too important a statistic. He was wrong, winning the award with 71 points compared to Marshall (54) and Bryant (50). Only Sandy Koufax and Bob Gibson had won more than one Cy Young Award prior to 1973. He was in select company.

"I'm surprised and happy," he said. "It goes to only one pitcher in the league and so it means an awful lot to me." Reporters asked if he was disappointed about the end-of-season results. Seaver said he was, citing fatigue, and pointed out that he started on short rest several times. With few exceptions, "I've pitched as well as I ever did in the big leagues." Surely for 8⅓ innings at Cincinnati and for seven innings versus Oakland, Seaver was as dominant in those two games as in any he ever pitched, or close to it. It was a conundrum, really, that both resulted in losses, but this was the way of baseball. In 1969 he pitched flat-out bad in the playoff opener at Atlanta, yet he won. In his career he pitched many, many more low-run, dominant games resulting in a loss or no-decision than did Steve Carlton, Bob Gibson, Catfish Hunter, Jim Palmer, or possibly any other pitcher. He was 1–2 in four World Series starts but should have been 3–1. He was 2–1 in three playoff starts. Flipping Atlanta (a win that could have been a loss, 1969) and Cincinnati (a loss that should have been a win, 1973), that was a fair statistic. He had 135 career wins. Using a conservative estimate, he should have won 30 more games over seven seasons. His lifetime earned run average was 2.41! Two point four one! Astounding. He was, to his club, the Franchise.

That winter, Seaver worked on correspondence courses he agreed to with USC, closing in on a bachelor's degree. He came from a family of college-educated people and had stuck with it, bound to achieve this goal. The media speculated on his place in the game's history. Would he become the best of all time? Would he reach 300 career wins? If he retired at the end of the 1973 season, he likely was already a Hall of Famer. What about after his playing career ended? Most were sure he would pursue broadcasting. Others speculated he would make a great manager, perhaps even the commissioner of baseball. Some on the Republican side of the aisle envisioned a political future, a run for governor or the U.S. Senate. Few could imagine Seaver schlepping about in an office lower than that.

"Life isn't very heavy for me," he observed. "I've made up my mind what I want to do. I'm happy when I pitch well, so I only do those things that help me be happy. I wouldn't be able to dedicate myself like this for money or glory, although they certainly are considerations. If I pitch well for 15 years, I'll be able to give my family security. But that isn't what motivates me. What motivates some pitchers is to be known as the fastest who ever lived. Some want to have the greatest season ever. All I want to do is to do the best I possibly can day after day, year after year. Pitching is the whole thing to me. I want to prove I am the best ever."

"One suspects that were the job not so suited for the isolated, aloof man, Tom Seaver would not love it nearly as well," wrote John Devaney.

11

THE BEST PITCHER IN BASEBALL: 1974–1977

IN THE SPRING OF 1974, TOM SEAVER COMPLETED HIS FINAL TERM paper for a geology course at the University of Southern California. The thesis of it was the consistency of National League infields. "Each team manicures its ball park to meet its strengths," he found. He mailed it in. Unable to attend the graduation ceremony due to his baseball schedule, a short time later he received his bachelor's degree from USC in the mail.

Tom Terrific was 29 years old, the best of the best. He seemed invincible. He signed a two-year, $173,000 contract. But a case of sciatica all but ruined the 1974 campaign. Finally in September he visited Dr. Kenneth Riland, who determined that his pelvic structure was out of order. After that the pain was miraculously gone. In his last start he struck out 14 to finish with 201, tying Walter Johnson's mark of seven consecutive 200-strikeout seasons. He finished 11–11.

In the winter of 1974–1975, Seaver studied film and reported to St. Petersburg buoyed by the fact he recovered his health and pitching effectiveness in late September of 1974. It was not an entirely lost season after all. He was 30 years old and had many goals to strive for.

"It would be shortsighted to think all this is never going to end, but I would like a long career," he told the writers.

During Spring Training, Seaver was playing catch with Jon Matlack. He started experimenting with grips. He wanted to develop a change of pace. He had the best fastball in the National League—a vote by his peers in *Parade* magazine verified it—a wicked slider, and a great curve but had never developed a true changeup. His motion made it problematic. He put so much into each pitch that when he threw a changeup he perceptibly altered his motion to slow the ball down. This meant he was courting a possible injury such as the sciatica that had plagued him in 1974, and it also was a tip-off to hitters. He wanted to be able to throw with the same motion as his fastball, only reducing the speed and hopefully even the trajectory of the pitch enough to be an effective big-league changeup.

By experimentation, really, Seaver created what eventually could be called the "circle change," which was effectuated by gripping the ball deep into his palms. "You got it," Matlack yelled to him when he saw the ball drift in at half the speed of his regular fastball. Seaver was a trendsetter once again, this coming on top of his role in the evolution of weight training in baseball and later his part in the five-man starting rotation, which by the mid-1970s was near universal.

Seaver was his club's player representative. His intelligence and reasonable attitude made him the perfect go-between to deal with both ownership and the union. The union was powerful by 1975, the year free agency kicked in. Seaver certainly was thinking about how it would affect him. He loved New York and wanted to be a Met, but he could not help considering the financial ramifications of the Curt Flood case, the original lawsuit filed by the Cardinals' former outfielder that eventually reached the Supreme Court, the result being that players were now free to move on once their contracts expired.

"And when everyone saw what a player's worth had become on the open market, it was inevitable that a new era would cross the moat and enter the castle" was how Seaver described it. "It took the decision of an arbitrator to make it happen, but it was destined to come about one way or another." Eventually "franchise values soared as never before. In 1943 the Philadelphia Phillies were sold for $80,000. In 1973, the Yankees were sold for $10 million. Both figures are bargains today, laughable almost." This started a "golden age of sports. . . . Free agency has gone through its infancy, and the Republic has survived."

When the clubs broke north and the season started, Seaver and the Mets were reinvigorated. Seaver was immediately successful, every bit as great as he had been prior to the sciatica injury. He was back, maybe better. There was no letup at all. The Mets climbed into the pennant race, and 1975 shaped up to be a great season. He was named to the All-Star team again but gave up his first runs, courtesy of a three-run homer by Boston's Carl Yastrzemski. Seaver had faced him in the 1967 All-Star Game, protecting a 2–1 lead in the 15th inning.

"Now, you never walk the tying run, so they say, but there was *no way* I was going to let Yaz hit one out there. It was good advice in 1967," Seaver recalled, adding he "still can picture Yastrzemski, that intimidating stance, holding the bat real high, and I knew right then that I wasn't going to allow him to swing the bat."

But in 1975 at Milwaukee County Stadium, as Seaver was protecting a 3–0 lead in the sixth inning, Yaz "got even." Seaver struck out two but the damage was done. The Nationals recovered, however, to win the game. His teammate Jon Matlack picked up the victory.

Nine days later Seaver faced the Cincinnati Reds in front of a packed house at Shea Stadium. Typically, his club failed to support him in a 2–1 loss to a pitcher, Fred Norman, who could not a hold a candle to Seaver. The 1975 Reds were one of the all-time best teams in the history of the game. They would go on to win 108 games, sweep the playoffs, and beat Boston in a memorable seven-game Fall Classic. Seaver struck out five and "fell" to 14–6 with another microscopic earned run average, 2.07.

On September 1, 45,991 fans arrived at Shea Stadium for a game with double meaning. A tense pennant race between the Mets and Pittsburgh for East Division supremacy was hot and heavy, but on that day Seaver struck out Manny Sanguillen to record his 200th strikeout. He was the first pitcher in history to record 200 strikeouts eight straight years, beating the record previously held by Johnson and Rube Waddell. Seaver went the distance in a sterling four-hit, 10-strikeout, 3–0 shutout. It was his 20th win of the season and his ERA was 2.06. He was as good as he had ever been.

Seaver was featured on the cover of *Sports Illustrated*, and a photo of him drinking champagne to celebrate the record and his 20th win appeared within the magazine. The game pulled New York (72–64) to within four games of Pittsburgh. As with past seasons, Seaver carried them on his back. On September 10, however, the Mets and Seaver's ERA suffered a major setback at Three Rivers Stadium in an 8–4 loss. Pittsburgh pulled away, and New York slumped to finish 82–80. Seaver beat Philadelphia on the last day of the season to finish 22–9 (.710), leading the league in victories. Thanks to the 8–4 loss at Pittsburgh, he did not finish first in earned run average but still maintained a 2.38 mark. In 280⅓ innings he led the league with 243 strikeouts in 36 starts, completing 15 (five shutouts). Always a picture of consistency, Seaver's 1975 ERA was the same as his earned run average between 1967 and 1975, an unreal 2.38.

In November Seaver and Baltimore's Jim Palmer in the American League won the Cy Young Awards. It was Seaver's third such honor. Only Sandy Koufax (1963, 1965, 1966) had won three Cy Youngs. Palmer, a future Hall of Famer, was generally considered the closest competition to Seaver for best pitcher in baseball.

"Jim Palmer is just an outstanding athlete and probably would have been a success in any sport," Tom recalled of his counterpart. "I've played golf with him a few times, and he appears as picture perfect on the golf course as he does on the pitching mound. He's really a very gifted person.

"Sometimes people compare us, because we're both right-handed, both have pitched about the same length of time, both have had good years together and some off-years together, both have been fortunate to win the Cy Young Award three times (twice in the same season), and both do broadcasting on occasion. . . . To me, it's a compliment to be compared with him, because he's been an outstanding pitcher for a long time . . . when you look at all of those 20-victory seasons."

A month after Tom won the 1975 Cy Young Award, Tom and Nancy's second child, daughter Anne Elizabeth, was born.

1976 turned out to be one of the most frustrating seasons in Tom Seaver's career. He was every bit as good as he had ever been, not dropping in effectiveness one iota. He was still the best pitcher in baseball. He threw just as hard, again leading the league in strikeouts with 235 in 271 innings. He extended his Major League record for most consecutive seasons with 200 strikeouts or more to an incredible run of nine. His average of 7.8 strikeouts per game was number one in the league. His sterling earned run average of 2.59, amazingly, *lifted* his lifetime ERA but was still awesome. He barely missed leading the league in that category. He tossed five shutout games and led the senior circuit in four specialized categories (adjusted pitching runs, adjusted pitching wins, based-out runs scored, and based-out wins). He again pitched in the All-Star Game, a 7–1 National League victory at Philadelphia.

"I faced Tom in the 1975 and 1976 All-Star Games," recalled Boston outfielder Fred Lynn. "In '75 I flied out in Milwaukee, but in '76 I homered off him, our only run in a 7–1 loss at Philadelphia. I think it's still on YouTube somewhere.

"Oddly, I never saw Tommy in Spring Training in Florida. I never saw Seaver when I was being recruited at USC. He had been there a number of years prior, but besides I was recruited by the football program. I was in the fold for football.

"In the spring of 1976 Tommy had won the Cy Young Award in 1975 and I was the MVP. We were both part of an alumni game. Coach Dedeaux took the alums. We had a really good turnout. Roy Smalley and a lot of big leaguers were on hand. It was like the highlight of USC baseball: perennial national champions, Dedeaux Field was almost new, and a galaxy of Major League alumni.

"Even though he was an SC guy, I would not go up to a pitcher. I did not talk to pitchers much because sooner or later you're gonna face 'em, and you've got to put your loyalty aside.

"Because Tommy had such a great personality, we all heard about him. Tom and Nancy Seaver were people you saw on TV a lot. He presented himself in a great way, a really professional manner.

"I never met Nancy Seaver but saw her on TV. They were very marketable, especially in New York. It's just understandable that others would get jealous; they had it all.

"I met Ron Swoboda a few times but never talked to him about Seaver. It's understandable that a position player could still learn the mental aspect of the game from a pitcher."

Tom Seaver should have won 22 or 23 games in 1976. He very well could have won his fourth Cy Young Award. In reality he won only 14 and finished eighth in the voting. A soft-tossing southpaw from Brea, California, named Randy Jones of the San Diego Padres, a figure barely recalled by history who also could not carry Seaver's dirty jockstrap, won the Cy Young that season (also finishing ahead of the great Steve Carlton). Seaver was the best pitcher in the game before Jones arrived and was still the best pitcher in baseball five years later when Jones was 1–8, on his last legs. Another great left-hander, Mickey Lolich, was Tom's teammate in 1976.

"Mickey pitched for the Mets near the end of his career, and it was always amazing to watch him work," Seaver recalled. "Nothing ever seemed to bother him. He'd ride his motorcycle to work, hang his helmet in his locker, get the uniform over that big belly, and go out and pitch. Whether it was Tuesday night, Thursday night, or Saturday night, he'd always give you the same game, and it was always a strong effort."

If in 1968, 1971, and 1973 the New York Mets failed to support their "franchise player," those teams were the Big Red Machine in comparison to the 1976 version. Incredibly, under manager Joe Frazier the Mets were competent that year (86–76, third in their division), but when Tom Seaver pitched they shut down their bats.

It looked as if Seaver would put together a season for the ages when he started 4–0, but over the summer the Franchise pitched seven games with four losses and three no-decisions, despite giving up less than two runs per game during this stretch. His ERA on the season at that point was a typically microscopic 2.13.

Seaver's lifetime earned run average was the lowest of any pitcher with 2,000 innings in all of baseball history. Greater than Cy Young, Christy Mathewson, Walter Johnson, Grover Alexander, Lefty Grove, Carl Hubbell, Bob Feller, Whitey Ford, Sandy Koufax, Don Drysdale, Bob Gibson, Juan Marichal, Jim Palmer, Catfish Hunter, Ferguson Jenkins, Gaylord Perry, Don Sutton, Steve Carlton, or any other hurler who had ever laced up cleats! By virtue of this singularly important pitching statistic, the record paid the most attention when gauging effectiveness, and further measured against a body of work, a career of longevity—consistency over many years, his stated goal—the argument could be made that Tom Seaver was not merely the best pitcher in baseball, he really was the greatest *ever*!

The only drawback to that argument was his own team's inability to score runs and pad his ultimate record for victories. Some detractors might point out that Seaver's postseason record was not quite as spectacular as those of Mathewson, Ford, Koufax, Gibson, and Hunter, but lack of runs cost him at least two victories, against the Reds and A's, in 1973. Ford, Gibson, and Hunter were all great clutch pitchers, but their respective teams supported them well in postseason competition. Ford, in particular, was given a plethora of runs to work with and was usually reserved for home games at the spacious Yankee Stadium by manager Casey Stengel in the 1950s.

Seaver was one of the highest-paid athletes in the commercial endorsement world. He wore Sears business suits, including one famous TV ad showing him pitching on the Shea Stadium mound in his suit, complete with his "drop and drive" and outfield wind sprints. He was a well-dressed, well-coiffed young man who dressed as an Ivy League prepster for most public appearances. He was like the athletes of old who wore a suit and tie off the field in an era in which athletes wore rags and sported long, scroungy hair. He was something from out of the Victorian age.

The birth of Anne Elizabeth eased his intensity of emotion. He called his entourage a "sorority house" and enjoyed taking his daughter to ballet practice. He read voraciously and with his brother, Charles, became an even greater devotee of the arts. Seaver was also a tremendous opera buff, a true New York sophisticate. He was a Renaissance man. Somehow, as he studied art, history, and dance, he was able to use this appreciation to ease the frustration he felt when his teammates failed to score runs for him in baseball games. His work ethic never wavered. He had a continued passion for pitching. He was also becoming a baseball philosopher.

"On the surface, baseball may seem like a simple game," he recalled. "Hit the ball, run the bases, score a run, pitch the ball so the batter can't hit it, catch it when he does.

"And on the Little League level, or America's sandlots throughout the long, hot summer, baseball is simple. And fun.

"But those of us talented enough or lucky enough to reach the Major Leagues quickly discover the harsh realities of America's national pastime. It may still be fun, but there's nothing simple about it.

"It's life under a microscope. Every move, both on the field and at the plate, is closely scrutinized while athletic strengths are applauded and weaknesses are exposed—and exploited."

He also came to grips with the fact he lacked teammate support over the years. "You also learn fairly quickly that you can't demand anything more from your teammates than their best. They're going to make mistakes behind you, mistakes that cost you dearly. They're also going to catch some of your mistakes. You have to live with both."

Seaver's position as a New York icon was further enhanced when the pop artist Andy Warhol created his portrait—six different renderings, each slightly different. A photo of Tom looking at them is telling. A traditionalist, he has a wry expression.

Money may not be the root of all evil, but as it says in the Holy Bible, the *love* of money is. Beginning in 1976, Tom Seaver achieved his stated goal of becoming a $200,000 ballplayer. He made $225,000 that season and the same in 1977. Seaver did not have a legion of detractors. In a sporting scene that included womanizers, drug addicts, alcoholics, criminals, reprobates, and all other forms of sinful human activity, his faults were minimal. However, his standards were not. He arrived, rosy-cheeked and innocent, a breath of fresh air infusing the comical Mets with good spirit and excellence. He led them to ultimate victory and, cultivated or not, achieved a reputation for uprightness and All-American good citizenship rarely if ever achieved in American sports.

From there, fault lines were detected. After all, he played in New York and was subject to all their tabloid investigations. So what had they found? Well, they found out he actually was faithful to his wife, and his teammates idolized him so much that some of them refrained from groupies as a form of homage. But they also found out that Tom Seaver offered no objection to being paid what he was worth. That Tom Seaver valued his privacy and protected his family. That Tom Seaver did not suffer fools. That Tom Seaver knew he was very intelligent. That Tom Seaver took losing hard. That Tom Seaver paid attention to his statistics and cared about his legacy. To the extent that these were faults, they were written about in the press. Few if any other athletes ever have had such "indiscretions" mentioned, but Seaver was so close to the ideal that they had to come up with some commentary.

While whatever "criticism" leveled at Seaver generally failed to stick because it was not valid, one aspect of the man resonated to some extent. Some called him "money hungry." Whether he was or not, he was a hard bargainer, as were his agents. He knew how much his contemporaries made. Seaver was less "greedy" than he was competitive; whatever Steve Carlton, Jim Palmer, Reggie Jackson, and Catfish Hunter made, *he* wanted to make. He was as good, better really, than any of them, so why not? He played in the Big Apple for a team that drew huge attendance and enormous TV ratings. The reason? Tom Seaver was the reason. He was the Franchise, their greatest all-time player, the face of the Mets, a true New York icon.

His $225,000 salary was a nice raise from his previous contract, $173,000, but the game had changed. Free agency, agents, an empowered players union, courts and arbitrators favoring players over "colluding" owners, creating skyrocketing salaries. This new world completely devastated owner Charlie O. Finley's great Oakland A's dynasty. In New York City, two former A's, Catfish Hunter and Reggie Jackson, had signed free agent contracts with Yankees owner

George Steinbrenner. Hunter made almost three times as much as Seaver. Jackson easily doubled the Met ace's pay.

"The sacred perpetual option that clubs had always claimed on players had ended," recalled Seaver. "The arbitrator, Peter Seitz, now recognized only a one-year reserve on a player contract.

"The big fish in that first draft was clearly Reginald Martinez Jackson. . . . Jackson was preeminent not only for his ability to grab headlines but for his ability on the field. . . .

"By today's ever-rising standards, the Yankees got a bargain in signing Reggie to a $2.6 million contract, spread over five seasons," which in those days "left people in awe." When Reggie courted the press, "It annoyed players, particularly after a losing game, to see one of their own conducting a press conference, evaluating one habit, and a lot of his teammates resented it. Although many individual writers are just fine people doing their jobs, there has always been a clubhouse mentality that they are 'outsiders' of sorts, peering into corners and seeing things they can't understand. So Reggie's courting these people, largely to enhance his own popularity, was not appreciated. . . .

"It's odd. When you think back, how the owners of baseball predicted that free agency would doom the game, how it would destroy the industry financially. What really happened was that people began to wonder how a ballplayer like Reggie Jackson could be worth a million dollars, and then they flooded the attendance gates to find out. Certainly other factors existed, but arguably free agency was the beginning of a 10- to 20-fold increase in the value of owners' franchises."

Reggie was great, Mr. October, but was he really a more valuable baseball commodity than Tom Seaver? No, he was not. Hunter? He was one heckuva pitcher, but the right-hander from North Carolina *was not as good as George Thomas Seaver.* Seaver wanted to be paid what he was worth. The Mets could not make the argument they were a "small market team." They were the darlings of New York. Steinbrenner had only recently begun to shift the allegiance the city had made to the Mets in the 1960s back to the Bronx Bombers.

In 1977 Seaver signed for a $225,000 base salary plus incentives. "But Tom Seaver's timing was bad," wrote Peter Golenbock. "When in the spring of 1977 he saw how high the owners were going to acquire some of the free agents, his deal began to look puny" compared to Jackson's.

"My welcome mat ran out with a guy I worked for named Donald Grant," said Seaver. "He didn't like me and I didn't like him. . . . [He had a] plantation mentality." Grant was already unpopular with the Mets because of his handling of the Cleon Jones incident, when he was caught in a van with a woman.

M. Donald Grant was the club's chairman of the board. He was a blue blood, a friend of future president George Herbert Walker Bush. Bush was the namesake of G. Herbert Walker, a nephew of Bush's father, U.S. Senator Prescott Bush (R.-Connecticut). Walker was one of the original owners of the Mets. When Seaver moved to Greenwich, and in particular when he and his family joined the elite Greenwich Country Club, M. Donald Grant turned up his nose at this upstart from Fresno, California, who had the temerity to think of himself as one of them.

"It was beneath my station," Seaver recalled of Grant's attitude.

He and Grant maintained a cool but professional relationship. They came to an uneasy agreement on a three-year contract, but when Seaver began to express a desire that he renegotiate so he could be paid money commensurate with his place in the game (i.e., as much as Hunter, Jackson, and the other new free agents), Grant accused the ex-Marine and conservative Republican from USC of disloyalty, calling him an "ingrate" and, most absurdly, "a Communist."

Seaver was also displeased when his club failed to sign any of the free agents on the market. They were a poor club by 1977, badly in need of offense. They failed to add any firepower to a lineup that for a decade had failed to support the great Seaver.

On the field, nothing changed. Seaver was the Opening Day starter for the 10th straight season, winning 5–3 over the Chicago Cubs. Five days later he completely shut down St. Louis, 4–0. On April 17 it was more of the same, a one-hit 6–0 shutout of Chicago. It was the 41st shutout of his incredible career. He had reached iconic status, not just with teammates (who worshipped him) or the fans (who also worshipped him) but among opponents, too. The name Tom Seaver was spoken in reverent tones.

But the usual doldrums came along, as they always did. In May he pitched brilliantly. His team slumped. The Dodgers, a first-place club and seemingly an unstoppable juggernaut in 1977, arrived at Shea. Seaver stopped them cold, but after he "worked my tail off," he left with the score 1–1 after nine innings in an eventual loss.

By the end of May the Mets were 11–20. Seaver had a winning record but was utterly drained. The city could care less. All attention was focused on the incredible show at Yankee Stadium, the infamous Bronx Zoo featuring George Steinbrenner, Billy Martin, and Reggie Jackson. Rumors of a Seaver trade were rampant. He was a "10 and 5" guy (10 years in the Major Leagues, 5 with the same club) who through collective bargaining could veto a trade or select which teams he was willing to be traded to. Seaver told Grant he would accept a trade to Los Angeles, Cincinnati, Philadelphia, or Pittsburgh. Jack Lang claimed a Seaver for Don Sutton trade. They negotiated with Sutton's agent, Larue Harcourt. Mets fans went crazy over speculation in the *Long Island Press*.

"Deep down, I don't think anything is going to happen," Seaver said. "Deep down, I don't want anything to happen."

On June 8 Seaver dominated Cincinnati, 8–0. Typically, he provided much of his own offense. He passed Sandy Koufax, striking out 10 to become number 13 on the all-time strikeout list with 2,397 while the Shea faithful chanted his name and gave him a five-minute standing ovation. Grant was on his feet with everybody else. Grant by this time had been given carte blanche by Mets management to do what he wished. He refused to negotiate. *New York Daily News* columnist Dick Young took the club's side, calling the ace "greedy."

"This was the way they were treating me after 10 good years with the club," Seaver recalled. "Why couldn't they have had the courtesy to give me a yes or no? They were trying to intimidate me if I didn't sign."

One day he just decided to speak to Joe McDonald face to face. "You know what he said to me?" said Seaver.

"No one is beyond being traded. I have one deal I can call back on right now."

"I was livid," said Seaver, who then used a swear word while daring McDonald to make the trade. "But he never moved. Suddenly it began to dawn on me. Everything I had done, everything I had meant to the team could go out the window with one phone call."

"When you have the best pitcher in the world, you sign him," Maury Allen wrote, adding that Grant is "cold and pompous."

Dick Young called Seaver a "clubhouse lawyer."

The trading deadline was June 15. On June 13 he beat Houston. It was his last game before the deadline. That night he had dinner with Koosman and Harrelson.

"I'm gone," he told them. "I don't think anything can save it."

On the 14th Seaver contacted Lorinda de Roulet, who had inherited the team from Joan Whitney Payson, in a final effort to save his Mets career. On the 15th an infamous Dick Young column hit. Seaver read it at the Atlanta Marriott. Young wrote an unattributed story claiming Seaver was influenced by Nancy. Mrs. Seaver, wrote Young, was jealous of Nolan Ryan's wife, Ruth, and the money paid Nolan by California Angels owner Gene "the Singin' Cowboy" Autry. Later Young admitted he was basing the column on rumor, not any hard fact.

"That Young column was the straw that broke the back," Seaver said. "Bringing your family into it with no truth whatsoever to what he wrote. I could not abide that. I had to go."

While the Young column was technically not coming from the Mets, Seaver was sure Grant had planted it there. This was not an uncommon practice. Melvin Durslag of the *Los Angeles Herald-Express* was known to do the bidding of certain patrons, such as Leo Durocher when he wanted to get back into baseball and Lakers owner Jack Kent Cooke during acrid contract talks with Jerry West.

The previous season, Seaver made his debut as a national broadcaster, doing color for the Championship Series won by Cincinnati over Philadelphia. He watched longingly as Cincinnati dominated, dreaming of pitching for a team that good. He interviewed and socialized with many Reds, among them Pete Rose and Johnny Bench. He loved New York, living in Greenwich, but he wanted to *win.*

"That's the number one goal you want when you play the game," he said. "That's what makes it all worthwhile."

Seaver demanded a trade away from New York. On the trading deadline of June 15, the Midnight Massacre sent Seaver to the Reds for Pat Zachry, Steve Henderson, Doug Flynn, and Dan Norman. His departure sparked sustained negative fan reaction. The Mets immediately became the league's worst team. The fans stayed away in droves. The Yankees won two straight World Series and completely recaptured Fun City. It ranks close to the sale of Babe Ruth from Boston to New York in 1920 among the worst trades ever. Fans and writers started calling Shea Stadium "Grant's tomb." It was also an unfortunate offshoot of the new economic dynamics of baseball: the immoralities of free agency, the union, agents, and greed.

Obviously it destroyed Grant's reputation in baseball. It also besmirched the memory of Dick Young, an acerbic yet respected columnist whose talents are lost to memory, replaced only by his foul role in a sordid event.

"He went turncoat against the players and went all-ownership," Koosman said of Young. Young's son-in-law, Thornton Geary, was given a job, and Young became a lackey. "We all felt he sold himself out. . . .

"And oh, yeah, he was on Grant's side. I felt the Mets bought him off. And Tom getting traded became Dick Young's legacy . . . he's never been forgiven for it in New York. . . . It was as if we lost our leader, our spokesman."

"I had no idea a player could have that much impact on a city, since Joe Namath, I guess," said teammate Lenny Randle. "And management was going to be the butt of the whole thing. It was a bad move."

"I don't know why the Mets would trade him," said Jon Matlack. "I don't think anybody could give many reasons that would explain what happened in '77, but nevertheless it did happen.

"Tommy went through a whole lot of hell, and to me much of it unwarranted. He couldn't get things worked out with the Mets, and all kinds of dirty stuff was being brought out in the press. And subsequently he was traded, and that was it. It was ridiculous, utterly ridiculous."

Oddly it was former detractor Ron Swoboda, now a TV sports personality in New York, who helped comfort Tom in his last moments as a Met, offering him condolences and sharing good memories of his ex-teammate's superstar career in the Big Apple.

On playing for one team throughout an entire career, Seaver said, "It didn't happen for Mays or Aaron or Rose or Jackson or even the guy the newspapers called the Franchise at Shea Stadium."

At Seaver's last news conference, he broke down, unable to finish. He had to write down a thank-you note to the fans, who always loved him. Tom Seaver may have been the most popular athlete in New York since Babe Ruth and Joe DiMaggio. Even such stalwarts as Lou Gehrig and Mickey Mantle had fought for fan approval at the beginning. Tom never heard a boo. From the most hardened, cynical iconoclasts in the sports world he engendered pure, unvarnished love and near-mystical appreciation of his talents. He was an iconic superstar. Teammates, management, and the press occasionally questioned how genuine he was; the fans never did. Had he chosen to run for mayor, the Senate, or the top job at Albany, John Lindsay or anybody else would have been toast, whether Seaver ran as a Republican or not. For a decade he rode astride the greatest city in the world like a Colossus. He was as big a celebrity as there was in 1977, a period of great angst and national malaise, when public figures were saddled by scandal. Tom Seaver was a rare hero in a world of villains. He was a guy whose fame was earned through honest, hard work and ability, not tainted in the slightest way by scandal or tabloidization, as was the case with the Yankees of the era. He was Tom Terrific. He was the Franchise. Now he was in Cincinnati.

12

THE HALL OF FAMER: 1977–1980

Tom Seaver was always a historian. "Funny thing was, after so many good years with New York, Mathewson was traded to Cincinnati, just like I eventually was," Seaver later wrote.

Tom Seaver's trade to Cincinnati began immediate speculation that the 32-year-old right-hander could win 30 games. It had been only nine years since Denny McLain had done it in Detroit. Every offensive slight of the Mets, the team that could not hit, was totally upended by the Reds, at the time still considered one of the greatest offensive powerhouses the game had ever known. All the countless 1–0 and 2–1 losses and no-decisions endured by the great Seaver would be replaced by 7–4 and 8–5 and 5–4 victories (on those rare occasions he was touched for three or four runs). He would win 30 in a season, easily get to 300 in his career. Given big leads he would coast to more shutouts instead of being forced to pitch tight in late-inning, low-scoring duels. He would be mentally freer to concentrate on the big picture.

Then there was his effect on the Reds. Winners of 108 games in 1975, back-to-back world champions the previous two seasons, they had done it with relatively mediocre starting pitching. Now they had the best ace in the game. They would challenge their old records, surpass the 1927 and 1961 Yankees, the 1970 Orioles, Stan Musial's Cardinals, and *The Boys of Summer* Dodgers for supremacy among all-time best dynasties.

Johnny Bench, Pete Rose, Joe Morgan, Dave Concepcion, George Foster, Ken Griffey, Dan Driessen—they were an unbelievably great team. Manager Sparky Anderson's praise of Seaver was so ebullient, so over the top, as to practically embarrass the right-hander. They had a Trojan connection in common. Seaver was a celebrated USC ace. Rumor had it Anderson's boyhood home once stood where home plate of the recently built Dedeaux Field now stood. Anderson was a USC batboy growing up. Sparky minced no words, predicting his new pitcher would win 30.

"This gives us the premier pitcher in baseball," Anderson said. "It will be like fielding an All-Star team. Seaver may be the all-time all-timer before he is through."

When the Ohio House of Representatives convened, the session opened with a prayer of thanks for the delivery of the great Tom Seaver. The reverend thanked the Mets for the gift, while angry protests roiled New York City.

Seaver's joining the Reds seemed just the shot in the arm they needed. Los Angeles was another powerhouse, a constant rival in the 1970s, and in 1977 they got off to an incredible start. By June they were leading in the West Division. Seaver's addition was immediately hailed as the equalizer. The Reds slumped a bit early in 1977, their place in the standings exacerbated by Los Angeles's winning streaks, but there was time to rally and win the West. Of course, this meant playoffs and World Series for Tom Seaver to star in. He would pitch in monumental games, defining the game, adding to his luster and place in history. He would go down as the finest hurler baseball had ever known.

Everything was in order when, on June 18, Seaver tossed a three-hit, 6–0 shutout at Montreal. He admitted a short time later when he appeared with Pete Rose on a panel of *The Mike Douglas Show* (along with *Star Wars* actors Harrison Ford and Carrie Fisher) that he had been extremely nervous. Asked how difficult it had been to leave New York, Seaver told Douglas it had been very difficult, that despite being Californians, he and his wife considered themselves "New Yorkers now." Then he talked about his first game as a Red.

"Joe Morgan came over after the first inning and told me to slow down," Seaver said. Seaver, given a chance to explain the predicament in New York, took the high road instead of demonizing Grant and the Mets. Rose was almost like a little boy, so excited was he to have a pitcher of Seaver's prowess on his side for once (not to mention not having to face him 60 feet, six inches away).

Morgan "could beat you in any one of three ways—with speed, with defense, or with the bat . . . he had an instinct, an ability to rise to the occasion," recalled Seaver of the Hall of Famer. "He knew when something needed to be done, and he'd do it. . . . He reminded me a lot of Lou Brock."

Now Seaver was teamed with his "rival," Johnny Bench, the man Seaver did not absolutely say was better than Jerry Grote, although Ron Swoboda stated when asked to clarify it that Seaver had said, "I wouldn't go that far."

"It was a pleasure to play with, and against, Johnny Bench," Seaver later wrote in one of his books about all-time greats. "He was the best all-around catcher I ever saw, truly an outstanding performer in every way. . . . Johnny was a pleasure to work with . . . he never got uptight and, as I discovered, had a great sense of humor."

Rose was "probably the best 'utility player' in history. . . . When he played third base at Cincinnati, at the time I was traded there, he took more balls at third during practice than anyone in the league, and he was an established superstar. . . .

"Pete wasn't a holler guy like most people think. He was actually quiet on the field. He hollered with his effort and his intensity."

Seaver also told a Pete Rose story in which he was standing with his buddy Tommy Helms around the cage during batting practice. For the amusement of the surrounding sportswriters, Pete leaned over and said, "Tommy, you know what the difference is between you and me? I can pick up the paper any day of the week and see what I'm hitting. You have to wait 'til Sunday."

Once Rose was 0-for-8 in a Sunday doubleheader. Seaver was showered, dressed, and headed out the tunnel at Riverfront Stadium to meet his family when "I heard the crack of a bat—somebody taking batting practice on the field." It was Rose. "Considering there are not many evenings during the season for a player to enjoy a barbeque or simply relax with his family, it is a telling story of Pete's dedication to his profession."

There were "two sides" of Rose as a person, but only one "Pete Rose: ballplayer . . . I don't think we ever saw an insecure Rose, one filled even briefly with self-doubt. And maybe the bravado was so genuine that it took him toward trouble, gave him a belief in himself so strong that he felt surely nothing bad could ever happen to him.

"I feel terrible for the misfortune that befell him after his playing days . . . he was my friend, my teammate. He paid a big price for his indulgences and his belief in his own infallibility."

Seaver chose to "dwell on the joy of Pete Rose on a baseball field. There was no one else like him in the years I played: a guy who couldn't run, couldn't throw, had no real position, had no power, and you couldn't win without him. He was a throwback, a fellow who could have played on the same field with Wee Willie Keeler and John McGraw, with Ty Cobb and Honus Wagner. He gave fans a chance to imagine what the game was like in baseball's 'dead ball' era, and he gave kids of average ability the message that with hustle and hard work, you could make it in the modern era.

"Perhaps the greatest tragedy of that sorry ending will be that in future years, instead of Peter Rose's name bringing a smile to faces, it will bring a sigh and a head shake, as though to say, 'Ah, Pete, you had so much going for you. What happened?'"

Seaver's trade engendered tremendous publicity, including a very positive *People* magazine cover feature of Tom and Nancy. The piece revealed that the Seavers had a dog named Boomer. Asked about New York he said, "That's all behind me now," but he could not resist a dig. "When they start writing rubbish about my family," Seaver snapped of the Young column, "that really makes me sick."

"I talk to Ruth Ryan about babies, not baseball," Nancy just said. Their image, Martha Smilgis wrote, was as "the squeakiest-clean couple in sports," adding, "Together they've popped up on TV on everything from Phillips 66 commercials to the Macy's Thanksgiving Day parade."

The *People* article showed Seaver doing a commercial for a Sears three-piece suit. Appropriately, after one Cincinnati merchant spotted Tom in his suit he cracked, "Seaver looks like a Procter & Gamble board member" (P&G was Cincinnati's biggest hometown company). There was also a photo of Tom and Nancy frolicking on the grass.

"Across the breakfast table in the Marco Polo Room of the Stouffer's Towers sits his wife, Nancy," at five feet, eight inches, 132 pounds, "blonde and chic in an immaculate white pantsuit," wrote Smilgis. She was holding down the fort at their $400,000-odd, seven-acre "dream house" in Greenwich.

New Greenwich resident Olympic champion Bruce Jenner's wife, Chrystie, met Nancy for the first time, complaining, "We're sick of being compared to Mr. and Mrs. Tom Seaver."

"I told her to be grateful," Nancy cooed. "It just means you appeal to the public."

"Nancy wouldn't have married me if she knew me better," Tom said, laughing.

The early years were "less glorious" for Nancy, who "wasted a lot of time waiting for Tom. I was afraid to go to movies alone and just sat around on the beach."

As she had said to Sara Davidson of *McCall's* after the 1969 season, she never "worried about predatory 'Baseball Annies' chasing her husband."

"The real groupies of baseball," she maintained, "are little 12-year-old boys."

"No one wants you but me," Tom cracked.

"That's what he thinks," she replied, adding, "When he finally comes home, his lawyer and agent get him first. I get him when he is tired."

"We want to have the same friends when we're 40," Tom said. Sarah, six at the time, was going back to her Greenwich Montessori school and, Nancy sighed, "doesn't really understand what getting traded means." Neither of their two children attended parochial school, though Nancy was raised as a Roman Catholic. Now, she jokes, "I go to doubleheaders instead of church on Sundays."

Johnny Bench joked, "He's welcome until he starts winning at poker," and offered to house-hunt with Tom before the Seavers found a suburban condominium. "Do I like him?" Bench asked. "I'm sharing my chewing tobacco with him." Pete Rose's wife, Karolyn, "mother hen of the players' wives," called Nancy early on to welcome her.

Both Seavers were already looking past baseball, wrote Smilgis, adding that Tom "is in fact a Ford Republican—though he alienated the Nixon administration by outspokenly opposing the Vietnam War." There was occasional talk about Seaver's future in politics.

"I started out with a young boy who has turned into a strong man" was the way Nancy described her husband's maturing. "I will have a career. I just found the guy I loved first."

"In some ways, Tom is the real stay-at-home in the Seaver family," wrote Smilgis.

"I could make a lot more money through endorsements," he pointed out, "but it would wreck my marriage. I don't want the children to accept that I'm always gone. Actually, I want roots more than Nancy does now."

On July 19 Seaver returned to New York City as a member of the National League All-Star team. He was received with a huge standing ovation by the 56,683 fans at Yankee Stadium, before the game and while pitching two innings in his league's 7–5 win. That was nothing compared to August 21 when he pitched against his old club at Shea Stadium. The Mets were a disaster, drawing flies. Every ounce and vestige of their glory days was gone, but the return of Seaver was a party, a carnival, with 46,265 people passing through the turnstiles. "It's like the old days," one Mets guard said wistfully. There are very, very few visiting players who ever garner big ovations in New York. Seaver was one of them.

Nancy was on hand. Seaver was very nervous. Harrelson visited with him before the game, but when he came to the plate, Bud was overmatched and struck out. Seaver managed to contain his emotions and pitched a brilliant game, winning 5–1. Each move he made was met with thunderous applause. The New York fans rooted openly for Seaver and the Cincinnati Reds. He struck out 11 and allowed six hits. It was a classic Tom Seaver effort.

"It's awfully nice to come home, but that way was no fun," he said afterward. "It was too emotional. I was aware they were up there at bat, but I tried to block it out of my mind, and now I'm awfully glad it's over."

Seaver encountered a new dynamic with the Reds. For the first time he had teammates who were stars, superstars, and celebrities in their own right. Seaver was as big a name as there was in baseball, but Bench, Morgan, and Rose were also huge stars. The three of them had won five National League Most Valuable Player awards in the previous seven seasons. In 1977 George Foster came into his own with 52 home runs and won the MVP award. Each had unique personalities. There were adjustments.

Seaver's teammates heard about his reputation, displayed on the cover of *People* and as one writer once put it, "the last of the non-adulterous ballplayers." Was this really true? Surely it was public relations. They discovered it was true. Seaver was one of the boys in most ways. He dipped and chewed tobacco. He drank beer. He played cards and engaged in elaborate practical jokes, always punctuated by his high-pitched laughter. He was already friends with many Reds stars from years of All-Star Games, as he famously cultivated relationships with the stars of other teams.

Bench was a notorious chick hound. Rose was technically still married but his dalliances were infamous and well known. Still, Seaver's faithfulness never resulted in recriminations. They went their way, he went his. Occasionally they hung out, took in a dinner or a social event, but when it came time to picking up on groupies, Tom made himself scarce. But Tom's sense of humor was still apparent. He was not raised in a cabbage patch. He was not naive. Once he pitched himself into a bases-loaded jam. Bench came out to the mound to try to relax the ace.

"Check out the blonde sitting behind the dugout," he told Tom.

"How do you think I got in this mess in the first place?" Seaver asked. Bench had to contain his laughter. Seaver gave a wry smile and proceeded to pitch out of trouble. The Reds pitchers, as with the Mets hurlers of past years, emulated, even idolized Seaver. They imitated his pitching style. A generation, 10, 20 Major League pitchers ranging from Jerry Koosman, Nolan Ryan, Gary Gentry, and Tom Hume to many others, copied Seaver's famed "drop and drive" style and approach. As in New York, some teammates took to refraining from adulterous sex as a paean to Tom Seaver. Foster, a devout Christian, welcomed a fellow Californian and moral man.

But there were personality adjustments. Bench was a tremendously proud fellow, as were his teammates. They were like the 101st Airborne Division when asked how they felt about being "rescued" during the Battle of the Bulge by General George Patton. They never felt they needed to be rescued, arguing they fought the Germans to a standstill on their own, thank you, and were prepared to hold out until victory was secure regardless of Patton's arrival.

When Seaver was presented as their "savior," Morgan and Rose pointed out they had gotten some hits off the guy and beaten him on more than one occasion. Seaver was asked about the great Bench. He loved Bench, but he also loved Jerry Grote. His response made it look as if he favored his old Mets receiver over the superstar, and Bench got his back up a little bit.

But Seaver's arrival in Cincinnati had a highly unexpected result. After his 6–0 shutout win in the first game against the Expos, everybody figured it would be like that. The Reds would score six, seven runs every time out, and Seaver would shut opponents down. The Reds would win games without mercy, catch Los Angeles, and coast to a third straight World Series victory. It did not happen.

Tony Perez, one of the great, underrated hitters of all time, had departed for Montreal. His bat was missed. Foster certainly made up for it, but incredibly, unbelievably, when Tom Seaver pitched *they did not score many runs.* It happened in a game or two, and everybody figured it was an aberration. Then it kept happening. It was not as bad as in New York, but Seaver had to pitch his heart out to win low-scoring contests, or he walked away with a no-decision after a superb performance. It was an old story. As Slim Pickens said in *Blazing Saddles,* "What in the wide, wide world of sports is goin' on here?"

The media wanted to know what was happening. Morgan was perplexed, trying to explain it. He said it was as if with the great Seaver on the mound they could relax; they did not need to score five or six runs as they so often did to give victory to the likes of Jack Billingham and Fred Norman. The next thing they knew, the score was tied 1–1 in the seventh and everybody was sweating it out, Seaver battling for every pitch, every out.

In the meantime, Los Angeles kept rolling. They slumped a little during the summer but never enough to blow their lead. Cincinnati finished in second place. The Reds won 14 of the 17 games Seaver pitched. Tom Terrific finished 21–6 overall. It was a great record, but it should have been even better! Certainly he did not fall in any way with the Reds. He was simply the best pitcher in baseball, that notion reinforced, his place in history utterly secure, but failing to make the playoffs was a bitter pill to swallow.

In 1977 Seaver tied the National League record for most one-hitters. When he tossed a three-hit shutout against Atlanta in September, he became a 20-game winner for the fifth time. He joined Ferguson Jenkins, Gaylord Perry, Jim Kaat, and Catfish Hunter as baseball's only active 200-game winners.

"If I can stay healthy and pitch five more years, I should win 300 with this club," he said.

Seaver's ERA was 2.58. He tossed 19 complete games on the year and led the league with seven shutouts. However, Steve Carlton of the East Division–champion Phillies (whose ERA was higher) and Tommy John of the National League–winning Dodgers (who won one fewer game) finished ahead of Seaver in the Cy Young balloting. Seaver was better. John in particular had no business finishing ahead of Tom Seaver in anything, but just as in 1976, Tom Terrific did not receive the award despite being the best of the best.

Sparky Anderson was asked to address the disappointment of losing the division race. It was crazy. His best stars did not perform at the same level in 1977 as they had in past seasons. Seaver came to town and was their biggest star, but as with the Mets, his teammates did not carry their end of the bargain.

"The whole club will be involved in turning it around, but Seaver is the basis for my feeling that we definitely will turn it around," he said when asked about 1978. "We're not going to fall behind right away, because we'll have the big honcho [Seaver] out there. He'll stop it. He won't let it happen."

Despite his new role as a Cincinnati Red, Seaver continued to be identified with the glorious sports history of New York City, in part due to events of October 1977. He was again tapped to be a member of the broadcast team, teamed with such luminaries as Howard Cosell and Keith Jackson, providing color commentary during the World Series between the Los Angeles Dodgers and the New York Yankees. As fate would have it, he was in the booth announcing during one of the greatest athletic events ever held.

In game six at Yankee Stadium, Reggie Jackson hit three home runs to secure victory. Mr. October had five homers in the Series. Seaver maintained his professionalism, but it had to be tough for him to watch. He and Jackson were in many ways the symbols of baseball in the 1970s, the faces of a new game with the passing of legends such as Mays, Aaron, Ernie Banks, and Juan Marichal. They had much in common. Each played at one of the two great college dynasties: Seaver at USC, Jackson at Arizona State. They were both articulate, both New York icons, both stars on the biggest stage, October heroes. But now it was Reggie basking in the limelight while Tom was forced to sit and watch. Still, it is Seaver's voice fans have heard for decades, as the game is one of the most replayed on the classic sports stations.

"The films of the moment show such happiness on Reggie's Teddy Roosevelt-look-alike face, such a burden lifted after his intense first season in New York" was how Tom remembered it.

The 1978 baseball season was a very strange and odd one. It did not comply with form. All hopes and dreams, all the expectations and aspirations that came with the June 1977 trade for Tom Seaver, went flat. The first sign came on Opening Day, when the Astros knocked Seaver out of the box early. He ended up with a no-decision in an 11–9 Reds win. His team scored 11 runs, and he did not get the win!

It was supposed to be a battle royal between the Reds and Dodgers, a grudge match of sorts to determine which of these giants were best in the West over the decade. Instead the Giants, as in San Francisco's unheralded club, took baseball by storm in the first half of the year. San Francisco had been a contender in the 1960s when Willie Mays, Willie McCovey, Juan Marichal, and Gaylord Perry were in their primes. But Los Angeles, led by Sandy Koufax and Don Drysdale, was always one step better. After Mays's departure, the veneer of respectability was stripped from the Giants. They were the joke of baseball, their stadium dirty, the city a corrupt laughingstock, a comic prop for a Dirty Harry movie.

The Dodgers and their city were glamorous. The Reds, representing a conservative town rejecting the 1960s and 1970s, produced excellence. But in 1978 the Giants rolled to a six-game lead by summer. The Dodgers and Reds were mired in slumps. It was as frustrating a season as Tom Seaver ever had. His great teammates, the superstars of 1975 and 1976, seemed to get old overnight. Seaver dispelled preseason predictions of a 30-win season, slumped early, recovered, but his team *could not score for him.* Every advantage supposedly gained by playing for Cincinnati was lost. They scored for the other guys, but not for Seaver. It was like 1973 or 1976 all over again.

"Seaver's getting old," said Houston pitcher J. R. Richard after the Astros defeated him on April 16. "You don't take anything away from him because he's a helluva pitcher and he was great in the past, but past years are past history."

"I got so jacked up over the winter," Seaver recalled. "I got so excited about our chances. I wanted to win the pennant in one day."

"Tom's the best I've ever seen at not taking one game to another," said his ex-teammate Buddy Harrelson. "But this must be a very difficult time for him."

Seaver was winless until May 6, then took matters into his own hands. On Friday, June 16, 38,216 fans arrived at Riverfront Stadium to watch Tom Seaver do battle with John Denny and the St. Louis Cardinals. The pitcher approaching the all-time record for most one-hitters finally tossed a no-hitter. He was not perfect, walking three, but Seaver struck out three in the 4–0 masterpiece. George Hendrick made the last out. Seaver's catcher that night was Don Werner, spelling Johnny Bench.

After the no-hitter, Nancy displayed "tears of joy. I burst out crying when Dan Driessen stepped on first base for the last out."

"I was aware of the possibility of a no-hitter in the third or fourth inning," said Tom. "If it happens, it happens, I thought. If you pitch long enough with enough good stuff, you are bound to pitch a no-hitter sooner or later."

He was 8–4, every victory hard fought, most of the losses and no-decisions symbols of frustration. His team struggled to stay close to first place. Would this be the spur they needed? It would not.

Seaver made his fourth straight and 11th of 12 All-Star Games, still another National League triumph, by a 7–3 score at San Diego. In the second half, the Giants finally faltered. Cincinnati eventually passed them, but it was Los Angeles under manager Tom Lasorda who surged to first place and a return to the Fall Classic. Tom Seaver pitched brilliantly in 1978. The frustration built up, game after game, as he gave it all he had only to lose or walk away without a decision. As in so many seasons throughout his illustrious career, he could have won 21 or 22 games. His team won 92 games but scored for Fred Norman or Bill Bonham, not Tom Seaver. His teammates were embarrassed, apologizing to him. Seaver understood, but just score runs. It was in vain.

He was all of 16–14, but his ERA was 2.88. He struck out 226 batters, walked 88, and allowed 217 hits in 259⅔ innings. Gaylord Perry of the Padres struck out 72 fewer hitters and his ERA was almost the same (2.73), but for some reason his mediocre team, as the Phillies did for Steve Carlton in 1972, scored runs for the man in bunches. Never had any team ever scored runs for Tom Seaver in bunches. Any hitter in the National League could have confirmed that Seaver was better, but Perry won the Cy Young Award. Polls consistently rated Seaver and J. R. Richard as the hardest-throwing pitchers in the league. While the "old" Seaver posted a 2.88 ERA in 1978, Richard—at the absolute apex of his career—finished at 3.11.

In the late 1970s Seaver hosted a TV program, *Greatest Sports Legends*. One of his guests was Ted Williams. During taping Williams went to dinner with Seaver and his parents, a big thrill for all concerned. Tom seemed to know everybody who was anybody, and not just know them but befriend them.

In 1979 John McNamara, a respected baseball man, replaced Sparky Anderson, the venerable future Hall of Famer. Anderson was very popular with both players and fans. The success he achieved with Detroit after he left the Reds indicated there was no better manager. The Reds were a mystery. Pete Rose was gone, an absolutely unthinkable concept. Money was too great a lure. A free agent, the Cincinnati native chose to become a Phillie, upping his contract from $750,000 to $3,225,000.

The question was whether Cincinnati was still the Big Red Machine, their great stars still stars, champions, or were they a club in transition, too old, over the hill, looking for an infusion of new life? Johnny Bench was 31, but the wear and tear of a career stretching back to 1967 was showing. Joe Morgan was 35 but a mere shadow of the two-time MVP of 1975–1976. The loss of Rose was an earthquake. He was no spring chicken, but Charlie Hustle was as great as he had ever been. The real star on offense now was 30-year-old George Foster, but the lineup was not nearly as imposing as it had been in their glory days.

Their undisputed ace was 34-year-old Tom Seaver. His 16 victories in 1978 looked to be a drop, but that was a fallacy. He was still the best. Jim Palmer was just about over the hill. Catfish Hunter sustained injuries that would end his career. Steve Carlton was still at his peak, as was Nolan Ryan, but the game was changing. A new generation of pitchers arrived on the scene: Ron Guidry in New York, J. R. Richard in Houston, Mike Flanagan in Baltimore. A golden age was slowly passing away. Free agency was chipping away at baseball. Stars were moving around. Tradition and loyalty were replaced by greed and suspicion. If Pete Rose could leave Cincinnati, anything was possible.

Seaver made $375,000 in 1979, but he was vastly underpaid in comparison with Rose and others. Seaver's reputation as a money man may or may not have been a valid one, but he could not be faulted for wanting to be paid as much as other athletes who were not as great as he was. It was to him a statistic just like ERA and victories, a comparison point.

Seaver was a super pitcher on a staff of journeymen, including starters Mike LaCoss, Fred Norman, and Bill Bonham (Seaver the Trojan and Bonham the UCLA Bruin). Tom Hume was now a closer, a spot he was well suited for. Hume was among the many pitchers who over Seaver's career revered the ace. Like others on the Reds, including Frank Pastore, Hume mimicked Seaver's style. He also copied his work ethic and even off-field habits. Hume was a talent but had struggled. Seaver advised that he become more aggressive, telling the young right-hander to become "an animal" on the mound and giving him a jolt of confidence.

The two-time defending National League champion Dodgers struggled badly in 1979. The Giants completely fell apart after their strong showing the previous season. On a veteran club past their prime, Seaver, Bench, and Morgan nevertheless realized they had a chance to make a run at it. Would it be their last shot at glory? It did not start out well, however, when Vida Blue and San Francisco knocked Seaver around in an 11–5 Opening Day loss. It was Seaver's 12th straight Opening Day start. The club played .500 ball throughout April. Houston was a talented young team off to a good start.

The odd malaise of Tom Seaver's career continued in 1979. Early in the season he was slowed by back and buttocks strains.

On June 9 in front of 36,207 at Riverfront Stadium, two ex-USC teammates squared off against each other. Montreal's Bill "Spaceman" Lee came in 5–3, but Seaver was 2–5. Outside of his lost 1974 season, when sciatica slowed him down, he had never struggled like this. Pundits wondered whether it was over, all that effort and exertion finally having taken its toll, but from that game on he was as good as ever. Seaver was brilliant, tossing a three-hit, no-walk, complete-game 7–1 victory over the Expos. His team was 32–26, two games out. Maybe for the first time, a Tom Seaver club was in contention despite him. His ERA was 4.62, but he was about to turn that around.

On June 15, Seaver beat Philadelphia, 6–3. On June 25, in what was the most important game of the season up to that point, Seaver and Houston's monster right-hander, the fireballer J. R. Richard, went head to head in front of 46,313 fans at the Astrodome. Seaver was back in form, evening his record at 5–5 with a masterful 2–1 win. From that point on, all talk that Seaver was past his prime was completely eliminated.

In the summer and fall of 1979 he was as good as he had been in 1969. The stakes were the same: a division on the line. He picked up and carried the Cincinnati Reds as he had done in New York in the pennant-winning seasons of 1969 and 1973. After losing to the Mets, 6–2, on June 4, Seaver was 14–1, the greatest win-loss run of his career. The Reds picked up their support for their ace but did not resemble their 1975–1976 champions. Mainly Seaver just stopped everybody cold.

In second place throughout the summer, the Reds fell behind by 10½ games on the Fourth of July, but the next day Seaver was the "stopper," besting Richard again. Slowly but surely, led by number 41, the Reds rallied. On August 28 they took over first place. They doggedly clung to a small lead in the last month.

"Pennant fever ran high in Cincinnati," wrote sportswriter Gene Schoor. "Cincinnati fans are among the most rabid, and loyal. They are also among the most vocal, and Tom Seaver became almost as much a hero in Ohio as he had been in New York. No city, of course, would worship Tom Terrific, could worship him, as much as did the city of New York."

On September 26 Seaver defeated San Diego's Randy Jones to put his club up by two-and-a-half games with just four days left. They hung on to finish 90–71, one-and-a-half over Houston.

As in other seasons, Seaver's final tally of 16 victories more likely should have been 20 or more. Alas, it was not, but his 16–6 record, resulting in a .727 percentage, was heretofore the best of his career. He still threw as hard as ever; perhaps his best fastball was not as consistent, but on his good days nobody could see any verifiable difference between Seaver in 1979 and the ace of a few years earlier. A testament to Seaver's remarkable career comes in the fact that his 3.14 ERA was, until then, the only time other than his injury-riddled 1974 campaign (3.20) when his earned run average was above 3.00. He featured a league-leading five shutouts.

He was as good as any starter in the senior circuit, among them Atlanta's Phil Niekro, his brother Joe (Astros), Chicago's Rick Reuschel, the Dodgers' Rick Sutcliffe, Carlton, and Richard. Cubs closer Bruce Sutter won the Cy Young Award.

"It was as though he came out of the woods with the ability to get everyone out," Seaver recalled of the unorthodox split-finger artist Sutter. "And he came out of nowhere, really. Nobody had heard of Bruce Sutter when he was in the minors."

As in most seasons, Seaver was as worthy of the honor as any other, lack of run support the principal reason he did not win. The Reds drew a healthy 2,356,933, many of those sellouts to watch Tom Terrific.

Now came the playoffs against the Pittsburgh Pirates. While Cincinnati's Big Red Machine of the mid-1970s was an offensive juggernaut, the Pirates' Lumber Company may have been every bit as daunting. Winners of 98 regular season games under charismatic manager Chuck Tanner, the Bucs were led by co-MVP Willie Stargell (tied with St. Louis's Keith Hernandez). Pops had picked up after the void left by Roberto Clemente's passing, the undisputed leader of his club, a dominant East Division powerhouse in the decade following the 1969 Miracle Mets. Stargell slugged 32 home runs with 105 runs batted in. Outfielder Dave Parker (.310, 94 RBIs), one of the best athletes in the world, was just as formidable. Tanner made liberal use of his bullpen, led by closer Kent Tekulve (31 saves). Pittsburgh was installed as the series favorite, but the prospect of Tom Seaver pitching the first and fifth games, as he did in 1973, seemed to even the odds. For years Tom Terrific had battled the great Pittsburgh sluggers, holding the decided advantage.

The first game, played before a packed house at Riverfront Stadium, goes down as one of Tom Seaver's underrated games. He was brilliant when he had to be against one of the best-hitting teams in years. In the third inning Phil Garner tagged Seaver for a home run. Omar Moreno tripled and scored on a sacrifice fly. In the fourth, George Foster's two-run home run evened things out. Seaver and John Candelaria settled into a pitcher's struggle.

For eight innings the great Seaver spread five Pittsburgh hits against five strikeouts and two walks, but in the bottom of the eighth he was removed for a pinch hitter.

"The scouting report on Stargell was basically 'Don't let him beat you; he can still do it,'" recalled the Reds' ace. "Before we had time to notice, it was over." Stargell did not beat Seaver, but he hit a three-run home run off Tom Hume in the 11th inning to win game one, 5–2. He was 5-for-11 (.455) with two homers to earn the MVP award of the NLCS while the dispirited Reds fell in three straight. Tom Seaver's chance at a third World Series was no more.

The Seavers maintained their farmhouse in Greenwich but also owned a home located right on a golf course in the Cincinnati area. Seaver had been a Cincinnati Red for a little more than two-and-a-half seasons but was probably already the greatest pitcher in the history of the club (just as he was indisputably the all-time greatest Met). His closest competition for this honor may have come from a fellow Fresno native, Jim Maloney.

In 1979, Yankee great Thurman Munson died in a private plane crash.

"I did have one long conversation with Thurman during a World Series when I was a broadcaster, but that was probably the only time we spent together," recalled Seaver. "It was always said about him, though, that he was a ballplayer's ballplayer and a terrific guy to have around. I'm sorry I never did know him better."

Seaver was 35 years old in 1980. It was a new decade and time for the ace right-hander to begin the approach toward retirement. He was focused on his legacy, namely the statistics that would define his place in history: the pursuit of 300 career wins, a lifetime ERA well below 3.00, his chase of Walter Johnson's all-time career strikeout mark, and his place at the top of the shutout list of active pitchers. He had three Cy Young Awards. Only Sandy Koufax and Jim Palmer matched that record. Seaver felt no reason he could not contend for a groundbreaking fourth award. He was unquestionably already a Hall of Famer, but how much higher in the pantheon could he go? Was he the best pitcher of his generation? The best since World War II? The best . . . ?

As great as the aces of the 1960s had been, a new crop of hurlers were putting up lifetime records that far exceeded those of Sandy Koufax, Don Drysdale, Bob Gibson, Juan Marichal, and Whitey Ford. Palmer was often the right-handed contemporary most often compared to Seaver, probably because they were on opposite sides in the memorable 1969 World Series and were both handsome, articulate men. But Palmer, a bit of a hypochondriac who always feuded with manager Earl Weaver, was a shell of his old self.

Baseball had changed. New methods of conditioning had taken hold. Strength training, which Seaver took to at the suggestion of USC classmate Jerry Merz and teammate Mike Garrett, was now commonplace. Nobody knew it at the time, but steroids may have already reared their ugly head a decade earlier than the Jose Canseco revelations would indicate. A look back at Brian Downing and Lance Parrish begs the question.

Philadelphia's Steve Carlton became a disciple of trainer Gus Hoefling, using unusual but highly effective methods to develop his legendary body strength. Nolan Ryan, who joined the Houston Astros in 1980, was already a legend. Don Sutton of Los Angeles seemingly snuck up on everybody and was still going strong. Tommy John of the New York Yankees underwent a surgery named after him, revitalizing his career better than ever. Gaylord Perry, once in the shadow of Marichal, was compiling gaudier lifetime numbers than the Dominican Dandy. Phil Niekro was an unsung star. These pitchers were all threatening to win the 300 games that Koufax, Drysdale, Gibson, Marichal, Ford, and Palmer all fell well short of.

Seaver might have lost some of the edge, the willingness to pay the price, but according to pitching coach Bill Monbouquette that never happened. He admired the superstar's work ethic, how much he ran, and said he never had to get on the pitchers to work hard. Seaver would do more than any of them and say, "Hey, let's go. We have a job to do here."

Monbouquette also recalled, "He wasn't afraid to throw the ball inside, or knock you off the plate. If one of your guys got drilled, he took care of business right away. And that's the way it's supposed to be. There wasn't any talk about it; it was just *done.*"

The 1980 season may have embodied just how important Seaver was to his teams over the course of his career. He was always "the man," the single player who carried the Mets and Reds. As Seaver went, so went his teams. The 1980 Reds were essentially the same team as the 1979 division champions, absent Joe Morgan (lost to free agency). Their 89–73 record was almost identical, but this time they finished third behind Houston and Los Angeles. The reason? Injuries, namely Tom Seaver's sore right shoulder.

Struggling with pain all season, Seaver was not as effective as in past seasons. As the summer played out, the hope was that their great ace would heal up, and when that happened, the team would make their surge. It never materialized. Instead, Tom Terrific suffered on the disabled list for the first time in his career (not even the sciatica of 1974 resulted in a stint on the DL), between July 1 and August 4, the heart of the season. Injuries to other key players prevented any one player from picking up the slack. Even the emergence of Hume—who gave all the credit to Seaver—as one of the best closers in baseball was not enough. Shortly before going on the disabled list, Seaver was beaten on June 30, 8–4 by San Francisco.

"I was recruited in 1976 and made my visit to USC along with Anthony Munoz, who was a baseball pitcher and later the All-Pro football lineman," recalled the pitcher who beat him that day, Bill Bordley. "That was the first time I met Tom Seaver.

"Rod ran me up to him. I found him very competitive, sure of himself, and gracious. Four years later, I pitched against him in 1980. I made my debut. I was with the Giants, and he was with Cincinnati, at Candlestick Park. He had a bad day. He was going through a rough spell. I was around 21 years old. I actually got a hit off him. I had not hit since high school with the DH. He's still throwing 97 miles an hour. He struck me out the second at-bat.

"After the game, Seaver came into our clubhouse. Willie Mays and Willie McCovey were both there. McCovey was retiring as I recall. Seaver shook my hand and kind of talked things over with Mays and McCovey.

"Ninety percent of his career was before I came along, but I was around with Nolan Ryan, Jerry Koosman, and pitchers who knew him, and they all said he was a step above the other pitchers.

"From what they said Seaver was just the best. I talked to Nolan Ryan about him. One of the things he said about Seaver was that he was, like Roger Clemens, a college pitcher who came into the league polished. I talked to Seaver, and he said he was not overpowering and had to learn how to pitch, so when he achieved his great fastball he was a complete pitcher.

"The biggest bonding thing I had with Seaver was that my draft was similar to Seaver's. I went in a special draft. Rod Dedeaux helped me with that, and from my situation did a very unselfish thing in helping me. In both cases the commissioner got involved. When I got in my situation, Rod called Bowie Kuhn.

"Seaver was a Marine and did all kinds of push-ups and sit-ups. He worked hard and was one of the first guys to really use weights. His delivery was absolutely symmetrical. He used his body perfectly in a very compact motion.

"If Tom knew you were an SC guy he would always come over and say hi; he'd give you a little extra attention. The last time I talked to him was at Rod's funeral in 2006. He said, 'You got one of the 205,' meaning one of the 205 games he lost."

Limited to 26 starts, five complete games, and one shutout, Seaver finished 10–8 with a 3.64 earned run average. He looked to be in trouble. Carlton won his third Cy Young Award in 1980, with Mike Schmidt named MVP while leading the Phillies to a World Series title. Sutton and Ryan were both outstanding. Seaver's chances at 300 lifetime wins and all the numbers defining his ranking in the pecking order of all-time greatness were in danger. However, the tall man they called Lefty (Carlton) had long before declared he would not speak to the media.

"In 1980 I was working for NBC, and I stopped by his locker before a game," recalled Seaver. "He raised a hand in midsentence and said, 'Are we talking as friends or in your capacity with NBC?' He needed to know where we stood." Carlton was "well liked by his teammates and is a generally likable person with a good sense of humor. I'm not going to judge him for his relationship with the press, but it's a pleasure to judge him on his pitching career, which has been . . . sensational."

"Mike Schmidt broke a lot of rules on the way to Cooperstown," including the "rules" of the free agent, said Seaver. "Just when we thought it was safe to say that Brooks Robinson had surpassed Pie Traynor as the best all-around third baseman ever, Mike Schmidt came along and complicated the argument. But that's what makes baseball so much fun."

13

THE 300-GAME WINNER: 1981–1987

THE 1981 BASEBALL SEASON REMAINS AMONG THE MOST FRUSTRATING and painful in the history of sports. It began with incredibly high hopes amid pure joy. A little-known left-handed pitcher from rural Mexico named Fernando Valenzuela lit up the baseball world when he began the season with an 8–0 record. He was seemingly unhittable, tossing shutouts and electrifying Dodger Stadium fans with his magnificent "screwball." The Dodgers' glorious ballpark had been built at Chavez Ravine, amid a certain amount of anger from the Mexican population claiming to be displaced in so doing. For years Dodgers crowds—as like the ones when Seaver attended games there in the '60s—were generally white males, business and Hollywood friendly, glamorous. The local Latino population had not adopted the team wholesale until "Fernandomania."

But in June the union forced a strike. The teams played no games between July 11 and August 10. They finally returned and after a delayed All-Star Game finished the "season." All was lost, however. Technically, Valenzuela finished 13–7, winning the Cy Young and MVP awards. The Dodgers won the playoffs and beat the New York Yankees in the World Series. It was all one big asterisk, the numbers skewed, the fans screwed over, the meaning of the whole thing nebulous.

This sad set of circumstances left nobody, *nobody*, a bigger loser than Tom Seaver and the Cincinnati Reds. Seaver's long, glorious career nevertheless is punctuated by incredible, unbelievable injustice. His consistent lack of run support, with very few exceptions, ran from the late 1960s all through the 1970s, encompassing his tenure with both the Mets and Reds, costing him games that pitchers on oft-hard-hitting teams (Carlton's Phillies, Sutton's Dodgers, Palmer's Orioles, Ryan's Angels, Catfish Hunter's A's and Yankees) were able to win with more support. Career statistics and milestones were all made much more difficult to attain.

It absolutely cost him the Cy Young Award in 1971 and very well could have cost him the honor, or at least a closer vote, in 1976, 1978, and 1979. Seaver was robbed blind of the 1969 Most Valuable Player award given to San Francisco's Willie McCovey when two writers decided to keep him off the ballot because they did not think pitchers should even be eligible for it.

But perhaps no other season heaped so much injustice upon a single player and his team as in 1981. A championship, a World Series perhaps, a 20-victory season, a Cy Young, perhaps an MVP award—all lost to the strike. The Reds voted for it like everybody else, so they were forced to stew in their juices amid further recriminations of what might have been.

Seaver increased his off-season throwing and hit the weights hard in 1980–1981. In an effort to counteract age and increasing physical ailments, he placed greater emphasis than ever on his physical conditioning. He always ran in the off-seasons, but that winter he ran harder than ever. He entered the campaign amid questions as to whether he was over the hill at 36. He answered that by putting together what may have been his greatest season. Perhaps he was not as spectacular as in 1969, when he turned the baseball world upside down; or 1970–1971, when he threw so hard and was so dominant; or 1973, when he put a mediocre club on his back and near-single-handedly carried them to the seventh game of the World Series. He was a different pitcher in 1981 than he had been then, but like John Elway when he propelled the Denver Broncos to consecutive Super Bowl championships in the late 1990s, Seaver may have been better than ever. He had, like the fine wines he cultivated such a taste for, grown better with age.

The 1981 Reds made some major breaks with their Big Red Machine past. Johnny Bench spent more time at first base than behind the plate. The team of Dave Concepcion and George Foster was as much now a team of Ray Knight and Dave Collins. McNamara probably did his best managerial job scrapping a successful club out of a team of disparate elements. Seaver, Mario Soto, and Tom Hume starred on a club that now did it with pitching.

The opener was an absolute classic: Steve Carlton and Philadelphia versus Seaver in front of a huge crowd at Riverfront Stadium. The two aces departed with the score tied at one, neither with a decision. The Reds pushed a run across in the bottom of the ninth to win it, 2–1. Five days later Seaver beat San Diego, 7–1. On April 18 Seaver lost to the Cardinals. On May 8 Seaver beat Don Sutton, now with the Houston Astros, in a masterful 4–0 shutout. On June 11, a sad day in the game's history, Seaver went the distance to beat the pitcher he was traded for, Pat Zachry, and the Mets, in a complete-game 5–2 win at New York. He was 7–1 with a 2.06 earned run average.

On that same day, Silvio Martinez of St. Louis outdueled Fernando Valenzuela, 2–1. Valenzuela was 9–4 with a 2.45 earned run average. He was 1–4 in his last five decisions, his ERA up from 0.50 on May 14. The Dodgers' record stood at 36–21 (.632). Cincinnati was 35–21 (.625). The vagaries of the schedule meant they had played one fewer game, which if they had played and won would have placed them in a flat tie. June 11 was the last day before they struck.

Because of the length of the strike, baseball commissioner Bowie Kuhn decided that the season would be divided into two halves. The team records of June 11 now represented the "first-half champions." The second half would be a "separate season." An extra playoff would be added between the two "winners." The Reds needed to win the second half in order to make the postseason.

When the strike finally ended, the All-Star Game was held in Cleveland on August 9. Valenzuela got the start for the Nationals and was succeeded by Seaver, who allowed a run in his one inning. The National League prevailed again (they had lost once since 1971) by a 5–4 score. On August 12 Seaver got his first start of the second half. Los Angeles roughed him up and won, 8–5. The winning pitcher was hard-throwing young right-hander Dave Stewart, who had potential but had not reached it yet. Seaver was 7–2. On August 18 Seaver beat Carlton again, 3–1. The Reds were battling for first place in the second-half West. The Dodgers faltered, but Houston, led by Tom's old teammate, Nolan Ryan, was hot. On September 2 Seaver beat Montreal, 7–0, but it was a struggle. The Reds trailed the Astros. Seaver picked his team up as he had so many times in past years, leading them to 11 wins in 13 games down the stretch.

On September 17 Seaver pitched one of the best games of his life, a spectacular 10-inning, 1–0 triumph over the Giants at Candlestick Park. He beat the Padres and the Braves down the stretch, but it was not enough. The Reds (31–21) had a better record than the Dodgers (27–26). Even San Francisco (29–23) had a better second-half mark than L.A. But Houston (33–20) was the second-half champion.

Overall, the Reds were 66–42. That was four games better than Los Angeles and six better than Houston. Both the Reds' first-half and second-half records would have won the East Division (won by Philadelphia and Montreal). Cincinnati's .611 percentage was the best not just in the league but in all of baseball (Oakland's 64–45 record was the best in the American League).

Somehow, someway, in a world turned upside down, in which black was white and white was black, in a season in which *a playoff series was added,* the Reds were the best team in baseball and left out of the postseason. They were not the only club that "wuz robbed." St. Louis featured the best overall record in the East Division and was rewarded with a trip home.

While the greatest injustice met the Cincinnati Reds, a similar injustice was Tom Seaver's "reward." At the very least, denied postseason glory at age 36, he deserved some awards. Valenzuela was mediocre after starting 8–0. He was 5–7 after that, all of 4–3 in the second half when his team tanked. He finished 13–7 with a 2.48

earned run average. Seaver led the league in wins at 14–2 with a 2.55 ERA. Had the players not struck, he surely would have won 22 or 23 games. Seaver's .875 percentage was the best since Roy Face of Pittsburgh in 1959.

Valenzuela was voted both MVP and the Cy Young Award. He was spectacular early in the season. Nobody could deny that he brought a community together in L.A., but it was a politically correct vote, as much affirmative action for his role as a Mexican as it was for great pitching. Fernando was a wonderful story and worthy fellow, but he was not in Seaver's class.

Valenzuela and Seaver both received eight first-place and six third-place votes. The difference was Valenzuela's eight second-place votes to Tom Terrific's seven. Had the Reds won either of the halves (the votes were all compiled prior to postseason games), Seaver almost assuredly would have won the Cy Young Award and very likely the Most Valuable Player trophy as well. It would have been redemption for the awards denied him in 1969 and 1971. He had to settle for his fourth selection to *The Sporting News* National League All-Star team (1969, 1973, 1975, 1981) and his second Comeback Player of the Year award (1975, 1981).

The utter unfairness of it all was not relegated to awards. Dave Concepcion, who had played all of 106 games for the 1981 Cincinnati Reds, was awarded a $5 million free agent contract. Seaver toiled away for $375,000. If Ron Swoboda was right in saying that Seaver was in it for money back in 1969–1970, that he cleaned up and got more than his fellow Mets, that dynamic most definitely turned around in a big way. By standards of the day, the free agent era, Seaver was one of the most underpaid athletes on the face of the earth!

For the great Tom Seaver, it was all grist for the mill. Time and time again, for all his records and accolades, he was given the short end of the stick. He should have been held to the same level of acclaim as in his 1969 fame. Everything he had been that year he continued to be for 12 years thereafter, but the serendipity, the magic, the sheer mojo was too often replaced by the failure of the world to truly recognize his greatness to its full extent, by bad luck, poor support, always something. Seaver just smiled and suffered it, satisfied he did all he could and grateful for what he had, rather than bitter over what had eluded him, fair or unfair. He was like the quiet heroes who face bias in academia and the media. They just smile, accept it as a fact of life they cannot change, and soldier on, convinced that in the end the truth shall make ye free!

In 1982 Seaver told attendees at a Boy Scouts event, "Concentration, hard work, and dedication. No one can lift your weights, do the sit-ups or any of the other work for you. I know it sounds egotistical, but Mets manager Gil Hodges didn't make me. Neither did my father or pitching coach Rube Walker. I am the person most responsible for my success."

Perhaps for the first time in his career, in 1982 Seaver was overpaid at $375,000. However, despite his awful record, it was not, as Reggie Jackson said in 1973, "the real Tom Seaver." He was beset by physical ailments. It all got turned sideways in Spring Training when the Reds' ace was sidelined by a lingering respiratory infection that sapped him of strength, will, and, of course, the ability to train and condition. No pitcher in the game—maybe in history—needed to run, strengthen his legs, and work so hard in order to be successful. It was everything to Seaver and had been since his freshman year at Fresno City College.

Seaver did not make a start until mid-April, never achieved effectiveness, and had to call it quits on the year by August 15 with an aching right shoulder after a game with Houston, when he faced a mere three batters.

Tom Hume was injured. Outside of Mario Soto the staff was bad. The veterans all got old fast, the youngsters—what there were of them—failed to deliver. Attendance in the poststrike year was abysmal, the club finished last in the division at 61–101, and everybody was happy to go home.

Seaver was 5–13 with a 5.50 ERA. About the only positive was the arrival of young catcher Dave Van Gorder, a fellow Trojan (Bench was almost through by then). When Los Angeles outfielder Ron Roenicke, a UCLA man (like Seaver and Van Gorder a former Alaska Goldpanner), came to bat, Dodgers announcer Vin Scully got a big kick out of telling his listeners that "it's a Trojan pitcher and a Trojan catcher with a Bruin at the plate." Los Angeles media personality Bud "the Steamer" Furillo called Tom "the noblest baseball Trojan of them all" during an interview in which one Fresno native called to remind the man once given the keys to the city and named "mayor for a day" after his rookie year of a hometown prep rivalry featuring the "pig and the little brown jug."

Despite a bad season, Seaver maintained his sense of humor and reputation as a clubhouse cutup. When some small-time radio reporters came by, Seaver waited until they turned on their microphones, then let out a torrent of expletives in order to "shock" them. On another occasion he was filming a TV commercial with a German director. Seaver started barking orders in his best *Hogan's Heroes* "German."

"You vill fix ze light, yes, Verner?" he asked, clicking his heels together. "And zen you vill do ziss right."

Once somebody asked him for help with a crossword puzzle. What, he was asked, was a five-letter word for pig? Looking at Johnny Bench and winking, Tom spelled out "B-E-N-C-H." He also went out of his way to mentor young players, especially pitching prospects.

"Tom Seaver is exactly like me," Pete Rose said. "He's tough and he's hard-nosed. If it's the right thing to do, he'll put you right down on your ass. Tom will always take the time for the younger ballplayers."

Seaver was little more than a month shy of his 38th birthday when the season mercifully came to a conclusion. It was a difficult time. Should he retire? Why continue if he could no longer pitch? Seaver had watched in horror while Willie Mays hung on, so obviously beyond the game, in 1973. He had it all. He could relax with Nancy, spend time with his family. So many athletes cite that as the reason to retire or quit or move on, but Seaver truly wanted to do just that. His future was laid out for him: a lucrative, rewarding career in national broadcasting. Others vied to get him to run as a Republican for office. His name in the past had been bandied about as a manager or even baseball commissioner, a job that was ready to open up in a few years.

But Tom Seaver was a competitor who wanted to go out on his own terms. Seaver had been underpaid for years, watching while teammates such as Pete Rose and Dave Concepcion, contemporaries such as Reggie Jackson and Catfish Hunter, all cashed in huge in free agency while he did not. There was, he believed, one last payday that would justify his career from a monetary standpoint, but more important, he still had statistical goals.

Seaver was chasing Walter Johnson in the all-time strikeouts category. In recent years Nolan Ryan and Steve Carlton had passed him and were in the process of passing Johnson—and each other several times—before Ryan eventually ran away with the record. Others would pass Seaver, but in 1982 he was still in very exclusive company.

He was still the active leader in shutouts and wanted to protect his status against such worthy competitors as Ryan, Carlton, Bert Blyleven, and Don Sutton. Most important, of course, were the 36 tantalizing victories he still needed to get to the magic 300 mark, that glorious number separating the great from the most elite of the great. Many fabulous pitchers had fallen shy of it. Given run support over the years he would have had it already, perhaps chasing down Warren Spahn (363), Christy Mathewson (373), and Grover Cleveland Alexander (373). They were out of his reach, but if he could get to 300 it would make up for the six years he was denied by poor support or a players' strike the chance of winning 20 games. His lifetime earned run average was 2.68, a statistic that almost defied belief.

Seaver looked about the baseball landscape, trying to determine his next move. His age, his bad year, and his salary, now viewed as a lot of money by the Reds, made him expendable. Cincinnati looked to trade him. Seaver was in control of his destiny. Los Angeles might have been a good destination—his home state, his old USC stomping grounds. But the Dodgers made a huge transition that season. They finally made the break with their old infield of Steve Garvey, Davey Lopes, Ron Cey, and Bill Russell in favor of a youth movement. A 38-year-old, probably washed-up pitcher did not fit in their plans. In 1965 they drafted Tom but offered a pittance that he turned down. In 1966 Buzzie Bavasi was too busy dealing with a Sandy Koufax-Don Drysdale holdout to draft Seaver, although he later claimed he got a bid in but Major

League Baseball failed to register it in time. If ever a player was born to be a Dodger, it was Seaver.

But Seaver was also a New Yorker. He identified himself and his wife as such on many occasions, even after the trade to Cincinnati, as he said on *The Mike Douglas Show* in 1977. He had a public in New York, a history, as much as any New York athlete. His departure had been acrimonious, but in 1983 the Mets were under new management. Nelson Doubleday was their owner, Frank Wilpon their president, Lou Gorman the vice president of baseball operations, Frank Cashen their general manager, and George Bamberger (Baltimore's pitching coach in the 1969 World Series) their manager. Gone was M. Donald Grant. Ironically, four years after vilifying Seaver for asking to renegotiate his contract, columnist Dick Young actually broke his, jumping from the *Daily News* to the *New York Post.*

The Mets were desperate to recapture lost glory. The 1977 Seaver trade was a disaster with a capital D. Their attendance was poor, their performance atrocious. The Yankees completely recaptured the city. Seaver convinced them he experienced a myriad of injuries in 1982 but was healthy. "The comeback" was effectuated via a trade for three virtual unknowns. Seaver could live in his Greenwich home during the season, making the old commute to Shea Stadium. Seaver "cashed in" with an $850,000 salary and figured he would achieve his career milestones and then retire a New York Met. A fairy tale ending.

Cashen tried to revive the Mets by purchasing several veteran stars. He was given a big checkbook to take full advantage of the free agent era. Mets fans were delirious. The media welcomed Tom back.

Onetime Mets hurler Al Leiter was a fan. "In '83 I was in junior high school. Tom Seaver did an appearance for the baseball coaches of New Jersey down at the Cherry Hill Hyatt," he said. Leiter was there, and "I was just looking up to him in complete awe."

"Tom Seaver has come home, and we are all of us young again," wrote Stephen Hanks. That spring, Seaver was effective despite sustaining nagging injuries. Seaver worked with young Mets Ed Lynch, Craig Swan, Carlos Diaz, and Jesse Orosco but was concerned about the club's bullpen. He knew he would not be able to complete games as in the past. The game had completely changed. The closer was now a key element. Rollie Fingers won the 1981 American League MVP award in that role.

"No pitcher can win and no team can win without a good bullpen," said Seaver. "Look at Rollie Fingers, Bruce Sutter, Rich Gossage, and Tom Hume. Those are the people who put the game away for you. And if I can go seven innings most times, I'd be happy to turn the game over to someone else."

Seaver's fastball was no longer the 99-mile-an-hour heater of the 1960s and 1970s. The Mets hoped he could still hop it up there at 93, but he was clocked at 87. "I can throw just as hard," Seaver quipped. "The ball just doesn't go as fast."

When the club broke north, they were given a big welcome home dinner the night before the opener. Tom was the honored guest, feted by an adoring public. The next day it was like old times, waking up in Greenwich on game day, only now his daughter Sarah Lynn was old enough to be a fan, while younger child Anne was concerned mostly with crayons. His family came in from California to cheer him on. Seaver arrived at Shea, where the excitement was palpable. A capacity crowd was on hand, and the banners unfurled: "WELCOME BACK, TOM TERRIFIC."

Seaver was given a huge ovation when he went to warm up. He had a nagging leg injury from Spring Training. Bamberger was concerned that it might act up and had Ed Lynch warm up alongside his veteran ace in case Seaver could not make it. Seaver pretended to hurt his leg, having Lynch thinking he was the substitute starter, incurring the wrath of fans there to see Seaver. Seaver just laughed. When the public announcer said, "Batting ninth and pitching, now warming up in the bullpen, number 41," the crowd went ballistic. Mets PR man Jay Horowitz asked him to walk in from the bullpen on the field instead of through the tunnel as he normally did, so the fans could serenade him.

"And then I started walking down the right-field line, and I realized what Jay was talking about," said Seaver. "The emotional reaction of the crowd . . . I have some pictures of that day. It was a terrific memory."

Amid a Diamond Vision highlight film of his great Mets career, Seaver went out to face ex-teammates Pete Rose and Joe Morgan of the Phillies. New York governor Mario Cuomo and mayor Ed Koch were on hand.

"It was a tremendously emotional moment," recalled Seaver. "I have so many wonderful memories here. It was great to be back but so emotional that I still had the jitters for two innings."

Rose was the first to face him. Seaver made no effort to fool him, raring back and throwing fastballs past him for a strikeout. The crowd exploded. He looked like the Seaver of old, his 87-mile-an-hour fastball suddenly, by virtue of pure adrenaline, coming in around 93 or 94. Morgan walked and made it to third, but Seaver got the great Mike Schmidt to get out of the inning. He threw all fastballs in the first two innings.

It was a replay of past classics: Tom Seaver versus Steve Carlton, a baseball game featuring four future Hall of Famers and one (Rose) who should be. He and the Phillie superstar matched zeroes through six innings. Rose in particular could not touch him. Seaver told Bamberger his leg was bothering him and came out after six innings. The Mets won, 2–0, but Tom did not get the victory. Still, it was an incredible homecoming.

"I knew it would be emotional, but I didn't think it would be that emotional," Seaver said. "It wasn't easy keeping cool, but I was pitching and I had to keep all that emotion bottled up. If I wasn't pitching, I would have cried."

"He's not the blower he was when he was here the first time, but he made some great pitches, about what you'd expect of a Hall of Fame pitcher," said Rose, who added he could not recall striking out twice in a game and that he had missed only two pitches in Spring Training. Morgan added that Seaver was "smarter."

But after that, none of it worked. The 1983 Mets were abominable. Bamberger was fired, Frank Howard brought on board, with no improvement. Veterans Dave Kingman and George Foster were past their primes. At the end of May, Seaver was struggling at 3–4 but was pitching effectively. It was the same old story: lack of support.

"When I look back at my career, I won't measure my success by the numbers," Seaver said when asked about the effect of years of bad offensive support. "And I'll never wonder what it would be like pitching for some other team. I've been through all that. And that's playing the numbers, too. . . . When I lose, it's not losing that bothers me as much as the *way* I lose." Seaver said he believed it was his job to pitch so well that he could make up for mistakes and the failure to score.

In June, Seaver pitched in a classic pitchers' duel with John Candelaria of Pittsburgh, but his bullpen blew it in a 2–1 loss. "This team has not hit well at all, and it seems that when Seaver is in there the hitting is at its worst," said new manager Frank Howard, echoing an old story.

As the season progressed, Seaver pitched valiantly, as in a hard-fought 5–4 win over the contending Expos. Slowly, the face of the Mets began to change. Young players such as Darryl Strawberry were coming into their own, and Keith Hernandez was obtained via a trade. The 1986 world champions were slowly being built, but Seaver was their past, not their future.

"In 1983, it wasn't easy being the Mets," said Hernandez. "You can read a losing team a mile away on and off the field, in the dugout, everywhere," he noted, adding that the team was "expecting to lose." Seaver called them the "Stems" (*Mets* spelled backward).

On August 21, legendary *Los Angeles Times* sports columnist Jim Murray tackled one of his greatest subjects, the superstar pitcher Tom Seaver. The title, "Almost Too Good to Be True," said it all, for Seaver was, even if apparently past his prime. As with his 1962 column on Willie Mays, it was the best meeting the best, a master writer given free rein to write about a larger than life subject. He began the piece exactly as he had with the Mays column 21 years earlier. "The first thing to do with a person like Tom Seaver is to establish that there is one." Seaver was a real-life inspiration from the boys' adventure stories of his youth. "You have to make sure he didn't just walk in off the pages of *A Lad's Pluck* or *How Frank Merriwell Saves the Day at Yale.*" Indeed Seaver was one of the rarest of all athletes—the absolute superstar, one of the greatest of the all-time greats yet possessing the intelligence of the secretary of state, "collar-ad good looks," and the All-American background of . . . Frank Merriwell.

Murray described a man almost like a statue made out of flesh and blood, the greatest pitcher in the game, arguably as good as Sandy Koufax, all the while comporting himself as if running for the U.S. Senate.

"You have to find out if he isn't a public relations hoax," Murray wrote of him. Many had thought early on he was "too good to be true," but by 1983 he was nearing the end, and indeed, he was that good, all the way around. Murray made the usual Seaver comparison with Christy Mathewson, one of baseball's earliest heroes, credited with giving the game respectability. Seaver never got thrown out of bars and did not pay alimony to two wives. It was probably not a coincidence Murray chose to write of Seaver in 1983, the same year he wrote of Walter Alston and Vin Scully, two other paragons of good character. It was an off year for the ace right-hander as he neared the end. His performance on the field was not what made him a feature story. Murray saw in the pitching great the same noble characteristics.

"What's a goody like him doing with a 97-mile-an-hour fastball?" he asked. His skin was clear. He did not even spit. With his tools he should look more "like Burleigh Grimes than Christy Mathewson." Seaver, Murray wrote, was that rarest of athletes, the true New York sports icon who "awed" the Big Apple, a place in awe of only the most elite of the elite, whether that be Babe Ruth, Dwight Eisenhower, or John Glenn. They called him "fearless, faultless, a hero out of the dime-novel era. The guy who would rescue the orphan from a burning building, warn the train trestle was out, capture the runaway horses with the heiress in the carriage. Thrash the bully. Tom Swift and his Electric fastball."

Seaver was as "motivated as a monk," who instead of discussing "booze [and] broads" enjoyed the merits of finger pressure and proper wrist snap. Now back with the Mets after a sojourn in Cincinnati, Seaver was closing in on 300 career victories. Murray displayed as much honest to goodness admiration of Seaver as any athlete he ever wrote about.

On September 15 Seaver lost a pitchers' duel with Neil Allen of St. Louis, 2–1. On September 20 he battled Pittsburgh, 2–2 through eight innings, but came away without a decision in a New York win. He was 8–14 but actually encouraged. He pitched relatively well in 1983 and decided not to retire. He told writers the young talent reminded him of the 1969 club, expressing the hope he could be part of their bright future.

They finished last in the league in attendance and last in the East with a record of 68–94. There were no highlights. There was, however, just a touch of hope for Tom Seaver. On a club that gave him no support offensively or defensively, he still managed a 9–14 record that could have been 14–9. His ERA of 3.55 was respectable. He pitched two shutouts.

"I know just where we are going in 1984, and what we're going to do to get there," Seaver said at season's end. He was certainly right. In 1984, Dwight Gooden emerged as a pitching sensation equal to the great Seaver of the late 1960s. Strawberry would become a star. Hernandez would capture ultimate glory. The Mets would contend for two years and, in 1986, win 108 games en route to a world championship and a place among baseball's greatest teams. But on the evening of January 23, 1984, Tom Seaver's chance to be part of this revival, to ride toward retirement in a cloud of glory with the team of his destiny, would end.

On that day he attended a sports convention in Chicago with one of his sponsors, Spalding, the iconic manufacturer of athletic equipment. While he was mingling with fans and buyers, the last vestige of "Mets magic" was being allowed to leave like unclaimed baggage.

The Chicago White Sox were for the most part a joke franchise. They won their last World Series in 1917, but that victory was completely overshadowed by the Black Sox scandal of 1919. They played in a dilapidated ballpark in a bad part of south Chicago. The Cubs were the toast of the Windy City. Owner Bill Veeck was forced to implement clown acts and crazy promotions in an effort to draw fans. In 1979 it all went awry when fans were invited to an ill-advised Disco Demolition Night, which turned into a riot forcing cancelation of a game when disco records were destroyed, causing fans to storm the field in a dangerous manner.

The club had the worst uniforms in baseball history, at one point wearing shirts that looked worse than softball outfits, even short pants. On the field they were usually also-rans but occasionally contended. From this perspective they were better than the Cubs, but not good enough to wrest popularity from the Northsiders.

But the club had a savvy general manager named Roland Hemond. In 1981 Eddie Einhorn and Jerry Reinsdorf bought the White Sox for $20 million. The club hired a sharp, young former bonus baby named Tony La Russa. La Russa, once a "can't miss" prospect, never succeeded as a player but was a law school graduate who used his smarts as a manager.

In the early 1980s the White Sox acquired veterans such as Carlton Fisk and Greg Luzinski. In 1983 they captured the American League West. Chicago did it the old-fashioned way, with great pitching in the form of LaMarr Hoyt, Richard Dotson, Britt Burns, and Floyd Bannister. Young stars included Harold Baines and Vern Law. But a playoff loss to Baltimore was a bitter pill to swallow. The thinking in Chicago was that the club needed one last piece to complete a puzzle that could result in a world championship in 1984.

While Tom Seaver schmoozed with sporting goods people at Chicago's Hyatt Hotel, Hemond, Reinsdorf, and Einhorn were studying teletypes. It was a list of protected players. The New York Mets had listed a number of names. Seaver's was not among them. The White Sox and Oakland A's were both eligible to select an unprotected player as compensation selections.

"When I first checked the list, I noticed Seaver's name wasn't included," said Hemond. "I went over the list once more and then again. Then I went over the list alphabetically. Seaver's name was not there.

"In our opinion, Tom Seaver was clearly the best player available, and we notified the baseball commissioner that we were selecting Seaver. We selected him not only because our scouts assured us he was still a top-notch pitcher, but because he is the sort of class guy we want on the Chicago White Sox."

Hemond had detailed reports on Seaver in part because he had scouts watching National League games in 1983 anticipating they would be in the World Series. Seaver had pitched a number of games against the contenders they scouted, and "they were mightily impressed," Hemond said, adding that if Seaver had been with Chicago in 1983, "we'd be celebrating a world championship instead of a division title."

The reaction in New York was nothing less than pure shock. For the second time in six years, management had allowed their ace to go to another club. The Mets apparently did not think he would be selected by a club as pitching-rich as the White Sox. The A's were focused on rebuilding with youth and not in a position to pay an aging veteran a big salary.

Hemond, however, was not willing to take that chance, selecting Seaver before the Athletics could pick the California native. "He is a great one," Hemond remarked. "And this was strictly a business decision."

But the selection of Seaver did not create a done deal. Einhorn kept calling Seaver's room at the Hyatt, but there was no answer. The Chisox brass had dinner at the Hyatt and decided to "stalk" the pitcher, figuring he might be contacted by another club. After that, anything could happen.

"We called Tom's room several times, and finally at about 10:30 p.m. he answered the phone," said Einhorn. Tom asked them to come to his room, and "we were flabbergasted when he asked us to produce some identification. It did not occur to us that Seaver wouldn't know us. Quite an embarrassment. Then, of course, he invited us to his suite.

"Now, this entire thing was a most delicate situation. Here was this truly great star, Tom Seaver, and we had to tell him that the Mets, a team that he had given his heart and soul to for more than 11 years, had not protected him, and the White Sox had selected him.

"He was in turn shocked, hurt, and angered, and after a few minutes, his first angry reaction: 'The hell with it all. Maybe I'll just retire.'"

The White Sox executives then told Seaver about the advantages of pitching for Chicago. The club was favored to win the division and perhaps the World Series. The designated hitter rule might help him win more games. He could pursue the coveted 300 victories he undoubtedly wanted very badly.

"When we ran through all these possibilities, he really listened and calmed down, and then we started to discuss a contract with him," said Einhorn.

Seaver promised to negotiate in good faith. The news hit the baseball world like a thunderbolt, the biggest of the 1983–1984 off-season. Seaver returned to New York and held a press conference.

"I got more upset as things went along," he said. "I am not here to blame the Mets. They just made a stupid mistake. When I came back here from Cincinnati, I expected to end my career in New York with the Mets. I still do not understand why I was not protected.

"What the Mets did was to disrupt my family life. I did have some idea I wasn't going to be protected. Bill Murray of the *Daily News* told me I was not on the list. But I really didn't believe it. I had pitched well the entire year, and I had not missed a start. I was 9–14, but with some help it could have easily been in reverse. Now I don't know what I'll do."

Seaver had an uncomfortable talk with Frank Cashen. Afterward he said he was glad his wife was not there because "she's got an Irish temper" and would not be "as kind as I have been."

Seaver's main trouble was not the baseball consideration. The White Sox had money and could pay him well. He would be with a contender, but he was so set on the fact he had brought his family back to Greenwich to finish his career at home that Chicago was hard for him to embrace. Sarah Lynn was 12, Anne 8. That said, his agent negotiated a sweet contract that would make it worth his while. Offers for Seaver to get into broadcasting were made, but Nancy began to see the value of becoming a White Sox.

Sarah, asked about disruptions to her horse and riding lessons in Connecticut, simply asked, "Will it be best for Daddy's career?"

"As a parent, you wonder if you're doing things correctly, if you're giving your children the right ideas," Seaver said. "I got tears in my eyes when I heard Sarah's reaction."

For a month Seaver and the White Sox went round and round. Seaver's phone bill was more than $1,000, but they eventually agreed to increase his existing $850,000 contract with a no-trade clause, incentives, and a club option in 1987.

"I sense an immediate feeling of winning here, the same kind of attitude we had in New York in 1969," Seaver told the press. "I talked with one of the players, who said that feeling of winning didn't just start last year, but was here a few years ago before that. I got the impression that all the guys wanted to keep playing in October last year. The White Sox had a taste of winning then, but not the whole mouthful. I hope I can help with that."

Seaver the baseball fan began to see other advantages. He had never been in Comiskey Park or Boston's Fenway Park and wanted to explore being an American Leaguer. "Maybe after all, the Mets did me one helluva favor," Seaver added, saying that the move to Chicago afforded him a strong shot at getting to 300 wins. He said he had always liked Chicago when he played there with the Mets and Reds, even though the Cubs had been fierce rivals. Seaver said he did not feel that way about all the cities he traveled to.

Seaver's arrival in Sarasota, Florida, for Spring Training resulted in tremendous press excitement. Seaver was matched with the legendary Carlton Fisk, a future Hall of Famer. Reinsdorf said, "I can truthfully say that seeing Tom Seaver in a White Sox uniform has to be one of the greatest moments of my life. I've never experienced anything like it." He added that Seaver was "a living legend, a certain Hall of Famer, whose exploits have filled the record books and sports pages for more than 18 years," and that "it just gives me goose bumps every time I look at him in uniform."

Seaver pitched well in the Grapefruit League, impressing the media, but he was more interested in impressing his new manager and teammates. "What this game is all about is simply proving things to your own teammates," he said.

LaMarr Hoyt, the reigning Cy Young Award winner, was given the first start of the season. This was one of the only openers Seaver had not started, but Hoyt was one of the best pitchers in baseball. The South Carolina native beat Baltimore, 5–2. On April 8 at Chicago, Seaver took the mound against Detroit.

The 1984 Tigers were one of the greatest teams in baseball history. They were off to one of the hottest starts of all time, and Seaver was unable to stop them. Kirk Gibson touched him for a two-run homer, and Seaver was a 7–3 loser before 20,478 fans on a cold, rainy day. Seaver was disappointed, describing his performance as "ragged."

Facing another powerhouse, the Brewers, in his next start before a capacity crowd in Milwaukee, Seaver was touched for three runs by Robin Yount and company—a decent performance but another loss. He told the writers he felt he pitched better, but "still, it's no fun to lose."

Seaver's next start drew more than 30,000 to Fenway Park. The fans sat through a long rain delay. When the game started, Seaver was masterful in dealing with the tough Boston lineup. Lacking his old overpowering stuff, he mixed speeds with location to emerge a 5–3 victor.

On May 9, Chicago and Milwaukee went 25 innings. Seaver was called on in relief, his first such appearance since 1976, and ended up the winner when Harold Baines hit a game-winning home run. Seaver's appearance came in the completion of a suspended game, and he ended up with two wins in the same day when he started the second game of the doubleheader, a 5–4 win over the Brewers.

Seaver captured his fourth win in a row with a 2–0 victory over Kansas City. The weather was warming up, and so was he. It was his 277th career win and 57th career shutout.

On May 19 Seaver lost to Toronto, 1–0. Seaver and Fisk worked well together. The great catcher knew Tom lacked the old heat and now guided him using guile, often utilizing intentional walks to their benefit. On June 5 Seaver tossed another shutout against the tough Angels and Reggie Jackson, 4–0. Seaver gained revenge for his loss to Detroit in April when he beat Jack Morris, and then he defeated Baltimore, 3–2.

In July Seaver beat Cleveland, 3–0, then the Red Sox, 7–0, and on August 4 beat Milwaukee, 7–3. He was 11–6. The White Sox struggled, but Seaver was their ace and one of the best pitchers in the American League. However, his teammates all seemed to falter. La Russa asked Seaver to address his new club. He told them they were playing like "contented fat calves." The season wound down, a disappointment. When all was said and done, Seaver was their brightest hero, finishing with an excellent 15–11 record. He could have won 20! Sometimes the bullpen blew his leads. Chicago was

74–88, a terrible letdown, but Seaver looked forward to 1985. He needed 12 wins to reach the magic 300 mark. He had 10 complete games.

"I said in Spring Training that if I won 15 games, I would be very happy," Tom said. "At this stage of my career, 15 wins and 225 to 230 innings should make me very happy." Seaver added that after he got to 300 wins, "I'll decide just how much longer I want to go on. I have been told my mechanics are so fluid that my arm would be fine at 45."

Seaver felt "fortunate to have spent most of my career in New York, which is a two-league town. It's meant there has never been a shortage of American League coverage in my newspapers or a lack of American League action on television." Seaver said he always watched AL action when the schedule allowed, and in Chicago he caught White Sox games at night in the hotel because the Cubs games were always played during the day. Overall he had "a lot of exposure to the American League."

A great player was great in any league, he felt. "A Yastrzemski, a Brooks Robinson, a Carew, any of them would have been big stars in the National League," he assessed.

Seaver also had the chance to compare Carlton Fisk with previous battery mates Johnny Bench and Jerry Grote. Few if any pitchers threw to such great catchers in their careers.

"It may have had something to do with the Vietnam War," Seaver said of baseball's apathetic fans of the early 1970s. "Anything steeped in the aura of 'establishment,' such as the national pastime, was out of favor with young people, who questioned many values the nation had taken for granted. Baseball was not attracting their attention. Attendance was stagnant, and the game wasn't being marketed with much imagination." He felt Carlton Fisk's 1975 World Series home run helped move fans back to the game.

"In his 40s he was still the best catcher in the league. We all call him Pudge," but few were "better conditioned" than Fisk.

Seaver did not merely bring pitching skill to Chicago. He brought a great sense of humor and highbrow intellectualism, which met each other courtesy of one of his best practical jokes—one that almost backfired. The man who quoted from Dickens,

Faulkner, Hugo, Chaucer, and Voltaire was also a devoted opera buff. One of his favorite tenors was Placido Domingo. They began a friendship.

Once Seaver invited Domingo to Comiskey Park. The opera star knew nothing of baseball customs. Tom told him it was a tradition for guests to be a "mascot for a day." He directed the great Domingo to don a huge white "sock," the uniform of the club's mascot. Domingo thought it odd but figured "when in Rome . . ."

Seaver held his laughter long enough to direct Domingo onto the field, where he was the object of delight in the eyes of the White Sox players. At around that time the man hired as the real mascot arrived to discover his white sock "uniform" was missing. He went out to the field, saw the "imposter," and directed the stadium police to apprehend Domingo. Seaver was doubled over in laughter observing this charade and was barely able to identify himself as the true culprit when explicating his friend from this sticky situation.

"I faced him with the White Sox," recalled Fred Lynn, who in the 1980s was with the California Angels. "He was not the same pitcher. He adjusted his style and was not the guy I remembered from 1976 when he threw everything hard and down, which was perfect for me because I was a lowball hitter. When I faced him again his fastball was more up in the zone with a lot of off-speed stuff. He threw breaking balls and had added something weird, a forkball or circle change.

"Power pitchers have to make adjustments. The only guy who could do it until he was much older was Ryan, and even he developed a weird pitch. The smart ones, the good ones, the Hall of Famers, make adjustments, just like the hitters, and it's a constantly evolving process.

"I had the opportunity during the 1999 All-Star Game in Boston, when the All-Century teams were announced, to work with Tom when we were representing Chase Manhattan Bank. I personally heard him speak in public, and he was very buttoned down, very polished, and I recall thinking, 'Here's two SC guys doing okay.' SC prepared us for the next stage.

"I saw Tom at the Rod Dedeaux funeral in 2006. It was sad, but there were hundreds of Trojans and we all told stories."

On November 17, 1984, Tom Seaver turned 40 years of age. That off-season, Hemond made an unpopular trade, sending Hoyt to San Diego for Ozzie Guillen and some other players. Seaver, who was paid $1,136,262 in 1985, arrived for Spring Training in tip-top physical condition. He knew he needed to work extra hard at his age. With Hoyt gone, Seaver was given the Opening Day start after going 4–1 with a 1.57 ERA in five Grapefruit League starts. It was his 15th Opening Day start, breaking another record previously held by Walter Johnson.

"It's just great if you win that first day, lousy if you lose," he said. He already held the National League record for Opening Day wins at six. He needed 105 strikeouts to overtake Johnson on the all-time list. For decades Johnson was number one at 3,509. That record seemed as impossible to surpass as his 110 career shutouts and 417 victories, but incredibly Seaver was not the only one to pass the record. Steve Carlton and Nolan Ryan also passed it, and Bert Blyleven was on their heels, as well.

"You reach a point in your career that you can't go back and reflect on the historical importance of such things because you lose perspective of what your everyday job is," said Seaver. "After you've been playing a few years you can look back. But who knows, maybe I'll have another Opening Day. I'm not finished yet." In front of 53,127 fans on a cold day at Milwaukee, Seaver pitched brilliantly in a 4–2 win.

"The big thing about being the starting pitcher in the opening game is to get the club on the right foot," Seaver said afterward. "That's the way I've always felt, to keep the game close so our club can possibly win the game." As for breaking Johnson's record, he said, "I'm very proud of it. It's terrific when you talk about something that no other pitcher in the history of the game has done. If we had been here now as a losing club, I wouldn't feel that way."

In his second start, April 15 at Boston, Seaver was effective, leaving with the score tied at three in an eventual 6–5 Chicago victory. On April 26 he stopped the surging Yankees, 4–2, at Chicago. As the season progressed, Seaver was marvelous. He beat Baltimore, 5–2, and Kansas City, 4–3. By June 17 he had his club sitting atop the West Division. Seaver, who was apparently still so good that "blind people come out to hear him pitch," struck out Reggie Jackson, the man who said it 12 years earlier during the 1973 Series, twice with men in scoring position in a 4–2 win over California.

Chicago slumped badly in July, losing eight straight. Kansas City surged to the front of the division. "We're so bad that Seaver lost his bid for his 296th win three times because our offense produced one, three, and three runs when he was pitching," commented Tony La Russa. Seaver shut out Cleveland, the 61st of his career, 1–0. On July 30 he beat Boston, 7–5. He was 11–8 with a 3.02 ERA. It was his 299th career win.

Seaver's next start was August 4. Where? Yankee Stadium in New York City. It was not the stadium where Tom forged his greatness, but it was the same city, in front of many, many of the same fans. It was, of course, the place where baseball greatness was most perfectly exemplified. It was a Sunday afternoon, and 54,032 fans came out. One of the rarest sights in all of sports occurred that day. All of Yankee Stadium cheered wildly for a pitcher facing the Yankees.

The crowd stomped and chanted, "*Sea-vuh! Sea-vuh!*" Tom was one of the few visiting players ever to receive huge ovations in New York, as he did when he returned with the Mets.

In the third, New York touched Seaver for a run when ex-teammate Ken Griffey singled home a man. In the sixth, Chicago pieced together four runs on five hits. As the game progressed, Seaver gained strength, as he so often had over so many wins. He was finishing strong, leading 4–1 while the New York fans pleaded for him to win his 300th game in front of them. He allowed a single and a walk in the ninth, but La Russa left him in. When Don Baylor flied out, Seaver won his 300th game by the same score as his uniform number, 4–1. In the dugout afterward, Seaver agreed with White Sox announcer Don Drysdale's question that it was the "biggest thrill" of his long career. "I think so," replied Tom.

Seaver finished the 1985 campaign with a 16–11 record and a 3.17 earned run average. He was the best pitcher on his team, undoubtedly still one of the best pitchers in the game of baseball. Seaver earned a $223,762 attendance bonus in 1985. He was second among active pitchers with 304 wins (Carlton had 314) and number one with an unbelievable 2.80 earned run average in 4,682 innings over 19 seasons. He had 61 career shutouts, also number one among active pitchers, with 3,537 strikeouts (third on the all-time list at the time). His winning percentage of .614 was third best among active pitchers. On November 17 he turned 41.

"You go to the ballpark and you see the pitcher standing there in the middle of the diamond," recalled Seaver of his great career. "He stands on a hill like a king with the grass of the infield cut away all around him. He's the center of attraction. He gets the third out and walks comfortably off the mound toward the dugout with the knowledge that he was better than the other side. Everybody else runs off the field, but the pitcher walks, lingering in the eye and the mind of the fans.

"It looks like fun.

"But think of what it took to get him there. If he's any good. If he's going to be better than the other side consistently and for very, very long, he had to be willing to give it an awful lot of his life. Maybe it's more than you're willing to give."

Bob Costas said Seaver was "always a thinking man's ballplayer."

On going to Chicago: "I wasn't especially happy about it, and I was more than just a little apprehensive about starting over in a new league at the age of 39," Seaver recalled. "But I look now at my two seasons with the White Sox with a special kind of fondness—happy that I could find success in a new league at an 'old' age, and delighted that I could experience the south side of Chicago and all that made it special.

"Chicago is one great baseball town! If only all teams could find a way to bottle the baseball formula from the Windy City, the game would go on to even greater prosperity."

In 1986 Seaver was paid $1,132,652. Finally, he was being paid commensurate with his greatness. Free agency had been in place for over a decade. Many stars were being paid for past performance. Seaver had never been a free agent, so he never cashed in on the big bucks as others had. But the system had completely changed the dynamics of sports economics. Cable television was now in place. Attendance was up, the game's popularity gaining year by year despite strikes and the mercenary nature of the players. Unquestionably, Tom Seaver and the 1969 Mets had played a major role in reversing the trend of poor attendance and lack of enthusiasm prior to their "miracle" year. The great pitcher was deserving of this reward.

But on the field, everything turned around. Seaver looked old, and his team floundered in the first half of the 1986 season. In June he was 2–6. Chicago was going nowhere fast. The White Sox certainly wanted to unload his salary and start over. Chicago looked to trade him, most likely to a contender looking to add veteran leadership down the stretch drive. In a pennant race, perhaps the great Seaver could muster one last . . . miracle.

The most obvious scenario seemed to be the Mets. Seaver's prediction at the end of the 1983 season came true in a big way. They contended in 1984 and 1985 and by 1986 were a fully formed juggernaut. Now under manager Davey Johnson, they were not the old Mets of Hodges and Seaver, underdogs playing over their heads. They were a team of young and veteran stars and superstars, a complete ball club with no weaknesses. The 1986 Mets would go all the way. They were also one of the most rambunctious groups of hard-partying, obnoxious, overpaid men-children of all time, their story detailed by Jeff Pearlman in *The Bad Guys Won! A Season of Brawling, Boozing, Bimbo-Chasing, and Championship Baseball* . . .

The Mets would win 108 regular season games. They did not need anything else. A Tom Seaver, family man, icon, may not have fit in on this club of testosterone-filled studs. The 1986 Mets were not the kind of guys to pay fealty to the idol of Tom Seaver as Tom Hume and the Reds pitchers had done in Cincinnati.

Mets general manager Frank Cashen was poised to make a midseason trade. However, Johnson—on the losing end to Seaver in the 1969 World Series—vetoed the idea, and for whatever reason, the trade was not consummated. Seaver instead ended his career with the Boston Red Sox after being traded for Steve Lyons on June 29, 1986. Thus did Seaver find himself part of one of the most dramatic stories in baseball history, one intertwined with the Mets.

Seaver's old skipper in Cincinnati, John McNamara, managed the Red Sox. Winners of 95 games and the American League title, they were led by a young right-hander who looked to be the next

Tom Seaver. Roger Clemens was a hard-throwing right-hander out of the University of Texas. Winner of his first 14 decisions of the season, he was having a year comparable to Seaver's in 1969, Ron Guidry's in 1978, and few others.

Clemens struck out 20 men in a single game and was practically unhittable, finishing 24–4 with 238 strikeouts and a 2.48 earned run average.

"Roger is an intense competitor, as all the great talents are. . . . In his intensity lies his greatness," Seaver said. He addressed the question of somebody striking out more than 20 batters.

"Many say no, but with expansion and the dilution of talent, and the likes of superb power pitchers . . . it could happen," he felt. "One day it could all come together—everything will work: every slider will be on the black, every fastball will flash past the batter—and maybe, just maybe, we'll have a new record."

Third baseman Wade Boggs was one of the greatest hitters of all time. Boston went wild over the Red Sox. For Tom Seaver, it was all quite strange. Here was a New York icon wearing the uniform of a Boston team, playing in front of fans who despise anything that has to do with New York City. But Seaver was such a respected figure, on and off the field, that he was welcomed with open arms. He started 16 games and was effective enough on a championship club, helping them win some key games during a tight pennant chase.

Seaver, still a baseball fan after all these years, understood the unique traits of all the teams, towns, and fans he played for.

"I had the opportunity to pitch for both of these 'jinxed' teams," he said of Chicago and Boston. "Pessimism is the common thread that seems to run between Chicago and Boston. From the sportswriter to the fan paying the price of admission at Fenway, Comiskey Park, or Wrigley Field, it's the train of thought that says, 'What will it be this year? We will be teased but in the end, the final step—the championship of a World Series—will escape us.' The histories of the organizations dictate this frustration."

On August 18 in front of 20,492 fans in Minneapolis's Metrodome, Seaver bested Frank Viola, one of the best pitchers in the game, 3–1. He pitched 8⅔ innings and struck out seven Twins. It was his last victory.

On Friday, September 19, he lost to Toronto in front of 40,494 fans at the old Exhibition Stadium by a 6–4 score. Seaver pitched four innings and surrendered three runs. His record on the season was 7–13, his ERA 4.03. Seaver was 5–7 with Boston, sporting a respectable 3.80 ERA since coming over from Chicago.

But a knee injury made him unavailable for the postseason. The prospects of the great Seaver winning one last huge October game, carrying still another team to glory, was not to be. Instead, he was a mere sidelight of one of the most exciting, eventful months the game has ever known. First Boston took on Reggie Jackson and the California Angels. Leading three games to one, the Angels seemed to have it won when relief pitcher Donnie Moore was tagged for a ninth-inning home run by Dave Henderson in Anaheim. Boston won in extra innings and then savaged the dejected Angels in two blowouts at Fenway Park.

Now it was Boston versus New York, the great rival cities of American sports, with Seaver wearing a Boston uniform. Before game one at Shea Stadium, another of the rarest of rare events occurred—a standing ovation from the Mets fans for Seaver. He tipped his cap, the announcers noted the event, and that was that. When actual baseball was played, Seaver was sidelined.

"So I was in no man's land, except for pulling for my teammates and watching in amazement as the gods of baseball once again looked over their shoulders at Shea Stadium to see that all was well in Metsville," Seaver recalled.

"It bears repeating again: Many Red Sox fans feel a curse has followed the franchise all these years, ever since Harry Frazee sold Ruth to New York to cover his debts. . . . They have had more heartbreaks than any franchise should have to endure. . . .

"As is always the case when Boston plays New York in anything, there are plenty of fans from the visiting side in attendance and plenty of rivalries on the field. Shea was jumping."

Perhaps had he been available it would have played out differently. Certainly the Red Sox came as close as a team can get without winning. Maybe it would have been Seaver on the mound in game six, trying to close it out instead of Calvin Schiraldi.

"So resigned to defeat were the Mets . . . that the electricians working the Mets' scoreboard accidentally flashed a 'CONGRATULATIONS TO THE RED SOX' sign on the board, visible for less than a second but seen by many," Seaver noted.

When the Mets put men on and would not die, "a buzz arose from the stands, and it sounded like, 'Things can still happen.'"

They did. Schiraldi looked like the proverbial "deer caught in the headlights," Bill Buckner allowed a ground ball to roll under his legs, and the Mets rallied to defeat Boston. Tom Seaver was denied membership on his second world championship club.

"It was simply human error," recalled Tom of his fellow Californian, the star-crossed Buckner (whose hometown, Vallejo, was the same as Tug McGraw's). "It could have happened to anyone. . . . That he should be remembered for this play is not so much unfair as it is a microcosm of life itself: Baseball can be cruel, just as life can be."

He said, "Game six was the one for the ages; game seven was almost an inevitability."

Asked who he rooted for he said, "To me the question has always seemed nonsensical . . . the name across the front of your uniform represents the efforts of all your teammates, those individuals with whom you have ridden the buses and airplanes and worked seven days a week. The professional ballplayer pulls for the team he is on, not the team he once represented—no matter how full of miracles that team may be."

Now he was at the end. He had seen this act before. Willie Mays in 1973. Johnny Bench and Joe Morgan were long retired. Pete Rose was at the end, a player-manager in Cincinnati. Only Seaver's great counterpart, Reggie Jackson, was making one last try in the place where it all started, Oakland. The Red Sox did not offer Seaver a contract to his liking for the 1987 season. His 1986 salary was $1 million; the Red Sox offered $500,000. Seaver declined. When no new contract was reached, Seaver was granted free agency on November 12, 1986.

Something still motivated Seaver. One last payday, a final pennant, whatever competitive drive an all-time great has left. In 1987, with their starting rotation decimated by injury, the Mets sought help from Seaver. Though no actual contract was signed, Seaver joined the club on June 6 and was hit hard in an exhibition game against the triple-A Tidewater Tides on June 11. After similarly poor outings on the 16th and 20th, he announced his retirement, saying, "I've used up all the competitive pitches in my arm!"

14

THE GREATEST PITCHER OF ALL TIME? 1967–1986

SEAVER'S CAREER DID NOT END UP THE WAY IT SHOULD HAVE, THE way he would have planned it out. He should have been with the 1986 Mets. After winning the World Series at Shea Stadium, he should have been given a last ticker-tape parade through Manhattan. He could have announced his retirement while still on top. Instead he finished in renegade manner, absent fanfare or glory. Few athletes ever go out on top. Seaver was not one of them. However, this did not in any way detract from his place in history.

Seaver's number was retired before 46,057 at Shea during a special Tom Seaver Day ceremony in 1988. He told the crowd, "I came to the decision a long time ago, if my number was retired, there was one way I wanted to say thank you. If you will allow me one moment, I want to say thank you in a very special way. If you know me and how much I love pitching, you'll know what this means to me."

Wearing a business suit on the mound he bowed to all sections of the stadium, blowing kisses, then joined his wife and family to drive the convertible they gave him through the center-field gate.

As of 2011, Seaver remains the only Mets player to have his uniform number retired. Casey Stengel and Gil Hodges had their numbers retired as Mets managers, and Jackie Robinson had his number retired by all teams. Their numbers—14 (Hodges), 37 (Stengel), 41 (Seaver), and 42 (Jackie Robinson)—were posted in large numerals on the outfield fence at Shea Stadium and are posted on the left-field corner wall at Citi Field. Seaver is unquestionably the greatest player in Mets history.

He was elected to the Baseball Hall of Fame on January 7, 1992. He received the highest-ever percentage of votes with 98.84 percent (on 425 of 430 ballots), higher than Nolan Ryan's 98.79 percent (491 of 497) and Ty Cobb's 98.23 percent (222 of 226). Reportedly, three of the five ballots that had omitted Seaver were blank, cast by writers protesting the Hall's decision to make Pete Rose ineligible for consideration. Seaver is the only player enshrined in the Hall of Fame with a Mets cap on his plaque.

"There are moments in an individual's life that he will take with him forever," Seaver said when told he was in. "This is one. . . . I don't suppose this is really going to hit me until I walk the halls of Cooperstown next August to look at the plaque of Christy Mathewson. My children will be able to take their children to the Hall of Fame and say, 'There's your grandfather. In his day he was pretty good.' It's a wonderful thing to think about."

He was also inducted into the New York Mets Hall of Fame in 1988, the Marine Corps Sports Hall of Fame in 2003 (he was in the Reserves until 1970), and the Cincinnati Reds Hall of Fame in 2006.

When Seaver officially called it quits in 1987, there was a very strong argument that he was the greatest pitcher since World War II, and if he was the greatest pitcher since World War II, then there was no reason he might not be the greatest pitcher of all time. Since 1987, a handful of pitching greats have made their marks. One or two of them have compiled statistics, records, and honors arguably placing them above Tom Seaver in the pantheon. However, these records, as with so many records of the past 20 years, must be viewed with suspicion, for this has been the infamous "steroid era."

After the 1981 season, Seaver's career ERA (2.55) established the National League career record among pitchers with 200 or more games won. At the time of his retirement Seaver was third on the all-time strikeout list (3,640), trailing only Nolan Ryan and Steve Carlton. His lifetime ERA of 2.86 was third among starting pitchers in the post "live ball" era, behind only Whitey Ford and Sandy Koufax. Seaver also holds the record for consecutive 200-strikeout seasons with nine (1968–1976).

He was the first pitcher to have 10 200-strikeout seasons. Seaver set the record for consecutive strikeouts with 10 against San Diego on April 22, 1970, a game in which he tied Steve Carlton's record for most strikeouts in a game with 19. He set the National League mark for strikeouts by a right-hander in 1970 with 283, then broke his own mark in 1971 with 289.

He retired with a .603 career winning percentage, the highest of any 300-game winner in the past half century (311–205). Had Seaver not chosen to pitch in his last season (1986), his lifetime record would have been 304–192. This would have put him in a very unique category: 300 wins and fewer than 200 losses. Instead, as with Mickey Mantle when he played long enough to see his lifetime batting average drop below .300 in 1968, it was most unfortunate that he did not achieve this mark.

Seaver was named the right-handed pitcher on *The Sporting News* National League All-Star team four times (1969, 1973, 1975, 1981) and was *The Sporting News* National League Pitcher of the Year three times (1969, 1973, 1975). Named Rookie of the Year in 1967, Seaver was *Sports Illustrated*'s Sportsman of the Year, *The Sporting News* Sportsman of the Year, and winner of the Hickok Belt as professional athlete of the year in 1969. He was named to 12 All-Star Games, striking out 16 hitters in 13 innings. Seaver was named Comeback Player of the Year in 1975 and 1981.

Seaver pitched in the 1969, 1973, and 1979 National League Championship Series, compiling a 2–1 record with a 2.84 ERA and 24 strikeouts in 31⅔ innings. In the 1969 and 1973 World Series he was 1–2, striking out 27 in 30 innings, with a 2.70 earned run average. He pitched one no-hitter and five one-hitters. It is not an exaggeration to state that Seaver was every bit as dominant in both 1969 and 1971 as any pitcher in the game's history.

Seaver ranked 32nd on *The Sporting News*' list of baseball's 100 greatest players, which came out toward the end of the 20th century around the time baseball announced its All-Century Team. He was the only player on the list to have spent a majority of his career with the Mets. Babe Ruth was number one, followed by Willie Mays, Ty Cobb, Walter Johnson, Hank Aaron, Lou Gehrig, and Christy Mathewson. Johnson, at number four, was the highest-rated pitcher.

His twice-set National League strikeout record for right-handers in a single season (283 in 1970, 289 in 1971) was subsequently broken. Ryan broke Seaver's record for most 200-strikeout seasons (10), reaching 200 strikeouts 15 times. In 2001 Roger Clemens recorded his 11th 200-strikeout campaign. Seaver's record for most consecutive strikeouts (10) against San Diego in 1970 has never been challenged. Several pitchers subsequently broke his record of 19 strikeouts in a game. His nine consecutive 200-strikeout seasons (1968–1976) remains the record. Seaver's 61 career shutouts tie him with Nolan Ryan for seventh all time. He earned three Cy Young Awards.

Not factoring in steroids, an honest assessment of Seaver probably ranks him second or third among all post–World War II pitchers, behind Roger Clemens, maybe Randy Johnson, "tied" with Steve Carlton, but ahead of Warren Spahn and Greg Maddux. However, most historians *do* factor in steroids. Sandy Koufax's name is most-often mentioned as the "best," but his short career simply fails to remotely compare with Seaver's lifetime stats. Bob Gibson evokes a sense of nostalgia for his 1968 high-mound Year of the Pitcher performance, but his career records fall far short of Tom Seaver's.

Statistically, few pitchers can "compete" with Cy Young, Walter Johnson, Christy Mathewson, and Grover Cleveland Alexander, but their records were compiled in the "dead ball" era. Logic and common sense dictate that a modern pitcher such as Seaver is "better" even than Walter Johnson, just as Kobe Bryant is "better" than Hank Luisetti; LaDainian Tomlinson is "better" than Bronko Nagurski; Michael Phelps is "better" than Johnny Weissmuller.

In the end, there is no real "proof" that Tom Seaver was the best pitcher since World War II, the best right-hander since the war, or the best pitcher ever. There is, however, enough statistical and anecdotal evidence to make a good argument on his behalf. This is all it is, an argument, a bar room discussion no more possible to settle than the question as to who the greatest president was; the best movie actor or film; the best general or writer or scientist or astronaut. Tom Seaver is part of the argument, and after all, as Seaver himself stated, "I like a good argument."

15

THE SHINING CITY ON A HILL: 1987–2011

WE NOW COME TO THE END OF OUR CINDERELLA STORY, AND IT concludes most appropriately with a man who may be flawed, ego driven, money hungry, and judgmental but nevertheless represents something very rare in sports, or anyplace else for that matter.

Call it virtue, call it old-fashioned values, call it true greatness, and call him a hero, call him an icon. They broke the mold when they made Tom Seaver. Guys like this are one in a lifetime. The first half of the century got Christy Mathewson; the second half got Tom Seaver. They are that rare.

It is precisely because Seaver was so close to perfection that his imperfections, scarcely noticed in other mortals, are used by the jealous to try to tear him down. Their efforts are as effective as the unimpressives throwing rocks at Mount Rushmore.

The combination of looks, intelligence, education, range of interests, character, family, luck, talent, and accomplishments is shared by Tom Seaver and . . . nobody. A Bill Bradley or a Pat Haden may be a Rhodes Scholar but not an accomplished athlete of his level. A Cal Ripken or a Tony Gwynn is a beloved man of character but not nearly as completely rounded as an individual.

Mathewson and Lou Gehrig possessed many of Seaver's traits. Seaver is a legend every bit as much as they are. Joe Namath was a shooting star. Seaver is a satellite, maintained by NASA year in and year out.

Other pitchers on the Mets and in later years treated him with hero worship. Seaver had a fallout with Cleon Jones, a carouser whom Seaver saw as taking "bread out of his mouth," according to one writer. For several years Nancy was viewed as "all Hollywood." Some players continued to resent her. Why, because she was beautiful and happy to apparently have a faithful, loving husband?

Various writers described Seaver to writer John Devaney as "an intellectual, interested in politics, art, music, good books, lots of money," who was not close with Jerry Koosman, who was more of a "farm boy." Seaver cultivated his future. In the early 1970s that future was seen as limitless: commissioner of baseball, political office, business, team ownership, or broadcasting. He spent a considerable amount of time around Ralph Kiner, Lindsey Nelson, and Bob Murphy, learning the tricks of the sportscasting trade. He made himself quite accessible to the electronic media. Some cynically viewed this as self-serving public relations more than friendly availability to media professionals.

He viewed broadcasters as equals in a sense, future partners. Writers were potential enemies to be wary of. He was especially available in Los Angeles, the city of his college years, many friendships, and potential contacts. Nancy continued to visit on the road more than other wives. Teammates who felt this domain was their private sanctuary to cheat on their wives resented the "perfect family." One writer called him "the last of the non-adulterous ball players."

Tom Seaver did reach the $200,000 salary he stated was his long-range goal in the 1969–1970 off-season. Free agency hit with all of its cataclysmic effect in the mid-1970s. Seaver was in his prime but curiously never took full advantage of it. Others were paid more. Finally, when he was past his prime with the Mets and White Sox from 1983 to 1986, he became one of the highest-paid athletes in the world, but for the better part of a decade, lesser stars were paid more. The $200,000 figure was of course passed, left in the dust as

Seaver and his fellow sports stars ascended toward the $1 million mark and well beyond.

By the mid-1980s, the money was exorbitant, although paling in comparison to 2000s figures. Still, Seaver was not part of that generation—Mays, Aaron—who looked back bitterly at the times passing them by. He had not come along too soon. He came along just in time to see big money. He negotiated hard, but teammates such as Ron Swoboda and detractors who said he was consumed by money were ultimately not proven correct.

Seaver was one of the most marketable athletes in the world throughout the late 1960s, 1970s, and 1980s. He has remained marketable since. He took 100 percent advantage of his New York base and reputation, doing numerous ads. One of his most memorable was for a line of clothes. It fit perfectly with Seaver's three-piece-suit image, depicting him pitching on the mound at Shea in business clothes, the tagline being that Seaver was a corporate tycoon on the mound. Or, as his college teammate Bill "Spaceman" Lee once said, "I was a pickup truck and a six-pack of beer. Even then Tom was a limo, champagne, and a big fat cigar."

During and after his career, he cowrote, and was the subject of, a number of books—some authorized, others not so. He cowrote a novel, *Beanball*, another book on baseball's great moments, and *How I Would Pitch to Babe Ruth*, in which he dissected mound strategies for various sluggers of history. Seaver was involved in various other literary projects, mainly what appear to be ghostwritten "scouting notebooks" in which he lent his name to the byline and authored an introduction, or various "pitching manuals" aimed at the youth market, none of which was guaranteed to make the *New York Times* Best Seller list.

In recent years book offers have been spurned by his agent, Matt Merola (who represents retired stars such as Reggie Jackson), who demanded larger sums of money than most publishers are willing to depart with in the Internet era, in which the publishing business has taken a hit. Merola claimed that "Tom can make more money sitting at home signing autographs" than he could writing a book, which may be true. For a man with a sense for baseball history like Seaver, however, it seemed odd he did not want it all on the historical record—his way, his words, once and for all.

Seaver benefited hugely from the enormous memorabilia market, which has always thrived in New York City. His memory and nostalgia for the 1969 Amazin' Mets remain golden. People line up for blocks, bidding large sums for those things attached to Seaver and the Mets. However, many have complained of Seaver.

"Seaver wants too much money" is the constant refrain of publishers, promoters, and those who wish to have him involved in various projects, autograph signings, appearances. On the one hand, he appears greedy; on the other, he is a good businessman who gets what he gets because people will pay for it, and he knows it. Perhaps he realizes that in the late 1970s and early 1980s, when he was still the best pitcher in the game, he was an underpaid superstar and wishes to make up some lost ground. Maybe it is not the money but the competitive approach he takes toward his price tag, his worth in the marketplace versus other legends.

In 2009 the Lyons Press, an imprint of the Globe Pequot Press, published *The 1969 Miracle Mets: The Improbable Story of the World's Greatest Underdog Team.* This lively account detailed the glories of that incredible summer and fall so long ago.

Discussions were entered about a movie version of the 1969 season or of Tom Seaver's life: perhaps a documentary or an HBO *Sports of the 20th Century* program like the Ted Williams special that aired in 2009. Seaver and the 1969 Mets, like most anything to do with the Yankees, the Red Sox mystique, Vince Lombardi's Green Bay Packers, Notre Dame football, or several other mythic sports genres, seem to have limitless potential, films and documentaries that are begging to be done by somebody. Curiously, the "quintessential Seaver book" was never written . . . until, finally, this one!

Tom Seaver started broadcasting while still playing, for channel two in New York (1975). He announced postseason games for ABC and NBC until 1984. In 1977, life imitated art at Yankee Stadium. Seaver was in the announcer's booth doing ABC color commentary, alongside sportscasting legends Howard Cosell and Keith Jackson. Reggie Jackson welcomed himself into the exclusive true New York icon club, pounding three home runs (five overall) to lead the Bronx Bombers to their first world championship since 1962, four games to two over Los Angeles. This event may well be the closest one to the 1969 Mets as an exciting sports story. Yankees fans surely would argue it was bigger.

At NBC, Seaver also broadcast professional golf. After retirement from playing, he broadcast the NBC Saturday *Game of the Week*, the preeminent weekly showcase in the days before Fox Sports, ESPN, and the proliferation of cable. Among his broadcast partners were Joe Garagiola and the legendary Vin Scully. When Garagiola left *Game of the Week*, Tom replaced him. Seaver's pairing with the great Scully was an honor and a privilege almost matching his accomplishments as an athlete.

From 1989 to 1993, Seaver was on the WPIX channel 11 broadcast team for the New York Yankees. In 1999, he rejoined the Mets as Gary Thorne's broadcast partner on WPIX. He is one of three sportscasters to be regular announcers for both the Mets and Yankees; the others are Fran Healy and Tim McCarver. He has also worked as a part-time scout and as a Spring Training pitching coach.

On September 28, 2006, Seaver was chosen as the "Hometown Hero" for the Mets franchise by ESPN. Seaver made a return to Shea Stadium during the "Shea Goodbye" closing ceremony on September 28, 2008, where he threw out the final pitch in the history of the stadium to Mike Piazza. He and Piazza then opened the Mets' new home, Citi Field, with the ceremonial first pitch on April 13, 2009.

Around 1977, while still in his pitching prime, Seaver's brother-in-law asked him what he intended to do when he retired. "I told him that I intended to go back to California and grow grapes," he said. "It just kind of emerged from the back of my mind, and I think there was an amalgam of reasons."

It was a return, literally, to Seaver's "roots" around the agricultural heartland of Fresno, the raisin capital of the world. He started sampling wines at USC. He and Nancy also took off-season bicycle trips through the wine regions of France.

"Nancy would ask me if I was sure I would like it," Seaver told longtime *Los Angeles Times* baseball writer Ross Newhan, "and I would tell her, 'No, but I know there's an itch.' I also knew that whatever I eventually did there had to be a physical involvement. Look at my [scarred] fingers and [dirtied] nails. I call it the red badge of courage. For me, sitting in front of a computer would be instant death. Nancy has the computer. I don't."

The Seavers live in the vibrantly green, sun-splashed Napa Valley wine country of Northern California. His "neighbors," which in this neck of the woods can be people 50 miles away, once included former San Francisco 49ers Hall of Fame quarterback Joe Montana, as well as Academy Award–winning director Francis Ford Coppola. It is a land of redwood forests, Douglas fir, manzanita, tanbark oak, and madrone.

"If I had a dream, it couldn't get any better than this," Seaver said.

Seaver operates a John Deere on a little slice of paradise called Diamond Mountain, 800 feet above the fertile Napa Valley. It is his shining city on a hill. His GTS Vineyard is the smallest, specializing in Cabernet (Sauvignon) grapes on 3.5 acres of a 115-acre maze of foliage and vistas.

"I've always said that I'd rather be lucky than good," he said. "It's like when you hang a slider with runners in scoring position, and the batter pops it up and everyone says to you, 'That was a great pitch in that situation,' and you kind of laugh to yourself knowing the truth."

Seaver found many similarities between baseball and wine growing, not unlike his observations to Pat Jordan on a winter day some 35 year earlier. "In many ways there is a sequential rhythm and analogous nature to the two seasons, and I'm sure that was a large part of the attraction for me," he theorized.

The Seavers' move back to California came only when daughters Sarah and Anne had finished Boston College. It involved a two-year search through San Luis Obispo, Apple Valley, Mendocino, Paso Robles, and even into Oregon. When they stopped at a realtor's office in St. Helena, one of the sales clips they were given was for the parcel on Diamond Mountain.

"I suspect that other potential buyers had been here before and never got out of their car," Seaver said. "I was in the Marines. Sometimes you have to put boots on the ground. This was the classic case of needing to see the forest through the trees."

The year was 1998, and the future was set. Boston architect Kenneth Kao designed a 7,000-square-foot house, blending into the hillside beige walls merging with the soil, contours and color of the roof, which looked just like the hills and trees. A patio and pool area oversees the panoramic view.

In 2000 the Seavers moved in. Nancy created a greenhouse and rose garden. Seaver had done his research, of course. He knew that grapes grow with southern exposure. Former teammate and restaurant owner Rusty Staub provided valuable advice. "How in the world did you find it?" Staub asked Seaver of his land. "This is what people are killing for out here."

"Sometimes you win, 7–6," Seaver replied.

"We're close, in year six, to a return on capital," he said in 2007 of his winery investment. "My game plan is to break even in 10 years, and we may beat that by a year.

"We're a drop in the bucket [compared to other wineries], but I'm talking quality and not quantity. It's Diamond Mountain Cabernet, south-facing slope. It has the potential to be drop-dead stuff."

They live in Calistoga. The vineyard, called the Seaver Family Vineyards, is 3.5 acres, located on a large estate. He presented his two Cabernets, Nancy's Fancy and GTS, in an April 2010 wine-tasting event in SoHo to positive reviews.

Seaver, the true New York sports icon who was idolized in the Big Apple like Joe DiMaggio and Joe Namath, said he could care less about getting his "face on the cover of *Wine Spectator* because I've had enough of all that." He wants the wine to stand on its own merits. The back of the labels reads, "May you enjoy this wine as much as I enjoy the journey bringing it to you. Day to day, month to month, season to season."

Seaver continued to do public relations work on a part-time basis for the Mets and became a familiar face at nearby San Francisco's AT&T Park, where he was one of the special guests honoring Willie Mays when the Giants held a day for the great star. Sandy

Koufax, Bob Gibson, Steve Carlton, and Don Baylor were among Seaver's guests, traveling to Diamond Mountain for wine and remembrance of past glories. They found the great star in repose, content with his life, his career, and his family.

He no longer needed the spotlight. He saw enough of that for 100 superstars, for 50 seasons, for 25 championship campaigns. He tasted glory as few, a very elite few, have ever tasted it. YouTube.com tributes to Seaver and the '69 Mets are easily found—mostly loving, homemade videos featuring melancholic old music of the era, evoking the lost days that men yearn to recapture and never can.

Others came after him, of course. "The beat," as they said in the 1960s, "goes on." New York saw a resurgence, as a city and among its sports teams: George Steinbrenner's Yankees of the 1970s, 1990s, and 2000s; the 1986 Mets; Bill Parcells's Giants. Great stars wore the N.Y. logo, some approaching Seaver's records and accomplishments, arguably none really surpassing them.

But something went missing after Seaver left—really, after his trade to Cincinnati in 1977, not found again in his brief return. Reggie lit up the sky, but he was a mercenary, paid oodles of Steinbrenner's dough, an Oakland Athletic, really, always arguing with Billy Martin. Lawrence Taylor fell from grace. Roger Clemens was something special, but he was a Boston Red Sox, now controversial.

Alex Rodriguez? There was something missing. Mariano Rivera? A thing of beauty, but to take the Big Apple by storm, to be a true American hero in a ticker-tape parade through the concrete canyons, as with a Neil Armstrong or a Douglas MacArthur, one must possess something that seems missing in all modern sports superstars, in all of society really. Something lost to an innocent age and never to be recaptured. Something Seaver had.

Then there was Derek Jeter. He had it all, the respect, the accolades, yet somehow in an age in which a Major League Baseball player is overpaid by 90 percent of his value to society, not even Jeter could be an icon in the true sense of the word, as was Ruth and Gehrig, DiMaggio and Mantle, Robinson and Mays, Gifford and Namath. And Tom Seaver.

So, the young Californian, who arrived so full of enthusiasm and wonder in a city begging for rebirth; who led a group of babes through the wilderness to a Pentecostal baseball rapture unlike any seen before or since; who rode astride our national pastime and the Big Apple like a Colossus, before Watergate, before free agency, almost as in an innocent Garden of Eden before the advent of original sin. Well, the last icon was really Tom Seaver.

The end.

TOM SEAVER'S CAREER STATISTICS

George Thomas Seaver (Tom Terrific)

Position: Pitcher Bats: Right Throws: Right Height: 6'1" Weight: 195 lb

Born: November 17, 1944, in Fresno, CA

High school: Fresno (Fresno, CA)

College: University of Southern California

(All Transactions)

Major League debut: April 13, 1967

Teams (by GP): Mets, Reds, White Sox, Red Sox, 1967–1986

[*]

Final game: September 19, 1986

Inducted into the Hall of Fame by BBWAA as a player in 1992 (425/430 ballots)

Year	Age	Tm	Lg	W	L	W-L%	ERA	G	GS	GF	CG	SHO	SV	IP	H	R	ER	HR
1967	22	NYM	NL	16	13	.552	2.76	35	34	1	18	2	0	251.0	224	85	77	19
1968	23	NYM	NL	16	12	.571	2.20	36	35	1	14	5	1	278.0	224	73	68	15
1969	24	NYM	NL	25	7	.781	2.21	36	35	1	18	5	0	273.1	202	75	67	24
1970	25	NYM	NL	18	12	.600	2.82	37	36	1	19	2	0	290.2	230	103	91	21
1971	26	NYM	NL	20	10	.667	1.76	36	35	1	21	4	0	286.1	210	61	56	18
1972	27	NYM	NL	21	12	.636	2.92	35	35	0	13	3	0	262.0	215	92	85	23
1973	28	NYM	NL	19	10	.655	2.08	36	36	0	18	3	0	290.0	219	74	67	23
1974	29	NYM	NL	11	11	.500	3.20	32	32	0	12	5	0	236.0	199	89	84	19
1975	30	NYM	NL	22	9	.710	2.38	36	36	0	15	5	0	280.1	217	81	74	11
1976	31	NYM	NL	14	11	.560	2.59	35	34	0	13	5	0	271.0	211	83	78	14
1977	32	TOT	NL	21	6	.778	2.58	33	33	0	19	7	0	261.1	199	78	75	19
1977	32	NYM	NL	7	3	.700	3.00	13	13	0	5	3	0	96.0	79	33	32	7
1977	32	CIN	NL	14	3	.824	2.34	20	20	0	14	4	0	165.1	120	45	43	12
1978	33	CIN	NL	16	14	.533	2.88	36	36	0	8	1	0	259.2	218	97	83	26
1979	34	CIN	NL	16	6	.727	3.14	32	32	0	9	5	0	215.0	187	85	75	16
1980	35	CIN	NL	10	8	.556	3.64	26	26	0	5	1	0	168.0	140	74	68	24
1981	36	CIN	NL	14	2	.875	2.54	23	23	0	6	1	0	166.1	120	51	47	10
1982	37	CIN	NL	5	13	.278	5.50	21	21	0	0	0	0	111.1	136	75	68	14
1983	38	NYM	NL	9	14	.391	3.55	34	34	0	5	2	0	231.0	201	104	91	18
1984	39	CHW	AL	15	11	.577	3.95	34	33	1	10	4	0	236.2	216	108	104	27
1985	40	CHW	AL	16	11	.593	3.17	35	33	0	6	1	0	238.2	223	103	84	22
1986	41	TOT	AL	7	13	.350	4.03	28	28	0	2	0	0	176.1	180	83	79	17
1986	41	CHW	AL	2	6	.250	4.38	12	12	0	1	0	0	72.0	66	37	35	9
1986	41	BOS	AL	5	7	.417	3.80	16	16	0	1	0	0	104.1	114	46	44	8
20 seasons				311	205	.603	2.86	656	647	6	231	61	1	4,783.0	3,971	1,674	1,521	380
162 game avg.				16	11	.603	2.86	34	34	0	12	3	0	250	207	87	79	20

	W	L	W-L%	ERA	G	GS	GF	CG	SHO	SV	IP	H	R	ER	HR
NYM (12 yr)	198	124	.615	2.57	401	395	5	171	44	1	3,045.2	2,431	953	870	212
CIN (6 yr)	75	46	.620	3.18	158	158	0	42	12	0	1,085.2	921	427	384	102
CHW (3 yr)	33	28	.541	3.67	81	78	1	17	5	0	547.1	505	248	223	58
BOS (1 yr)	5	7	.417	3.80	16	16	0	1	0	0	104.1	114	46	44	8
NL (17 yr)	273	170	.616	2.73	559	553	5	213	56	1	4,131.1	3,352	1,380	1,254	314
AL (3 yr)	38	35	.521	3.69	97	94	1	18	5	0	651.2	619	294	267	66

BB	IBB	SO	HBP	BK	WP	BF	ERA+	WHIP	H/9	HR/9	BB/9	SO/9	SO/BB	Awards
78	6	170	5	0	5	1,029	122	1.203	8.0	0.7	2.8	6.1	2.18	AS,MVP-22,RoY-1
48	5	205	8	1	8	1,088	137	0.978	7.3	0.5	1.6	6.6	4.27	AS
82	9	208	7	1	8	1,089	165	1.039	6.7	0.8	2.7	6.8	2.54	AS,CYA-1,MVP-2
83	8	283	4	0	6	1,173	143	1.077	7.1	0.7	2.6	8.8	3.41	AS,CYA-7,MVP-29
61	2	289	4	1	5	1,103	194	0.946	6.6	0.6	1.9	9.1	4.74	AS,CYA-2,MVP-9
77	2	249	5	0	8	1,060	115	1.115	7.4	0.8	2.6	8.6	3.23	AS,CYA-5,MVP-25
64	5	251	4	0	5	1,147	175	0.976	6.8	0.7	2.0	7.8	3.92	AS,CYA-1,MVP-8
75	10	201	3	2	4	956	112	1.161	7.6	0.7	2.9	7.7	2.68	
88	6	243	4	1	7	1,115	146	1.088	7.0	0.4	2.8	7.8	2.76	AS,CYA-1,MVP-9
77	9	235	4	0	12	1,079	127	1.063	7.0	0.5	2.6	7.8	3.05	AS,CYA-8
66	6	196	0	1	7	1,031	150	1.014	6.9	0.7	2.3	6.8	2.97	AS,CYA-3,MVP-25
28	3	72	0	1	3	390	124	1.115	7.4	0.7	2.6	6.8	2.57	
38	3	124	0	0	4	641	169	0.956	6.5	0.7	2.1	6.8	3.26	
89	11	226	0	1	6	1,075	125	1.182	7.6	0.9	3.1	7.8	2.54	AS
61	6	131	0	0	4	868	121	1.153	7.8	0.7	2.6	5.5	2.15	CYA-4,MVP-21
59	3	101	1	0	4	692	99	1.185	7.5	1.3	3.2	5.4	1.71	
66	8	87	3	0	5	671	140	1.118	6.5	0.5	3.6	4.7	1.32	AS,CYA-2,MVP-10
44	4	62	3	0	3	501	67	1.617	11.0	1.1	3.6	5.0	1.41	
86	5	135	4	0	10	962	103	1.242	7.8	0.7	3.4	5.3	1.57	
61	3	131	2	0	5	978	105	1.170	8.2	1.0	2.3	5.0	2.15	
69	6	134	8	0	10	993	136	1.223	8.4	0.8	2.6	5.1	1.94	
56	2	103	7	0	4	759	106	1.338	9.2	0.9	2.9	5.3	1.84	
27	1	31	5	0	1	309	100	1.292	8.3	1.1	3.4	3.9	1.15	
29	1	72	2	0	3	450	111	1.371	9.8	0.7	2.5	6.2	2.48	
1,390	116	3,640	76	8	126	19,369	128	1.121	7.5	0.7	2.6	6.8	2.62	
73	6	190	4	0	7	1,011	128	1.121	7.5	0.7	2.6	6.8	2.62	
BB	**IBB**	**SO**	**HBP**	**BK**	**WP**	**BF**	**ERA+**	**WHIP**	**H/9**	**HR/9**	**BB/9**	**SO/9**	**SO/BB**	**Awards**
847	70	2,541	52	7	81	12,191	136	1.076	7.2	0.6	2.5	7.5	3.00	
357	35	731	7	1	26	4,448	116	1.177	7.6	0.8	3.0	6.1	2.05	
157	10	296	15	0	16	2,280	116	1.210	8.3	1.0	2.6	4.9	1.89	
29	1	72	2	0	3	450	111	1.371	9.8	0.7	2.5	6.2	2.48	
1,204	105	3,272	59	8	107	16,639	130	1.103	7.3	0.7	2.6	7.1	2.72	
186	11	368	17	0	19	2,730	115	1.235	8.5	0.9	2.6	5.1	1.98	

Year	Age	Tm	Lg	Series	Rslt	Opp	W	L	W-L%	ERA	G	GS	GF	CG	SHO	SV	IP
1969	24	NYM	NL	NLCS	W	ATL	1	0	1.000	6.43	1	1	0	0	0	0	7.0
1969	24	NYM	NL	WS	W	BAL	1	1	.500	3.00	2	2	0	1	0	0	15.0
1973	28	NYM	NL	NLCS	W	CIN	1	1	.500	1.62	2	2	0	1	0	0	16.2
1973	28	NYM	NL	WS	L	OAK	0	1	.000	2.40	2	2	0	0	0	0	15.0
1979	34	CIN	NL	NLCS	L	PIT	0	0		2.25	1	1	0	0	0	0	8.0
3 seasons (5 series)							3	3	.500	2.77	8	8	0	2	0	0	61.2
3 NLCS							2	1	.667	2.84	4	4	0	1	0	0	31.2
2 WS							1	2	.333	2.70	4	4	0	1	0	0	30.0

H	R	ER	HR	BB	IBB	SO	HBP	BK	WP	BF	WHIP	H/9	HR/9	BB/9	SO/9	SO/BB
8	5	5	2	3	2	2	1	0	0	33	1.571	10.3	2.6	3.9	2.6	0.67
12	5	5	1	3	0	9	0	0	0	61	1.000	7.2	0.6	1.8	5.4	3.00
13	4	3	2	5	2	17	1	0	1	69	1.080	7.0	1.1	2.7	9.2	3.40
13	4	4	0	3	0	18	0	0	1	62	1.067	7.8	0.0	1.8	10.8	6.00
5	2	2	1	2	0	5	0	0	0	30	0.875	5.6	1.1	2.3	5.6	2.50
51	20	19	6	16	4	51	2	0	2	255	1.086	7.4	0.9	2.3	7.4	3.19
26	11	10	5	10	4	24	2	0	1	132	1.137	7.4	1.4	2.8	6.8	2.40
25	9	9	1	6	0	27	0	0	1	123	1.033	7.5	0.3	1.8	8.1	4.50

Year	Age	Tm	Lg	IP	GS	R	R*rep*	R*def*	aLI	RAR	WAR	Salary	Awards
1967	22	NYM	NL	251.0	34	85	138	–6	1.1	53	6.4	$7,500	AS,MVP-22,RoY-1
1968	23	NYM	NL	277.2	35	73	131	1	1.1	58	7.5		AS
1969	24	NYM	NL	273.1	35	75	142	10	1.1	67	7.6	$38,000	AS,CYA-1,MVP-2
1970	25	NYM	NL	290.2	36	103	160	8	1.0	57	6.0	$80,000	AS,CYA-7,MVP-29
1971	26	NYM	NL	286.1	35	61	143	1	0.9	82	9.2	$90,000	AS,CYA-2,MVP-9
1972	27	NYM	NL	262.0	35	92	139	–9	1.1	47	5.8	$120,000	AS,CYA-5,MVP-25
1973	28	NYM	NL	290.0	36	74	161	–1	1.0	87	9.5	$130,000	AS,CYA-1,MVP-8
1974	29	NYM	NL	236.0	32	89	141	–9	1.0	52	5.7	$173,000	
1975	30	NYM	NL	280.1	36	81	148	0	1.0	67	7.7	$173,000	AS,CYA-1,MVP-9
1976	31	NYM	NL	271.0	34	83	131	2	1.0	48	5.7	$225,000	AS,CYA-8
1977	32	NYM	NL	96.0	13	33	55	0	0.9	22	2.2	$225,000	AS,CYA-3,MVP-25
1977	32	CIN	NL	165.1	20	45	96	0	1.0	51	5.4		AS,CYA-3,MVP-25
1978	33	CIN	NL	259.2	36	97	139	–5	1.0	42	4.8		AS
1979	34	CIN	NL	215.0	32	85	116	1	1.0	31	3.4	$375,000	CYA-4,MVP-21
1980	35	CIN	NL	168.0	26	74	88	0	1.0	14	1.6	$375,000	
1981	36	CIN	NL	166.1	23	51	86	–1	1.1	35	4.2	$375,000	AS,CYA-2,MVP-10
1982	37	CIN	NL	111.1	21	75	67	–4	0.9	–8	–0.8	$375,000	
1983	38	NYM	NL	231.0	34	104	127	0	1.0	23	2.5	$850,000	
1984	39	CHW	AL	236.2	33	108	144	2	1.0	36	3.7		
1985	40	CHW	AL	238.2	33	103	150	0	1.0	47	4.8	$1,136,262	
1986	41	CHW	AL	72.0	12	37	42	3	0.9	5	0.5	$1,132,652	
1986	41	BOS	AL	104.1	16	46	65	0	1.0	19	1.9		
20 seasons				4,782.2	647	1,674	2,609	–7	1.0	935	105.3	$5,880,414	
				IP	**GS**	**R**	**R*rep***	**R*def***	**aLI**	**RAR**	**WAR**	**Salary**	**Awards**
NYM (12 yr)				3,045.1	395	953	1,616	–3	1.0	663	75.8	$2,111,500	
CIN (6 yr)				1,085.2	158	427	592	–9	1.0	165	18.6	$1,500,000	
CHW (3 yr)				547.4	78	248	336	5	1.0	88	9.0	$2,268,914	
BOS (1 yr)				104.1	16	46	65	0	1.0	19	1.9		

BIBLIOGRAPHY

2001 New York Mets Information Guide. New York: Mets Media Relations Dept., 2001.

Adell, Ross, and Ken Samelson. *Amazing Mets Trivia.* Lanham, MD: Taylor Trade, 2004.

Alston, Walter, and Don Weiskopf. *The Complete Baseball Handbook.* Boston: Allyn and Bacon, 1972.

Angell, Roger. *Five Seasons.* New York: Simon & Schuster, 1977.

———. *Game Time: A Baseball Companion.* Orlando, FL: Harcourt, 2003.

———. *Late Innings: A Baseball Companion.* New York: Simon & Schuster, 1972.

———. *The Summer Game.* New York: Viking, 1972.

Appel, Marty. *Yogi Berra.* New York: Chelsea House, 1992.

Archibald, Joe. *Right Field Rookie.* Philadelphia: MacRae Smith, 1967.

Baseball Encyclopedia, The. New York: Macmillan, 1996.

Biskind, Peter. *Easy Riders, Raging Bulls: How the Sex-Drugs-and-Rock 'n' Roll Generation Saved Hollywood.* New York: Simon & Schuster, 1998.

Bjarkman, Peter C. *The New York Mets Encyclopedia.* Champaign, IL: Sports Publishing, 2003.

Bouton, Jim. *Ball Four.* New York: World Publishing, 1970.

Bouton, Jim, with Neil Offen. *I Managed Good, but Boy Did They Play Bad.* New York: Dell, 1973.

Breslin, Jimmy. *Can't Anybody Here Play This Game?* New York: Viking, 1963.

Brosnan, Jim. *Great Rookies of the Major Leagues.* New York: Random House, 1966.

Cramer, Richard Ben. *Joe DiMaggio: The Hero's Life.* New York: Simon & Schuster, 2000.

Creamer, Robert. *Stengel: His Life and Times.* New York: Simon & Schuster, 1984.

Dearborn, Mary V. *Mailer.* New York: Houghton Mifflin, 1999.

Devaney, John. *Tom Seaver.* New York: Popular Library, 1974.

DiMaggio, Joe. *Lucky to Be a Yankee.* New York: Grosset & Dunlap, 1947.

Drucker, Malka, with Tom Seaver. *Tom Seaver: Portrait of a Pitcher.* New York: Holiday House, 1978.

Eig, Jonathan. *Luckiest Man: The Life and Death of Lou Gehrig.* New York: Simon & Schuster, 2005.

Einstein, Charles. *Willie's Time.* New York: Lippincott, 1979.

Enders, Eric. *100 Years of the World Series.* Barnes & Noble, 2003.

Fox, Bucky. *The Mets Fan's Little Book of Wisdom.* Lanham, MD: Taylor Trade, 2006.

Fox, Larry. *Broadway Joe and his Super Jets.* New York: Coward-McCann, 1969.

Golenbock, Peter. *Amazin': The Miraculous History of New York's Most Beloved Baseball Team.* New York: St. Martin's Press, 2002.

Grabowski, John. *Willie Mays.* New York: Chelsea House, 1990.

Graham, Jr., Frank. *Great Pennant Races of the Major Leagues.* New York: Random House, 1967.

Gutman, Bill. *Miracle Year 1969: Amazing Mets and Super Jets.* Champaign, IL: Sports Publishing, 2004.

Helyar, John. *Lords of the Realm.* New York: Villard Books, 1994.

Hodges, Gil, with Frank Slocum. *The Game of Baseball.* New York: Crown, 1969.

Holy Bible. National Publishing, 1970.

Honig, Donald. *The National League.* New York: Crown, 1983.

Jordan, Pat. "Tom Terrific and His Mystic Talent." *Sports Illustrated,* July 24, 1972. Available: http://sportsillustrated.cnn.com/vault/article/magazine/MAG1086339/4/index.htm#ixzz169JfNOZ4.

Kuenster, John, ed. *From Cobb to Catfish.* Chicago: Rand McNally, 1975.

Lee, Bill, with Richard Lally. *The Wrong Stuff.* New York: Viking, 1983.

Leventhal, Josh. *The World Series.* New York: Tess Press, 2004.

Lichtenstein, Michael. *Ya Gotta Believe!* New York: St. Martin's Griffin, 2002.

Macht, Norman L. *Tom Seaver.* New York: Chelsea House, 1994.

Markusen, Bruce. *Tales from the Mets Dugout.* Champaign, IL: Sports Publishing, 2005.

Mays, Willie, as told to Charles Einstein. *Willie Mays: My Life In and Out of Baseball.* New York: Dutton, 1966.

New York Times Book of Baseball History, The. Foreword by Red Smith. New York: New York Times Book Co., 1975.

Newhan, Ross. "Vintage Seaver." *Los Angeles Times,* July 5, 2007. Available: http://articles.latimes.com/2007/jul/05/sports/sp-seaver5.

Official 1969 Baseball Guide. St. Louis: *The Sporting News,* 1969.

Official 1970 Baseball Guide. St. Louis: *The Sporting News,* 1970.

Official 1971 Baseball Guide. St. Louis: *The Sporting News,* 1971.

Parrott, Harold. *The Lords of Baseball.* New York: Praeger, 1976.

Pearlman, Jeff. *The Bad Guys Won!* New York: HarperCollins, 2004.

Reichler, Joseph. *Baseball's Great Moments.* New York: Crown, 1974.

Ritter, Lawrence. *The Glory of Their Times.* New York: Macmillan, 1966.

Ritter, Lawrence, and Donald Honig. *The Image of Their Greatness.* New York: Crown, 1979.

Robinson, Ray, ed. *Baseball Stars of 1965.* New York: Pyramid, 1965.

———, ed. *Baseball Stars of 1970.* New York: Pyramid, 1970.

Schoor, Gene. *Seaver.* Chicago: Contemporary Books, 1986.

Seaver, Tom, with Alice Siegel and Margo McLoone-Basta. *Tom Seaver's Baseball Cards.* New York: Wanderer, 1985.

Seaver, Tom, with Dick Schaap. *The Perfect Game.* New York: Dutton, 1970.

Seaver, Tom, with Herb Resnicow. *Beanball.* New York: Morrow, 1989.

Seaver, Tom, with Lee Lowenfish. *The Art of Pitching.* New York: Mountain Lion Books, 1984.

Seaver, Tom, with Marty Appel. *Great Moments in Baseball.* New York: Carol, 1992.

———. *Tom Seaver's All-Time Baseball Greats.* New York: Wanderer, 1984.

Seaver, Tom, with Rick Hummel and Bob Nightengale. *Tom Seaver's 1989 Scouting Notebook.* St. Louis: *The Sporting News,* 1989.

Seaver, Tom, with Steve Jacobsen. *Pitching with Tom Seaver.* Englewood Cliffs, N.J.: Prentice-Hall, 1973.

Shamsky, Art, with Barry Zeman. *The Magnificent Seasons: How the Jets, Mets, and Knicks Made Sports History and Uplifted a City and the Country.* New York: Dunne, 2004.

Smilgis, Martha. "A Tale of Two Cities." *People,* July 25, 1977.

Smith, Robert. *Baseball.* New York: Simon & Schuster, 1947.

Stout, Glenn. *The Dodgers: 120 Years of Dodgers Baseball.* New York: Houghton Mifflin, 2004.

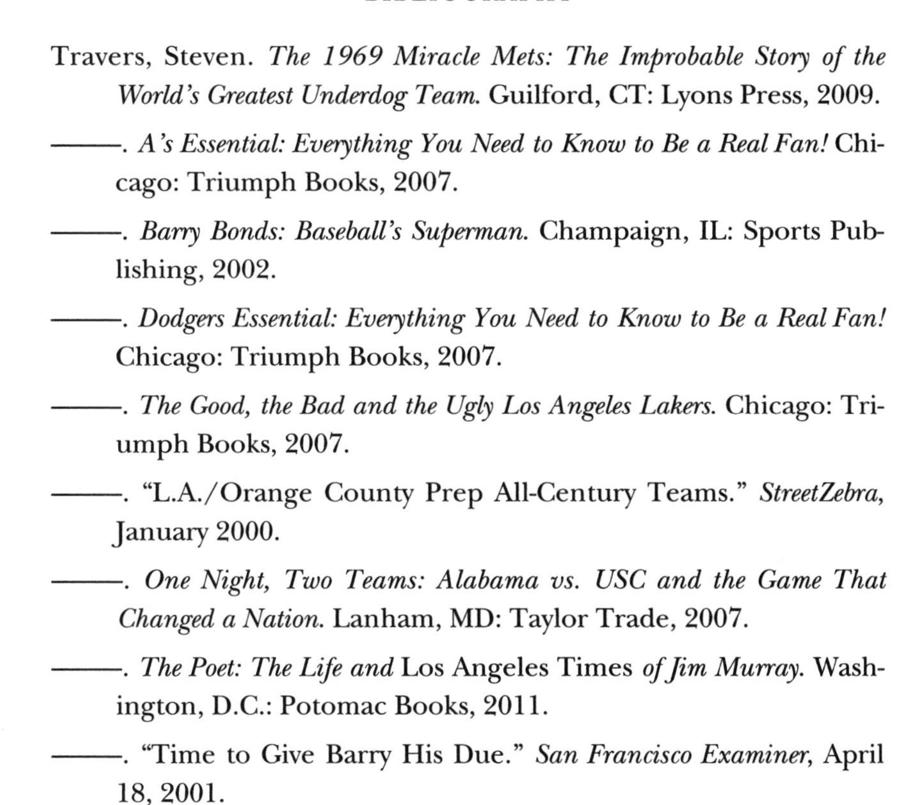

Travers, Steven. *The 1969 Miracle Mets: The Improbable Story of the World's Greatest Underdog Team.* Guilford, CT: Lyons Press, 2009.

———. *A's Essential: Everything You Need to Know to Be a Real Fan!* Chicago: Triumph Books, 2007.

———. *Barry Bonds: Baseball's Superman.* Champaign, IL: Sports Publishing, 2002.

———. *Dodgers Essential: Everything You Need to Know to Be a Real Fan!* Chicago: Triumph Books, 2007.

———. *The Good, the Bad and the Ugly Los Angeles Lakers.* Chicago: Triumph Books, 2007.

———. "L.A./Orange County Prep All-Century Teams." *StreetZebra,* January 2000.

———. *One Night, Two Teams: Alabama vs. USC and the Game That Changed a Nation.* Lanham, MD: Taylor Trade, 2007.

———. *The Poet: The Life and* Los Angeles Times *of Jim Murray.* Washington, D.C.: Potomac Books, 2011.

———. "Time to Give Barry His Due." *San Francisco Examiner,* April 18, 2001.

Whittingham, Richard. *Illustrated History of the Dodgers.* Chicago: Triumph Books, 2005.

Will, George. *Bunts.* New York: Touchstone, 1999.

Wise, Bill, ed. *1963 Official Baseball Almanac.* Greenwich, Conn.: Fawcett Publications.

Zimmerman, Paul D., and Dick Schaap. *The Year the Mets Lost Last Place.* New York: World Publishing, 1969.

INDEX